The Priority of Love

NEW FORUM BOOKS   Robert P. George, Series Editor

A list of titles in the series
appears at the back of the book

The Priority of Love

CHRISTIAN CHARITY AND
SOCIAL JUSTICE

Timothy P. Jackson

PRINCETON UNIVERSITY PRESS

PRINCETON AND OXFORD

COPYRIGHT © 2003 BY PRINCETON UNIVERSITY PRESS
PUBLISHED BY PRINCETON UNIVERSITY PRESS, 41 WILLIAM STREET,
PRINCETON, NEW JERSEY 08540
IN THE UNITED KINGDOM: PRINCETON UNIVERSITY PRESS,
3 MARKET PLACE, WOODSTOCK, OXFORDSHIRE OX20 1SY
ALL RIGHTS RESERVED

LIBRARY OF CONGRESS CATALOGING-IN-PUBLICATION DATA

JACKSON, TIMOTHY P. (TIMOTHY PATRICK)
THE PRIORITY OF LOVE : CHRISTIAN CHARITY AND SOCIAL JUSTICE /
TIMOTHY P. JACKSON.
P.   CM.   — (NEW FORUM BOOKS)
INCLUDES BIBLIOGRAPHICAL REFERENCES AND INDEX.
ISBN 0-691-05085-6 (ALK. PAPER)
1. AGAPE.   2. CHRISTIANITY AND JUSTICE.   I. TITLE.   II. SERIES.

BV4639 .J34 2003
241'.4—DC21   2002023666

BRITISH LIBRARY CATALOGING-IN-PUBLICATION DATA IS AVAILABLE

THIS BOOK HAS BEEN COMPOSED IN GALLIARD

PRINTED ON ACID-FREE PAPER. ∞

WWW.PUPRESS.PRINCETON.EDU

PRINTED IN THE UNITED STATES OF AMERICA

1   3   5   7   9   10   8   6   4   2

To My Parents, James P. and Katherine G. Jackson

You would know our Lord's meaning in this thing? Know it well.

Love was his meaning. Who showed it you? Love.

What did he show you? Love. Why did he show it?

For love.

—*Julian of Norwich*

Contents

Preface

In an academic text, even one dedicated to practical issues, an author is usually reluctant to ground his or her judgments existentially. Lest one seem too confessional or self-absorbed, accent falls on objective argument rather than autobiography. This tendency is understandable: few things are less edifying than the self-indulgent narration of a life, and there is no substitute in ethics for sound reasoning and appropriate evidence. This preface assumes, nevertheless, that it is neither irrelevant nor fallacious to try to forge a link between lived experiences and normative theses. On the one hand, true-life tales, well told, can be more interesting than abstract theories. On the other hand, and more important, finely crafted memoirs can help clarify what a writer wants to say about a moral issue, as well as why he or she wants to say it. If a new text emerges, or is thought to emerge, solely as a response to older academic texts, what meaning can it have for those who have not read or cared about the traditional books? If a text flows, and is shown to flow, at least partially from "experimental" engagement with the world and its problems, however, it may be accessible to many more readers. Hence this brief history of my highest times, a prelude to the more detached analysis and argument in the chapters that follow.

Three experiences in particular have decidedly formed my moral opinions. The first involved the force of inanimate nature; the second, an encounter with conscious but nonrational life; the third, a conversation with a memorable human personality. Each of these experiences led me to revise my understanding of love and justice, especially the relation between personal and impersonal goods. I relate the incidents here, not because they are rare or mysterious, but because, however idiosyncratic in some respects, they point to more accessible truths that are the inspiration of this book.

October 17, 1989 was to bring my first World Series game seen in person, and I was agreeably lost in the excitement of the moment. Two friends and I had just made our way to our upper-tier seats in Candlestick Park, having watched from field level the Giants and A's (including Rickey Henderson and Mark McGwire) take batting practice. Then the entire stadium began to sway from side to side as if on wheels, like a carnival ride. The low rumbling and massive rocking were not unpleasant; in fact, they inspired awe. They lasted long enough for me to make eye contact with the woman sitting in front of me, who, it turned out, was watching over her shoulder for her husband who had gone for a hot dog. We exchanged a glance that said "What are we supposed to do?" and I heard myself reply out loud, "There is not a thing we can do except ride it out." Almost everybody I could see was surprisingly calm.

When the earthquake reached a crescendo and abruptly stopped, the normal psychic barriers dropped and virtually everyone was talking to strangers as if they were old friends. We had been through a common, if brief, trial. We did not first admire one another's courage and then decide on solidarity; we had been literally thrown together by chance, given some communion as a gift without a giver. The sense of human smallness and dependence before natural phenomena was palpable, and this seemed to explain the lack of general panic. One is most afraid when one's fate is at least partly under one's control. If I can act, I might fail. Against an ongoing 7.2 earthquake in the middle of a crowded stadium, in contrast, there is nothing to be done. Wonder is then the overriding emotion, rather than fear. Those near an exit no doubt felt anxiety, but my companions and I were many rows in and so mainly exhilarated. Exhilarated, that is, until we saw in the distance the plume of smoke rising over San Francisco.

After the game was called off and we made our way back to the parking lot, the full extent of the devastation began to be known. People with radios reported that the Bay Bridge was down, and one couple with a mini-TV showed us pictures of the Marina District in ruins. Clearly there had been loss of human life, and suddenly a "noumenal experience" turned sour in my mouth. The quake of '89 had a terrible natural beauty, which I will always remember, but it was a human calamity. The release of seismic pressure along the Loma Prieta fault spelled disaster and death for many people, and the tectonics involved seemed a manifestly amoral system, something devoid of ethical value however physically powerful. Human ideals, including justice and compassion for suffering, seemed fragile yet essential reeds in a contingent and often dangerous world. The subsequent television image of a tired and confused Joe DiMaggio, waiting in line to see if his Marina home was still standing, has ever since summed up for me the sheer arbitrariness of material fortune. Earthquakes are no respecters of persons.

A second notable experience, this time involving an animal, had come some ten years previously. Walking dully along Temple Street in New Haven, one March day in 1979, I awoke from a rationalist's dream. I heard from over my right shoulder the screeching of tires, then a loud "Thump!" followed by horrific howling. I turned to see a beautiful black Labrador retriever staggering along the side of the road with blood dripping from its nose and mouth. It was instantly clear, to me and the other pedestrians transfixed on the sidewalk, that this dog was doomed. Its internal injuries from being hit by the car, which did not stop, were so severe that nothing could be done. It was only a matter of time . . .

and time seemed to clot more and more slowly with each high-pitched "Yelp!" from the beast. It obviously did not know how to die, because it came up to two of us in front of Timothy Dwight College and seemed to look imploringly into our eyes for some sort of explanation. I suddenly felt the need to beg pardon.

Partly inspired by Kant's speculation that animal subjectivity is "less even than a dream," I had just two months before written a graduate seminar paper arguing that animals don't feel morally significant pain. Since meaningful pain requires the ability to be self-conscious, to know oneself as the ongoing subject of intentions and sensations across time, I reasoned, no sub-human brute can technically be said to suffer. Aversive behavior is best seen on the model of stimulus-response, I concluded, and our concern not to "harm" animals is best accounted for in aesthetic or prudential categories rather than strictly ethical ones. How can one wrongly injure what is not fully sentient or personal? Now, confronted by the Lab's agony, I saw how absurdly callous and callow this opinion was. I did not go through any elaborate process of reasoning; I simply felt for the dying dog so obviously in pain and so needlessly undone. As it slumped down in a patch of grass, I was touched by its misery and viscerally ashamed of myself.

Several emotions overtook me, made more powerful by my inability to act on them. I wanted to apologize to the dog for the hit and run driver, as well as for my own moral stupidity. I wanted to upbraid God, in whom I was not sure I believed, for making creatures so vulnerable and people so careless. Throughout it all, I kept saying to myself, "I am watching my own death. There is no reason why this should not be me, and one day it *will* be." This reaction was akin to a Rortian "solidarity with fellow sufferers,"[1] but, to my vast surprise, with a difference. For out of nowhere but immediately everywhere, I intuited an infinitely loving Presence watching and upholding us all. I seemed to hear a still, but not so small voice, intone: "Take care of my children!"

Immediately, my academic convictions about projection theory were turned on their heads: I was the created, projected personality, while the Other was the really real, the paradigmatic Person. At that moment, I could not doubt that I was addressed by a One larger than anything human or natural, individual or collective—One on whom I, the dog, the bystanders, the heedless driver, the blades of bloody grass, the very stones in the pavement utterly depended. And I knew more surely than I knew my own name that, should this One withhold for a moment its unconditional love for me and the world, we would instantly cease to exist. My own and others' stories were sustained by a Storyteller of ineff-

---

[1] See Richard Rorty, *Contingency, Irony, and Solidarity* (Cambridge: Cambridge University Press, 1989), esp. chap. 9.

able beauty and goodness. And S/He expected something of me! More accurately, I felt charged with sin, forgiven, then charged with acting as forgiven for others.

The dog finally keeled over completely, exhaled with a low rattle, and died. Here was neither a happy ending nor a fulfilled theodicy, but my life had been changed. I had no answer to "the problem of evil," but I had been given a glimpse of a Love that makes evil at once intolerable and endurable, a Love that is a goad to action yet also a remedy for sorrow. I did not begin to believe in a just God in spite of natural tragedy and human wickedness; rather, I sensed a divine anguish yet sublime resoluteness in the midst of these dark realities. I did not begin to have faith in personal immortality in spite of physical death; rather, I was temporarily delivered from the overwhelming worry that death renders life pointless.

Over nineteen years after the fact, it is no more yet no less possible to construe the Temple Street "visitation" as illusory. But whether one speaks with Teresa of Avila of "a divine locution" or with Ebenezer Scrooge of "an undigested bit of beef," I learned something that day that I now connect with the events in Candlestick Park a decade later. From the black Lab, I learned that strong agapists can and should love the creatures of the world for their own sakes, not merely for God's or the neighbor's or one's own. Call it "autonomous value," "intrinsicality," or whatever, nonrational life matters as such. (Even lives that *really* cannot feel pain, e.g., redwood trees, have an integrity that must be honored.) Since the 1989 earthquake, nonetheless, I have subscribed more emphatically to a metaphysical hierarchy in which the highest good remains God, and God's goodness is not reducible to the animal, vegetable, or mineral phenomena of the world—however intricate and awesome. I remain a supernaturalist who believes in a real Deity partly because of, but partly in spite of, the natural world and natural forces. The same can be said of the human world and human forces.

A stable faith begins, I am convinced, with trust in the holiness of God, experienced in the Spirit, then presumes the world at least potentially good and orderly because fashioned by a loving Creator and inhabited by creatures made in that Creator's Image. In creating and sustaining human agency, as well as the material world, God's love (*agape*) precedes both social justice and physical laws. If we try to begin with "projective nature" for a grounding of our moral values,[2] we will likely

[2] See Theodore W. Nunez's "Rolston, Lonergan, and the Intrinsic Value of Nature," *Journal of Religious Ethics* 27, no. 1 (spring 1999): 105–28; and my reply, "Ambivalences about Nature and Naturalism," in the same number. See also Jackson, "Naturalism, Formalism, and Supernaturalism: Moral Epistemology and Comparative Ethics," *Journal of Religious Ethics* 27, no. 3 (fall 1999): 477–506.

end up worshiping sex and/or death, the two strongest natural powers. When that happens, it does not matter much whether one calls oneself a "realist" or a "pragmatist," one will be a cad—or worse.

This brings me to a third instructive experience, this time involving a highly charismatic personality. On April 21, 1994, I had the good fortune to meet Tenzin Gyatso, the Fourteenth Dalai Lama. I began by saying that I welcomed the chance to talk about ethics, especially charity, with "The Buddha of Compassion"—but he immediately broke in and informed me that he does not call himself that. Although many of his followers apply the title to him, he does not use it himself, he made clear, because the phrase connotes divinity. Feeling like an obtuse novice, I nevertheless forged ahead, asking him, "If Buddhism teaches that the substantive self and its suffering are illusions (*maya*), then shouldn't the enlightened one seek to be liberated from attitudes that assume the reality of persons and their pain? Should not the Bodhisattva find deliverance from such 'virtues' as compassion for the afflicted and forgiveness for victimizers, since these imply that there are real and enduring selves that either experience distress and loss or perpetrate violence and tyranny? Indeed, are not both love and justice rather dubious notions within Mahayana Buddhism, ideas precluded by the realization of Nirvana?"

I suspected that these were standard queries for an Eastern Master, but I wanted to hear what could be said in response. Similar questions haunt the genesis of Western philosophy—how can a philosopher be a king? Why should someone who apprehends the Good reenter Plato's/Socrates' cave and again concern himself with such ephemeral things as material bodies and political relations?—yet here was a twist. Whereas the gadfly of Athens pined for self-sufficiency and permanence, I knew the refugee from Tibet to teach the interrelation and impermanence of all things. Just so, I halfway expected the Dalai Lama to say something like: "Yes, fully to escape *Samsara*, the wheel of reincarnation, is to be beyond ethics because such distinctions as right and wrong, pleasure and pain, self and others disappear into the white light of infinity." To my surprise, however, His Holiness insisted most emphatically that compassion is always a virtue, for both Buddhas and Bodhisattvas. "Because the sufferer himself thinks that his soul and its affliction are real," he explained, "the Bodhichitta takes these seriously and acts to help relieve them. It is the lived experience that touches the enlightened mind."[3]

[3] I paraphrase here, to the best of my recollection, but the Dalai Lama has published similar sentiments:

> If beings have no real existence, who is in pain? Why try to dispel suffering? Although the "I" does not truly exist, in relative truth everyone wants to avoid suffering. This is sufficient reason for dispelling the sufferings of others as well as our own. What is the use in discriminating?

As the Dalai Lama has subsequently written, true liberation makes one more sensitive to others' needs rather than less.[4] Moreover, this sensitivity is not preoccupied with the metaphysics of selfhood or even the rights of rational agents. Love is fundamental across the scale of wisdom—no one is ever above or beyond it—and in the end compassion encompasses "all other sentient beings."[5] Compassion is "unconditional, undifferentiated, and universal in scope,"[6] enfolding even the impersonal world of plants and animals. Rightly or wrongly, I took His Holiness's remarks (in conversation and later in print) to resonate with Christian accounts of *agape*. His emphasis on sentient need rather than abstract rules or philosophical theories seemed to echo Jesus' own spontaneity and iconoclasm. One need not claim a simpleminded identity for their teachings to see that both preach a message of peace and service to others that delivers auditors from fear and self-absorption. For both Christ and the Dalai Lama, compassion does not insist on reciprocity or even comprehension for a motive to give of itself. Neither figure nihilistically denies the import of pain and injustice, but each attends to the present moment and its prospects for grace and cooperation.[7] "Sufficient unto the day is the evil thereof," says Jesus (Matt. 6:34, KJV), and the joyful equanimity with which the Dalai Lama speaks makes most modern accounts of love-as-self-gratification and justice-as-rational-self-interest seem otiose.

My Christian faith, as well as my experience of the Loving Presence with the black Lab, move me to see the source of charity as both personal and supernatural; here I part company with most Buddhists, including Tenzin Gyatso. All three experiences described above suggest, nonetheless, that both nature and culture, both the impersonal and the personal, depend on love to guide them and give them content. I am as much a fan of natural beauty, individual autonomy, and intellectual aptitude as the next person; in their places, they are real and important goods. But each is inadequate as the touchstone for virtue. "Nature is red in tooth

See *A Flash of Lightning in the Dark of Night: A Guide to the Bodhisattva's Way of Life* (Boston and London: Shambhala, 1994), p. 103.

[4] In *Ethics for the New Millennium* (New York: Riverhead, 1999), p. 124, the Dalai Lama makes the point explicitly:

When we enhance our sensitivity toward others' suffering through deliberately opening ourselves up to it, it is believed that we can gradually extend out compassion to the point where the individual feels so moved by even the subtlest suffering of others that they come to have an overwhelming sense of responsibility toward those others. This causes the one who is compassionate to dedicate themselves entirely to helping others overcome both their suffering and the causes of their suffering. In Tibetan, this ultimate level of attainment is called *nying je chenmo*, literally "great compassion."

[5] Ibid., p. 123.
[6] Ibid.
[7] See, for instance, ibid., pp. 125 and 45.

and claw" (Tennyson); self-governance without a standard beyond consistency is hollow; and reason divorced from substantive sympathies becomes instrumental manipulation. Without love, one forgets the delicacy and neediness of all earthly life, including one's own.

In spite of the communication among von Frisch's bees, Tinbergen's gulls, and de Waal's chimpanzees, animals are comparatively inarticulate; in spite of the lapses of communication identified with Baron Munchausen, Calvin Coolidge, and Yogi Berra, undamaged people are more or less capable of informative conversation; yet these facts ought not occasion an invidious contrast between those beings possessing moral worth and those not. The difference is one of degree.[8] More to the point, moral subjects do not require rational objects, any more than those subjects can take their primary lead from the nonrational. Moral subjects often care for the prerational, postrational, or nonrational, and the bestowal of love is not premised on a calculating justice in which one consciously agrees to a tit for tat. Otherwise, those who love would give nothing to animals, infants, retarded adults, and future generations. Such an evasion of care would eventually mean the end of all human infants and adults, as well as of most domesticated animals.

The *logos* of love can address, to their benefit, all manner of "beast" and "human," and some form of "care" must precede any individual of any sentient species. (Christians believe that the creative Word of God called even the mute minerals into being.) Thus personal autonomy and rationality are not the only goods; if we make freedom or self-consciousness our exclusive moral priority, we will refuse divine grace and ignore those creaturely needs and potentials that have nothing to do with "personhood." When the precarious unity of all life is lost sight of, it does not matter much whether one calls oneself a "Christian" or a "Buddhist," one will be a clod—or worse. Or so I will argue in these pages.

This book is the companion volume to my *Love Disconsoled: Meditations on Christian Charity* (Cambridge, 1999). I dedicate this work to my

---

[8] The most touching form of nonverbal communication, by an animal, of which I am aware is reported by Dian Fossey. She recounts how Coco, a young mountain gorilla brought into Fossey's camp after her (Coco's) entire family was killed by poachers, "began to sob and shed actual tears" upon gazing out at her former mountain home. The story is quoted in Frans de Waal's *Good Natured: The Origins of Right and Wrong in Humans and Other Animals* (Cambridge, Mass.: Harvard University Press, 1996), p. 228, n. 19. De Waal admits "profound skepticism" concerning the "tears"—could they have been due to "excessive perspiration" (p. 227)?—but he relates the account nevertheless out of respect for Fossey's powers of observation. Assuming the accuracy of Fossey's characterization, one imagines that Coco's tears would have been intelligible to both humans and other gorillas. De Waal himself tells a number of stories that suggest the reality of "empathy" among apes (e.g., pp. 19–20 and 56–57).

parents, James P. and Katherine G. Jackson. I am most grateful for the priority of their loves. Special acknowledgment is owed to several others: Grace Ascue, Robert Audi, Michael Baxter, Michael Berger, Elizabeth Bounds, David Bromwich, Irene Browne, Terence Cuneo, Malcolm Diamond (RIP), Nancy Eiesland, Jean Bethke Elshtain, Margaret Farley, Robert Fogelin, Nicholas Fotion, Sarah Freeman, Hans Frei (RIP), Jon Gunnemann, Vigen Guroian, James Gustafson, Stanley Hauerwas, Richard Hays, Jennifer Herdt, Carol Holbert, Paul Holmer, Kevin Jackson, Mary Jackson, Luke Johnson, Cathy Kaveny, John Kelsay, David Kelsey, Robert McCauley, Gilbert Meilaender, Thomas Nagel, Carol Newsom, Gene Outka, Michael Perry, Jean Porter, Wayne Proudfoot, Paul Ramsey (RIP), Inger Ravn, Jock Reeder, Tanya Sudia Robinson, Richard Rorty, Maura Ryan, Edmund Santurri, Thomas Söderqvist, Jeffrey Stout, Steve Strange, John Taylor, Steven Tipton, Sumner Twiss, Paul Weithman, Jonathan Wells, Lucy Wells, Rulon Wells, William Werpehowski, Cornel West, Sondra Wheeler, Todd Whitmore, Steve Wilson, John Witte, Nicholas Wolterstorff, Diane Yeager, and Lee Yearley. Each of these teachers, colleagues, family-members, and friends commented on significant portions of the manuscript and/or shaped central provinces of my soul.

The undergraduate, divinity, and doctoral students who have influenced my thinking over the years are too numerous to name in full, but explicit recognition is due to the Stanford "Sons of *Agape*," who helped me better understand God's grace over Monday-night Bible study and Thursday-night poker: Andrew Cuneo, Bruce Huber, William Inboden, Brian Lee, C. E. Smith, Terry Taylor, and Bailey White.

I also wish to thank for their generous support The Center of Theological Inquiry in Princeton, New Jersey, and The Whitney Humanities Center at Yale University. I spent part of a semester at the former in 1989, and a full year's leave at the latter in 1992–93. During both periods, I worked on the literature of Christian charity and social justice; during both periods, I came to appreciate a very rare scholarly community.

Shorter versions of two chapters in this volume have been published elsewhere. Chapter 2 originally appeared in *Faith and Philosophy* 12, no. 3 (July 1995): 393–408; while chapter 3 was first printed in *The Love Commandments: Agape and Moral Philosophy*, ed. by Edmund Santurri and William Werpehowski (Washington, D.C.: Georgetown University Press, 1992). Much of the autobiographical portion of this preface was initially published in my "Ambivalences about Nature and Naturalism: A Supernaturalist Response to Theodore W. Nunez," *Journal of Religious Ethics* 27, no.1 (spring 1999): 137–44.

I am indebted to the senior fellows of The Center for the Interdisciplinary Study of Religion at Emory University for their critical reading of portions of my text. The Center is supported by The Pew Charitable

Trusts, to which I am also grateful. (The opinions expressed in this book are those of the author, of course, and do not necessarily reflect the views of either my colleagues or The Pew Charitable Trusts.) Finally, I wish to register my gratitude to The McCormick Art Museum of Princeton University for permitting me to reproduce Hieronymus Bosch's "Christ before Pilate," both within chapter 4 and on the cover of this volume.

The Priority of Love

INTRODUCTION
The Fate of Charity

And now faith, hope, and love abide, these three;
and the greatest of these is love.
—1 Corinthians 13:13[1]

THE ECLIPSE OF CHRISTIAN CHARITY

Saint Paul put love first among the enduring virtues, and love has had a central place in much subsequent Christian ethics.[2] Paul's words in 1 Corinthians did not announce a moral departure; Jesus himself had summarized the Mosaic Law and Hebrew prophets in terms of the two primary commandments to love God and neighbor (Matt. 22:37–40; Mark 12:28–31; Luke 10:25–28). No end of ink, sweat, tears, and blood has since been spilled in trying to fathom what, concretely, love demands of individuals and groups. Nonetheless, for all this, the distinctive *priority* of the virtue has not always been clear in the Christian ethical tradition. Hence the two key questions for this book: First, what does it mean to call love of God "the *greatest* and *first* commandment" (Matt. 22:38), or to call love simpliciter "the *greatest* of these" (1 Cor. 13:13)? Second, how does love's primacy relate to other human values, within and without the Christian church, often associated with love? For both Jesus and Paul, love is intimately related to openness to self-sacrifice, to take a controversial example, yet several influences have combined in this century to give self-sacrifice a bad name. "Love" continues to permeate culture, high and low, but the word signifies very different things (from erotism to friendship to altruism) to very diverse people.

My concern, then, is with the preeminently commanded Christian excellence, what *New Testament* Greek calls *agape* and I will frequently

---

[1] Unless otherwise noted, all biblical quotations are from *The New Oxford Annotated Bible with the Apocrypha*, New Revised Standard Version (NRSV), ed. by Bruce M. Metzger and Roland E. Murphy (Oxford: Oxford University Press, 1991). I do occasionally cite the Revised Standard Version (RSV), the King James Version (KJV), and the New International Version (NIV), when these translations are preferable for my purposes.

[2] Edward Collins Vacek, S.J., holds that "love has *not* been central in most Christian ethics and dogmatic theology." See Vacek, *Love, Human and Divine: The Heart of Christian Ethics* (Washington, D.C.: Georgetown University Press, 1994), p. xiii. Stanley Hauerwas and Richard Hays, in contrast, have taken exception to what they perceive as the *overemphasis* on love in Christian moral reflection. I respond to Hauerwas and Hays in the third section of this introduction.

refer to as "charity," "neighbor-love," or simply "love."[3] *Agape* resonates with a number of non-Christian virtues, from Stoic *misericordia* to Buddhist *mahakaruna*, but it remains distinctive and assigning it priority may even appear paradoxical. One paradox, Christianly understood, is this: all human beings are created for agapic love, to give it and receive it, to be fulfilled by it as first virtue, yet much of human life is unloved and unloving. Pauline sensibilities seem not to abide with us. Of course, even first-century Christians did not always embody the radical teachings of Jesus, and the twentieth century was not monolithic in its rejection of a costly benevolence.[4] (One thinks of Bonhoeffer, King, and Mother Teresa from the West; Gandhi and the Dalai Lama from the East.) But the robust ideal of love is largely alien to our elites and their public discourse. Once connoting an unconditional love of neighbor binding on all, the word "charity" is now commonly construed to mean supererogatory philanthropy, optional almsgiving. Traditional versions of "taking up the cross" or "sharing patiently in affliction" tend to be rejected as impossible (thus dispiriting) ideals or reviled as fanatical (even masochistic) compulsions. At a minimum, an individual ethic of health and prudential adjustment and a political ethos of autonomy and procedural justice are strong competitors with a more ancient ideal of personal compassion and social solidarity. "Self-realization" vies with "saintliness," the two no longer being equated.

What accounts for the relative eclipse of charity, even at times within the confessing Christian community? The norm of suffering love has always had its detractors—Jesus went to the cross, after all—but Nietzsche's late-nineteenth-century charge that Christianity is inspired by *ressentiment* was a watershed. For Nietzsche, self-assertion rather than self-denial was the principle most to be extolled. Freud sounded similar themes early in the twentieth century by characterizing *agape* as basically unjust and deluded, although he offset Nietzsche's aestheticism somewhat by accenting distinctively ethical concerns (e.g., social justice).[5]

---

[3] I use "charity," "love," "personal care," "loving care," and *agape* more or less interchangeably, as I make clear below.

[4] Vacek has maintained that love should not be equated with either beneficence, doing good deeds, or benevolence, which he defines as the disposition to do such deeds. He reminds us (1) that one might assist another with an ulterior, even an insidious, motive and thus not embody benevolence as a trait of character, and (2) that one might love others (e.g., a statue or deceased parents) without being able or even disposed to care for their needs (see *Love, Human and Divine*, pp. 35–36). I interpret benevolence more broadly, however, as consistently willing another's good, whatever that entails: not a mere abstract well-wishing but an emotional engagement, not an intrusive agenda but an ever-attentive commitment. Thus I associate it with agapic love.

[5] See Sigmund Freud, *Civilization and Its Discontents*, trans. and ed. by James Strachey (New York: W. W. Norton, 1961), esp. chaps. III and IV.

Both men doubted what Nietzsche called "the value of the 'unegoistic,'"[6] and both built on Machiavelli's critique of the ideal of personal innocence as inevitably leading to social impotence. Although there are significant differences between them, both Nietzsche and Freud sought, in sum, to dethrone *agape* and give priority to some variant of controlled erotic instinct.

Other, less purely textual, factors might be cited. The Nazi Holocaust seared the conscience of an era with what many perceived as Christian and Jewish passivity before a radical, altogether worldly, evil. Recently some feminists have been wary of any moral outlook, religious or secular, that recommends a forgiving mildness, much less self-abnegation. Such qualities are frequently thought to retard personal development and reinforce political oppression. They may even be lethal. Carol Gilligan is eloquent and representative when she writes:

> The notion that virtue for women lies in self-sacrifice has complicated the course of women's development by pitting the moral issue of goodness against the adult questions of responsibility and choice. In addition, the ethic of self-sacrifice is directly in conflict with the concept of rights that has, in the past century, supported women's claim to a fair share of social justice.[7]

In light of such earnest concerns, it is difficult indeed to praise the charisma of goodness as self-giving. In the extreme, it may seem that will to power and political competition define us most deeply after all. Neither postmodernism nor a too wary feminism is the main cause of charity's decline, however. For all their rhetorical power and influence, Nietzsche and Freud represent a more flamboyant rejection of the ideals of obedience to God and love of neighbor than is evident in Western popular culture.[8] I have responded elsewhere to Nietzsche and Freud, as

[6] Friedrich Nietzsche, *The Genealogy of Morals*, preface, sec. 5, in *Basic Writings*, ed. and trans. by Walter Kaufmann (New York: Modern Library, 1968), p. 455.

[7] Gilligan, *In a Different Voice* (Cambridge, Mass.: Harvard University Press, 1982), p. 132. On Christian calls for self-sacrifice as reinforcing female "guilt," see Mary Daly, *Pure Lust: Elemental Feminist Philosophy* (San Francisco: HarperSanFrancisco, 1984), pp. 213–16. For a summary of some of the theological literature, see Barbara Hilkert Andolsen, "*Agape* in Feminist Ethics," in *Feminist Theological Ethics*, ed. by Lois K. Daly (Louisville: Westminster/John Knox, 1994). Andolsen's thesis is succinctly stated: "*Agape* defined exclusively as other-regard or self-sacrifice is not an appropriate virtue for women who are prone to excessive selflessness" (p. 151). It should be clear that my definition of *agape* is not so "exclusive."

[8] The extent to which U.S. society has been secularized is hotly contested, and there is no doubt some slippage between theoretical self-image and practical reality. Nonetheless, two statistics are often cited as representative of current commitments: over 90 percent of Americans claim to believe in God, and over 70 percent claim to participate in or give to charitable organizations. On the difficulty of interpreting American religious practices, see

well as to such talented scions as Michel Foucault and Richard Rorty,[9] but the eclipse of charity is not to be traced primarily to these authors. They stand too completely outside the Judeo-Christian[10] tradition to be responsible for any basic loss of inspiration.

For its part, the best of feminism, Christian and non-Christian, looks to women's lives and relationships for models of nurturing care that are stifled in patriarchal society. Here something like *agape* is retrieved as an ideal instead of abandoned. Admittedly, many Christian feminists are reluctant to extol self-sacrifice as at the heart of Jesus' gospel, lest this encourage victims of injustice to accept their lot or traditionally self-effacing groups to stifle their moral agency. The good news is most fundamentally about joy and fulfillment, they maintain, rather than self-denial. Gail O'Day, for instance, finds good exegetical grounds for avoiding talk of "sacrifice":

> The love to which Jesus summons the community [in John] is not the giving *up* of one's life, but the giving *away* of one's life. The distinction between these prepositions is important, because the love that Jesus embodies is grace, not sacrifice. Jesus gave his life to his disciples as an expression of the fullness of his relationship with God and of God's love for the world. Jesus' death in love, therefore, was not an act of self-denial, but an act of fullness, of living out his life and identity fully, even when that living out would ultimately lead to death.[11]

This is an eloquent reminder, first, that Jesus is not willing death for its own sake, and, second, that his Passion is a gift to others given out of strength rather than a flight from himself indulged in weakness. Death on the cross is a precious fruit of his inspired personality, not its thwarting. That said, however, an additional word of caution—or is it closer to abandon?—is in order.

For all the redemptive power and uncanny resolution behind Jesus' crucifixion, it still represents the acceptance of real vulnerability and loss. Though sinless, he experiences dread before the prospect of a shameful and agonizing death, and he even asks the Father, "if it is possible, let this cup pass from me" (Matt. 26:39). The Gospel of John has Jesus say

---

the "Survey of U.S. Church Attendance," *American Sociological Review* 63, no. 1 (February 1998); and Robert Wuthnow, *Learning to Care* (Oxford: Oxford University Press, 1995).

[9] See my *Love Disconsoled: Meditations on Christian Charity* (Cambridge: Cambridge University Press, 1999), esp. chap. 3.

[10] Some object that the adjective "Judeo-Christian" is misleading or triumphalist, but the common biblical wellspring in the love of God (*ḥésed*) makes the term sufficiently comprehensible, I believe, when used with discretion.

[11] O'Day, "The Gospel of John," in *The New Interpreter's Bible*, vol. 9, ed. by Leander Keck (Nashville: Abingdon, 1995), p. 734.

from the cross the wondrously self-possessed, "It is finished" (19:30), but Matthew has him cry out the pathos-filled, "My God, my God, why have you forsaken me?" (27:46). We must not lose sight of either dimension of the Messiah, the divine or the human. Only a dualistic Socrates lets the body go without regret, and only a docetic Christ is beyond pain and suffering. Although Jesus' death is a revelation of his steadfast love and a fulfillment of God's saving purpose, it also comes at a cost that must be knowingly embraced.[12]

Far from being masochistic, agapic love of God and neighbor is what we were made for, according to Scripture; but far from being synonymous with either *eros* or prudence, such love is not premised on temporal merit or motivated by temporal reward. "Reward" is spoken of by the *New Testament* Jesus as a *result* of virtue, but it is usually "in heaven" and seldom the primary *motivation* for keeping a commandment.[13] Nor does virtue depend on human will-power alone: "not my will but yours [God] be done" (Luke 22:42). The thought that virtue is commanded by a supernatural power is, at best, ticklish for postmoderns. But Christians hold that when *agape* is commanded, however irksome the gesture, this empowers rather than retards spiritual health, rather like a doctor ordering a patient to exercise. To be commanded by God and to keep a commandment of God is to have an intimate relation with God.[14] Moreover, to be related to God in love is invariably to come into loving relation with oneself and others. We can even love our enemies (Matt. 5:44; Luke 6:27–28) because, being forgiven by God in Christ, we can forgive ourselves.

Even when self-directed, forgiveness is a form of sacrifice (chapter 4), since one is refusing a just claim that might otherwise be pressed. But all self-sacrifice must be voluntary and constructive, as charitable feminists contend. If it is to remain an expression of *agape*, sacrifice cannot be the upshot of coercion, masochism, or mere profligacy. In the best of feminism, nonetheless, loving concern, including empathy with and effort to

[12] O'Day is well aware of this, and she fittingly employs the more conventional language of sacrifice at times: "the threat of martyrdom will present the disciples with the same situation that Jesus faced: the giving up of one's life for one's friends ([John] 15:13; cf. 10:11, 15, 17)." See ibid., p. 766.

[13] References to "reward" are overwhelmingly Matthean: the Greek noun (*misthos*) occurs nine times in Matthew, with the Greek verb (*apodidomi*) appearing three times; no other canonical Gospel uses the verb "to reward," and the noun appears only once in Mark and only twice in Luke. The author of the Gospel of Matthew is unknown, but she or he may have used sayings collected by the apostle Matthew. If so, given Matthew's original métier (tax collector), we should not be surprised by the more frequent use of language of payment and exchange.

[14] As O'Day makes clear; see her commentary on "The Gospel of John," esp. pp. 732–33.

abolish suffering, is upheld and clarified as a human (and divine) ideal.[15] "Postmodernism" is a crude label for a symptom rather than a disease, in short, and the deepest insights of feminism are decidedly part of the solution to love's eclipse rather than the problem.

The contemporary fate of charity was sealed not so much by direct attacks on agapic love itself as by ill-considered defenses of three related virtues: prudence, freedom, and justice. (These defenses have been offered both by Christians and by those who see themselves as secular heirs to the Christian moral tradition.) Prudence, defined as healthy attention to one's peace and future prosperity; freedom, defined as absence of arbitrary or coercive external restraint; and justice, defined as keeping contracts civilly and distributing basic goods based on merit, all have their place. Indeed, it is the chief glory of liberal democracy to have deployed the language of "rights and duties" in an effort to safeguard these three essentials. But neither prudence, nor freedom, nor justice alone can do the work of agapic love, and in the absence of such love, all three of these other goods wither. When exponents of other virtues suggest (explicitly or implicitly) that they can *supplant* charity in some quarter of life, they cut morality's root in all quarters.[16] Yet when either exponents or opponents of *agape* argue that it is "*directly in conflict*" with rights and duties, or with social justice generally, they pluck morality's modern flower.[17]

---

[15] See, among Christian theologians, Dorothee Soelle, *Suffering* (Philadelphia: Fortress, 1975); and Lisa Sowle Cahill, *Sex, Gender, and Christian Ethics* (Cambridge: Cambridge University Press, 1996), esp. chap. 6. Among works by secular philosophers, Eva Feder Kittay's *Love's Labor: Essays on Women, Equality, and Dependency* (New York and London: Routledge, 1999) is especially insightful on the place of vulnerability and service in human life: rather than assuming the equality of autonomous individuals, she emphasizes that "no one escapes dependency in a lifetime, and many must care for dependents in the course of a life" (p. xiii). Nel Noddings's *Caring: A Feminine Approach to Ethics and Moral Education* (Berkeley: University of California Press, 1984) offers an ethic based on natural tenderness and maternal nurture that is in some respects similar to putting charity first. Noddings is highly doubtful, however, of the language of "self-sacrifice" (p. 99), and she declines to call her position "agapism," even as she rejects "the notion of universal love" as "a source of distraction" (pp. 28–29). For criticisms of a gender dualism found by some in both Noddings and Carol Gilligan, see *An Ethic of Care: Feminist and Interdisciplinary Perspectives*, ed. by Mary Jeanne Larrabee (New York and London: Routledge, 1993). For her part, Kittay maintains that, at present, "it is mostly women who are dependency workers" but "there is nothing inherently gendered about the work of care" (p. xiii).

[16] Various feminists have provided powerful analyses of the limits of justice in particular. See, e.g., Iris Marion Young, *Justice and the Politics of Difference* (Princeton: Princeton University Press, 1990), esp. chap. 1; and Agnes Heller, *Beyond Justice* (Oxford: Basil Blackwell, 1987). Heller argues that "all claims to justice are rooted in certain values other than justice itself—namely, in 'freedom' and 'life'" and that "while justice may well be a precondition of the good life, the good life is something beyond justice" (p. v). As indebted as I am to Heller, her central focus on rational freedom is alien to strong *agape*, as defined below.

[17] Stanley Hauerwas has written that "the current emphasis on justice and rights as the

Consider two prominent cases. John Rawls has claimed that justice is "the first virtue of social institutions, as truth is of systems of thought."[18] Susan Moller Okin has defended this thesis, explaining that "justice takes primacy because it is the most *essential*, not because it is the *highest*, of virtues."[19] For Okin, generosity and the other higher moral sentiments are forms of "supererogation," while "justice is needed as the primary, meaning most fundamental, moral virtue *even* in social groupings [such as the family] in which aims are largely common and affection frequently prevails."[20] Okin's views are especially surprising in light of her own observation that "contemporary theorists of justice, with few exceptions, have paid little or no attention to the question of moral development—of how we are to *become* just."[21] If the most fundamental virtue is that which is most indispensable to the growth of moral persons, however, it seems clear that (agapic) love is prior to justice. For moral persons only evolve over time and with a good deal of "parental" care that is not premised on the reciprocity characteristic of justice. Our adult capacity for balancing competing interests and for keeping valid contracts comes only after our unconditional nurturance by others while we are weak and dependent children, incapable of either stating our interests or entering into binding agreements.

Empathy, defined as "the capacity . . . to see things from the perspective of others," is indeed "crucial for a sense of justice," as Okin suggests,[22] but empathy is more akin to the necessary condition for justice than to justice itself. Better put, empathy and compassion are required to direct the neutrality (the "blindness") of justice; true empathy does not merely apprehend what others feel or need, it affirms and acts on these conditions for the others' sake. In short, fair play within the economies typical

---

primary norms guiding the social witness of Christians is in fact a mistake." See his *After Christendom?* (Nashville: Abingdon, 1991), p. 45. Given the qualifying adjective "primary," this claim resonates well with my theses about the priority of agapic love in Christian ethics. At times, however, Hauerwas goes further and seems to suggest that Christians should see liberal democratic accounts of justice, perhaps *any* account that refers to reciprocity or contract, as *antithetical* to Christianity—as when he subtitles *After Christendom? How the Church Is to Behave if Freedom, Justice, and a Christian Nation Are Bad Ideas.* A dualistic opposition between love and justice, the language of *agape* and that of "rights," is very far from what I have in mind. Again, reciprocal justice cannot simply replace agapic love, and there can even be tensions between them; but once the priority of that love is recognized, it allows the best modern appeals to prudence, freedom, and justice to find their limited yet proper place.

[18] Rawls, *A Theory of Justice* (Cambridge, Mass.: Harvard University Press, 1971), p. 3.

[19] Okin, *Justice, Gender, and the Family* (New York: Basic, 1989), p. 28.

[20] Ibid., p. 29.

[21] Ibid., p. 21.

[22] Ibid.

of justice depends on love as the unconditional willing of the good for would-be players, rather than the other way around.[23]

Ironically, nineteenth- and twentieth-century champions of prudence, freedom, and justice have done such an able job that the stage is now set for a corrective: a critical defense of the priority of love, defined as *agape*'s primacy among divine gifts and human goods. A fatal misunderstanding must be preempted at the outset, however. I offer here a defense of the "priority of love," but the "love" in question (*agape*) must not be identified with any purely human achievement or even with any strictly human aspiration. My case is mounted in terms both contrasted with and borrowed from Occidental philosophy,[24] but my starting point is decisively theological.[25] The key to love is provided by neither the cosmos as a whole nor human nature in particular, but rather by God's supernatural holiness. God *is* love (1 John 4:8), and we are dependent on God's gracious self-revelation for a rudimentary understanding of and participation in this Goodness. Since God is the Creator of all that is, God's loving nature cannot be totally alien to—much less contradictory of—creatures, especially those made in the divine Image. But to seek to ground an account of agapic love in the rhythms of the material universe or the recesses of the human heart is to travel down the now dead-end of immanence. Or so I have argued elsewhere.[26]

Natural processes are too arbitrary and amoral to be the chief inspiration for virtue, and human instincts are too frail and fallible. Naturalism runs aground on the devastation and ugliness left behind by earthquakes

---

[23] The inspiration behind Okin's position is her understandable insistence that "intimate" associations like the family not fall below justice even while claiming to rise majestically above it. Her discussion of the "legal fiction" of coverture—whereby upon marriage a wife's property, children, and legal rights became her husband's—is a devastating indictment of marriage law in the eighteenth century, and beyond (see ibid., pp. 30–31). Moreover, Okin is surely correct to contend that love and justice are not simply at odds. But it seems best to say that love is not independent of justice or that love must not be guilty of injustice, rather than that justice has "moral primacy" (p. 32). Again, *because* human beings only emerge as agents by virtue of being shown a gratuitous care, agapic love has chronological priority; and because a harmony that is without scarcity and conflict is our highest ideal, agapic love also has moral priority.

[24] Perhaps the most magisterial recent effort to fathom love's mysteries, philosophically, is Irving Singer's three-volume *The Nature of Love* (Chicago: University of Chicago Press, 1984–87). My uses of the words "appraisal" and "bestowal" (and their variants) in this introduction and throughout this book are adapted from Singer's first volume, *Plato to Luther* (1984).

[25] My debt to Anders Nygren is considerable; see his *Agape and Eros*, originally published in three volumes in the 1930s, trans. by Philip S. Watson (New York: Harper and Row, 1969).

[26] See my "Ambivalences About Nature and Naturalism: A Supernaturalist Response to Theodore W. Nunez"; "Naturalism, Formalism, and Supernaturalism: Moral Epistemology and Comparative Ethics"; as well as the preface to this volume.

and diseases, for instance, while a reliance on human personality alone comes to smash on guilt and mortality. Love often comes to us sinners unsought, and, in any case, we did not create our own natures. (Whether we were created by God or are the result of blind chance is, of course, the subject of continued debate.)[27] Kant turned to noumenal agency to escape the amorality of a purely phenomenal world of Newtonian mechanism—How is moral responsibility possible in an apparently necessitated universe?—and he memorably associated human dignity with "the moral law within." (Whether Kant is best seen as discovering dignity or as constructing it is also much disputed.) But Kant struggled with the radicality of human evil and the poverty of an ethic of consistency alone. He never could cope, I believe, with a thoroughgoing fanatic who regularly rejects his own and others' (putative) dignity. The *New Testament* maintains, at any rate, that self-reliance is not enough: a supernatural gift is called for if human beings are to practice charity. Conversion from above is the one thing needful, not analysis of the external world or introspection of one's internal powers.

As von Balthasar has observed, God's *agape* liberates the world, but it comes originally as scandal and indictment. As the fullest disclosure of

[27] Two accessible defenses of the latter, neo-Darwinian alternative are Richard Dawkins's *The Blind Watchmaker: Why the Evidence of Evolution Reveals a Universe Without Design* (New York and London: W. W. Norton, 1987) and Daniel C. Dennett's *Darwin's Dangerous Idea: Evolution and the Meaning of Life* (New York: Simon and Schuster, 1995). Dawkins' and Dennett's books are too complicated to respond to in detail here, but they seem entirely successful in establishing two things: that variation occurs within individual species and that speciation occurs across species over time. The causal mechanism at work, however—the how behind these empirical thats—remains debatable. The issue, as Dennett emphasizes, is whether Mind can be understood as an effect rather than a First Cause, as the result of purposeless forces rather than their antecedent author (*Darwin's Dangerous Idea*, p. 66). Evolution by natural selection *may* be the sole cause of human origins, in which case Christian theism is false, but random mutation as an ingredient in explaining how "descent with modification" has led to present-day complexity and diversity seems a nonstarter. Coupling random mutation with natural selection does no better, since the latter idea is notoriously hard to define without circularity. For their part, both Dawkins and Dennett charge that the theistic appeal to an intelligent Creator is vacuous. As Dawkins puts it, "To explain the origin of the DNA/protein machine by invoking a supernatural Designer is to explain precisely nothing, for it leaves unexplained the origin of the Designer" (*The Blind Watchmaker*, p. 141). One wonders if Dawkins quite appreciates the point of referring to God as a transcendent, necessary Being, but, as I say, the debate continues. Theists will begin with their supernaturalist premise (a loving God) and reason *to* design, while Darwinians will begin with their naturalist premise (random mutation plus natural selection) and reason to *no* design, at least no intentional design. For critiques of neo-Darwinism, see Phillip E. Johnson's *Darwin on Trial* (Washington, D.C.: Regnery Gateway, 1991) and Jonathan Wells's *Icons of Evolution: Science or Myth?* (Washington, D.C.: Regnery Gateway, 2000). For an interesting discussion of love in relation to evolutionary biology, see Stephen J. Pope, *The Evolution of Altruism and the Ordering of Love* (Washington, D.C.: Georgetown University Press, 1994), esp. chaps. 4 and 5.

God's love, the cross of Christ is both pitfall and rescue. Having first cast him into the pit of dread and self-doubt, God's love

> goes in search of man in order to lift him out of the pit, free him from his bonds and place him in the freedom of the divine love that is now human as well. . . . Stumbling into the pit, [man] learns two things: that the love offered him is quite unlike anything he knows as love; and that the scandal exists in order to make him see the uniqueness of this new love—and by its light to reveal and lay bare to him his own love for what it is, lack of love.[28]

Strictly speaking, neither God nor *agape* requires an apologia, but I try to do three things in this book: to define an ethic of Christian love, to refine it through criticism of the tradition from whence it comes, and to show in detail how it differs from some significant competitors. This volume is not a systematic argument. Two of the chapters originally appeared as self-contained essays, and I have made no attempt to relate the chapters generally as steps in a single deductive line. I offer no sustained theory of *agape*, judging the subject unconducive to such treatment, but rather provide kaleidoscopic perspectives on Christian love with special reference to its relation to social justice. Social justice is a fruit of the redemption issuing from God's love, but it is not that love itself.

Throughout these pages I defend a position I call "strong *agape*." Let me elaborate on both words in the quoted phrase. When viewed interpersonally, as the conversion of human relations wrought by the grace of God, *agape* involves three basic features: (1) unconditional willing of the good for the other, (2) equal regard for the well-being of the other, and (3) passionate service open to self-sacrifice for the sake of the other. Lest the first two features seem to refer only to internal dispositions, the third puts an explicit premium on a particular action: bearing one another's burdens (cf. Gal. 6:2). The word "strong," in turn, implies that agapic love is a metavalue, that virtue without which one has no substantive access to other goods, either moral or nonmoral.[29] Other goods are genuine, so there is no question of denigrating norms of justice or of vilifying aesthetic pleasures and personal happiness. Moreover, the strong agapist does not claim the kind of self-sufficiency or invulnerability claimed by some (e.g., Socrates) who advocate a life of moral rigor. Such a claim is untrue to the social needs and ethical fragilities experienced in the flesh.[30] Nonetheless, *agape* has a unique priority; it is the necessary condi-

---

[28] Hans Urs von Balthasar, *Love Alone: The Way of Revelation* (London: Sheed and Ward, 1968), p. 60.

[29] I borrow the term "metavalue" from Gerald Doppelt, "Is Rawls's Kantian Liberalism Coherent and Defensible?" *Ethics* 99, no. 4 (July 1989): 823–24.

[30] See *Love Disconsoled*, esp. chap. 5. I argue there, in effect, that accent on the priority of agapic love must be preceded by that same love's disconsolation, lest we venerate a cruel or dogmatic sentimentality.

tion to realizing and sustaining other human values in any adequate form. As Saint Paul affirms so famously in 1 Corinthians 13:1–3,

> If I speak in the tongues of mortals and of angels, but do not have love [*agape*], I am a noisy gong or a clanging cymbal. And if I have prophetic powers, and understand all mysteries and all knowledge, and if I have all faith, so as to remove mountains, but do not have love, I am nothing. If I give away all my possessions, and if I hand over my body so that I may boast [or, to be burned], but do not have love, I gain nothing.

Note that outward actions of service and sacrifice are futile if unmotivated by love. Indeed, virtually any temporal good one can think of tends to go over into its opposite without charity, as romantic lovers who end up hating each other can attest.

My title, *The Priority of Love*, is a double entendre. On the one hand, as suggested, I argue that love is antecedent (axiologically and chronologically) to other goods in being the necessary condition for their full enjoyment. On the other hand, I argue that love has an internal *telos* or proclivity in tending to bring about caring personalities: *agape* generates itself as its first priority. *Agape* does not bestow *only* itself or aim at extirpating other passions—erotic desire is not, as such, an enemy—but charity does take precedence in persons and give precedence to developing persons. Love of others, first and foremost the Holy Other, is the chief means and end of self-realization. Self-love is compatible with or even part of *agape*, broadly construed,[31] but proper self-love comes only through self-transcendence. Self-realization comes, that is, via interpersonal service that does not look first to personal gain. We must attend to ourselves and our neighbors, but we often care best for ourselves by forgetting the ego and nurturing the other with patience. We cannot return to "the Golden Age, before mankind was burdened with sin and sorrow, and before pleasure had been darkened with those shadows that bring it into high relief, and make it happiness;"[32] but Christians, in turn, wisely decline to equate what now passes for happiness with the highest virtue.

Two More Limited Senses of "Charity"

As noted, I treat "charity" as a synonym for *agape*. In contemporary contexts, however, "charity" often means something considerably more limited: assistance to the poor, either personal generosity shown to an indigent few or socially organized philanthropy aimed at the needy more

---

[31] Here I part company with Nygren, *Agape and Eros*, p. 100ff.

[32] Nathaniel Hawthorne, *The Marble Faun*, in *The Complete Novels and Selected Tales of Nathaniel Hawthorne*, ed. by Norman Holmes Pearson (New York: Random House, 1937), p. 637.

systematically. One speaks here of "charit*ies*," referring to private institutions that distribute staples like food and clothing or that provide basic
services like health care and education. This form of charity is analogous
to medieval almsgiving. The key difference, however, is that private charity is now frequently thought admirable but morally optional—a matter
of pure supererogation—whereas Thomas Aquinas, for instance, considered almsgiving "a matter of precept."[33] Even today, when the agencies
of support are branches of local or national government, terms such as
"public aid" or "social welfare" are more likely to be used than "charity,"
and then the support is more likely to be seen as a right than as a gift.
But when aid to the unfortunate (private or public) is construed as morally optional, this represents a significant narrowing of the biblical and
medieval meanings traditionally assigned to the term "charity." However
much biblical and medieval contexts may have differed, both held that
giving assistance to the poor and afflicted was an obligatory expression of
love of neighbor, at least for Christians.

A second specific sense of charity points toward mercy or forgiveness,
that facet of *agape* that used to be called "meekness." When understood
as an act, this charity is the pardoning of another for some offense (or
pehaps the commuting of his or her punishment), the releasing of another from a debt (or at least the reduction of its amount), and so on.
When construed as a trait of character, in turn, such charity is the disposition to be patient and long-suffering. A charitable person is habitually
compassionate, showing others leniency and understanding, giving them
the benefit of the doubt, being slow to anger and quick to reconcile, and
so on. Whether an action or a virtue, this second sense of charity accents
willing the good for another in ways that go beyond strict calculation of
what is (normally) considered his or her right. Here charity fosters another's well-being beyond what is contractually required and often at real
cost to oneself. An enduring question for those who commend charity in
this sense is how it relates to justice, particularly secular or naturalistic
conceptions of it.

If justice is defined as giving persons their due (*suum cuique*, in Cicero's Latin), is charity antithetical to it, distinct from but compatible with
it, altogether unrelated to it, or somehow even identical with it? Is mercy
or forgiveness to be seen as unjust, for instance, or rather as more than
just? Does charity so eschew retaliation as to be incompatible with all
retributive justice, personal and political, or does even "meekness" at

---

[33] Aquinas, *Summa Theologiae* [1256–72], trans. by the Fathers of the English Domincan
Province (Westminster, Md.: Christian Classics/Benziger Brothers, 1981), vol. 3, II-II, Q.
32, art. 5, p. 1321. As Thomas elaborates, "we are bound to give alms of our surplus, as
also to give alms to one whose need is extreme" (ibid., p. 1322); see also *ST*, II-II, Q. 66,
art. 2.

times take up the sword to defend the innocent and rebuke the guilty? I attempt to answer these questions in detail, but this much can be said at the outset. Being the "root of all virtue," a metavalue, makes charity too important, too fundamental, to count as a (mere) duty of justice. Charity is the wellspring of rights and duties, justice, and the like, but it is not itself a right or a duty in the modern sense. *Agape* is beyond all economies of exchange, all questions of desert or contract, at least when human beings are the subjects and objects of love. Being fallen, no human being has a straightforward claim to be loved purely on his or her merits. No doubt, God deserves to be loved as a function of His supreme beauty and goodness, but we sinful folks cannot insist that we ought to be loved as a matter of justice (defined as *suum cuique*). We are loved by God, and if we are lucky by one another, via a spontaneous and long-suffering gift. God commands the giving of love to our neighbors, but such a command is not premised on the objective worthiness of human beings but rather on God's own expansive holiness and humanity's neediness and sacred potential. We love the neighbor agapically to build her up and to participate in the life of God.

WHY SHOULD LOVE, OR ANY ONE VIRTUE, HAVE PRIORITY?
The Question of Anti-essentialism

In asserting love's priority I may seem to betray the anti-essentialist spirit that leads me to literature and art (chapter 4) more readily than to abstract theories for a useable picture of the good life. Putting charity first may seem a regression to a narrow and dogmatic ethics that equates a single, rather idiosyncratic, activity with the fundamental good for all humanity. Past efforts to define a supreme, universal good have at times been beautiful and awe-inspiring, and their influence on Western civilization can hardly be overestimated. But there is an emerging consensus that the more foundationalist of these efforts have not worked out well. The trouble with the foundationalist quest for singlemindedness and purity of heart is that it tends radically to underestimate the multiplicity and uncertainty of our moral concerns; it tempts us to be insufficiently pluralistic about value and insufficiently fallibilist about knowledge.[34] It may move us, most basically, to deny the extent to which culture and the good are human creations, even if divinely inspired. Thus the putative

---

[34] For a general critique of foundationalism, see my "The Possibilities of Scepticisms: Philosophy and Theology Without Apology," *Metaphilosophy* 21, no. 4 (October 1990): 303–21. For a fine sampling of the spectrum of views on moral universalism, see Gene Outka and John P. Reeder, Jr., eds., *Prospects for a Common Morality* (Princeton: Princeton University Press, 1993).

supreme good (e.g., reason) becomes a tyrant, dominating rather than complementing other human faculties (e.g., emotion and imagination) and enticing exponents to fanaticism.[35] Why should putting charity first be any different?

The moral alternatives open to individuals are so dependent upon context, and the range of permissible options is so broad even within a given context, that putting any particular virtue or principle ahead of all others may seem an exercise in oversimplification, if not self-deception. Why not be content with individuals who are dutiful spouses and parents in the morning, ruthless politicians during the day, and carefree aesthetes at night—indviduals who make little effort to rank their several interests and activities or to integrate their public and private selves? Human lives do not run along a single set of ethical tracks, and the attempt to formulate a first principle of practical reason binding on all seems inevitably vacuous ("Good is to be sought and promoted, evil to be shunned") or stultifying ("*Semper Fidelis!*"). Why should love be the fundamental normative force—constant, apprehensible, and overriding—rather than justice or even self-assertion? Why shouldn't *agape* itself be as relative and doubtful as any other human standard? With these questions we approach the heart of the matter.

The answer I defend, a characteristically Christian answer, is that charity is a participation in the very life of God and, as such, the foundation of all virtues for those made in the Image of God. Scriptural warrants can be adduced for this answer—for example, the two great love commandments (Matt. 22:37–40), Paul's panegyric on "the greatest of these" (1 Corinthians 13) and his promise that "the God of love and peace will be with you" (2 Cor. 13:11), John's declaration that "God is love" (1 John 4:8), and so on—but in the end many evidences will tend to be autobiographical. The Bible is not self-interpreting, and there are no knockdown arguments (exegetical, empirical, or metaphysical) convincing to all. Strong agapists are those who feel themselves touched by an infinitely loving Presence that allows them to be present to others and themselves, an ineffably kind Word that echoes in the words with which they explain the world. Here is no works righteousness, to repeat, since the immediate impact of the Present Word is indictment for sin. Gratitude for the serendipitous and forgiving love of God, the *ens realissimum*, is where strong *agape* begins, rather than where it ends, both existentially and

---

[35] John Rawls considers Christian purity of heart—for example, Aquinas's subordination of all human aims to a dominant end (God)—to be irrational, even mad; see his *A Theory of Justice* (Cambridge, Mass.: Belknap/Harvard University Press, 1971), p. 554. For a response to Rawls, see my "To Bedlam and Part Way Back: John Rawls and Christian Justice," *Faith and Philosophy* 8, no. 4 (October 1991): 423–47; and "The Return of the Prodigal? Liberal Theory and Religious Pluralism," in *Religion and Contemporary Liberalism*, ed. by Paul J. Weithman (Notre Dame: University of Notre Dame Press, 1997).

logically. The God who is love simply invites and empowers a response in kind.

More prosaically, there are two reasons why strong *agape* is not undone by the anti-essentialist comments and questions rehearsed above. First, strong *agape* acknowledges a broad and complex range of traits, values, and action-guides as legitimate, even indispensable, for a well-lived life. The metaphysical comfort that comes from reducing ethical reflection to an algorithmic science, proof from uncertainty, or from vilifying certain goods (e.g., erotic gratification) because they are subject to the vicissitudes of time and chance, is resisted out of love itself. Love appreciates the plenitude and ambiguity of the world, balancing affirmation of what is believed to be worthy or sacred with resistance to what is believed to be ugly or evil. Love itself is the greatest, but not the only, good; nor can it obviate all need to choose between goods in cases of scarcity or conflict. Second, strong *agape* emphasizes *putting* charity first as personal action and disposition rather than merely *discovering* it to *be* first as human capacity and need. There is a performative aspect to love; it is productive rather than merely appraisive. One does not determine love to be the universal human good the way one might discover a dime in one's pocket. Love *makes* itself the good by enriching whomever it touches, and the egalitarian assumption that this performative capacity is shared by all persons makes love a natural ally of liberal democracy. The liberalism I have in mind, however, will be prophetic rather than bourgeois, based first on charity rather than a calculating justice (chapter 1).

Love seeks to elicit those virtues in self and others without which human flourishing is impossible; and without this eliciting, the virtues remain as unrealized as seeds that go unwatered. Love in particular is a passive potential that must be sparked from without by an initially gratuitous care. (This is the partial truth in the romantic emphasis on ethical creativity.) By awakening others' benevolence, charity makes the world valuable in ways not otherwise realizable; the interactions designed to display love are in fact necessary to produce it. Persons must be cultivated as and by lovers, and without the care extended to human beings in infancy, life itself is not possible (chapter 5). It is worth reemphasizing, even so, that the potential to be built up by love is itself an intrinsic feature of human nature that must be recognized rather than invented. For all its drive to bestow value, human charity does not create all good ex nihilo: creatures are not God.

Other Christian Foci?

Thus far, I have written as though objections to putting charity first come most potently, if not exclusively, from modern or postmodern secularists. Stanley Hauerwas and Richard Hays, both United Methodist professors at Duke Divinity School, are important exceptions to this rule. Hauerwas writes that "if Christianity is primarily an ethic of love I think that it is clearly wrong and ought to be given up, since our moral experience reveals that such an ethic is not sufficient to give form to our moral behavior."[36] Hays has recently defended both the general thesis "that no single principle can account for the unity of the New Testament writings" and the specific thesis "that the concept of love is insufficient as a ground of coherence for the New Testament moral vision."[37] These claims may seem to cut against my project, but I do not argue that (human) love alone is *sufficient* for ethics (Christian or otherwise). I suggest, instead, that the love awakened in us by God's own love has *priority* in relation to other basic values, that it is their *necessary* source and end. Other virtues are indispensable to the good life (e.g., justice), and the cross is central to the Good Book (Matt. 10:38). But agapic love, I maintain, has primacy in animating our moral characters as well as in explaining the meaning of sacrifice.

If Hauerwas and Hays confined themselves to noting that "love's not all you need," there would be no dispute. But Hauerwas allows that *emphasis* on love "is bad theology which results in bad ethics, or it is bad ethics that results in bad theology."[38] Hays does not simply reject the thesis that love is the *one and only* Christian ethical ground; he writes that "for several reasons love cannot serve as *a* focal image for the synthetic task of New Testament ethics."[39] Reading these intimations of love's eclipse, I am reminded of the quarrel between W. H. Auden and e.e. cummings over the language of songbirds. How ironic that English-speaking poets should take natural beauty as the occasion for argument; how sad that Bible-believing ethicists should take supernatural goodness as a similar occasion. Yet important issues are at stake here, and I pay my respects to colleagues in the faith by responding at some length.

Culling arguments from the two champions of "the Duke school," one finds perhaps six main challenges to the priority of love. The first three are from Hauerwas:

1. "While it is true that God in his essence is charity, love cannot be assumed as an end in itself—i.e., that love is the purpose of God's eternal will. God is not the God of love because he wills love but because he is the truth of our existence. God's identity is prior to his presence and the love we find in his presence is possi-

---

[36] Hauerwas, "Love's Not All You Need," *Cross Currents* 24 (summer 1972): 227.
[37] Hays, *The Moral Vision of the New Testament* (San Francisco: HarperCollins, 1996), p. 5.
[38] Hauerwas, "Love's Not All You Need," p. 226.
[39] Hays, *The Moral Vision of the New Testament*, p. 200; emphasis mine.

ble only because he stands for goods prior to such presence. . . .
God can come to us in love only because he comes to us as God,
the creator, sustainer, and redeemer of our existence."[40]

2. "As an ethic of love the Gospels would be an ethic at our disposal
since we could fill in the context of love by our wishes, but as a
story we cannot control it for one can tell stories only as the story
is allowed to tell itself through us."[41]

3. "Christian ethics as an ethics of love reinforces our illusions by
retreating into an ethic of interpersonal understanding and acceptance as if becoming an I to a Thou is the height of human
attainment. But ethically our life involves more than person-to-
person interaction; we exist as social creatures, and as such we
confront social problems that require not love but justice. . . .
good will is no less tyrannical than bad will in its continued control of the other."[42]

Thesis (1) is about what love is and is not; (2) is about how love is and is
not known; (3) is about what is and is not worth knowing.

When Hauerwas denies in (1) that love is "an end in itself," and then
contrasts God's "identity" with God's "presence," he is chiefly warning
us not to idolize *human* love, not to equate ethics with our own amor-
phous velleities. He is surely right when he insists that God's will that we
love him "is not love directed at *any* being, but the particular God of
Israel whose freedom is the power and the weakness, of redemption on
the cross."[43] As I emphasize in chapter 3, Christian ethicists owe Hauerwas a massive debt for bringing them back to the distinctiveness of biblical stories, in contrast to speculative moral rules or fashionable cultural
trends. But he makes too much of a good thing. When he writes, for
instance, that "Jesus comes not to tell us to love one another, but to
establish the condition that makes love possible," and that "the Gospel is
not about love, but it is about this man, Jesus Christ," he sets up misleading dichotomies.[44] To say that the meaning of love for Christians
cannot be separated from the story of Jesus is not to say that love is not
an end in itself. It is rather to say that the end of relation to Jesus is
personal knowledge of love, and vice versa. Coming to know God is a
matter of recognizing and serving a living Person, rather than of analyz-

[40] Hauerwas, "Love's Not All You Need," p. 227.
[41] Ibid., p. 228.
[42] Ibid., p. 230.
[43] Ibid., pp. 227–28.
[44] Ibid., p. 228.

ing an inanimate object or comprehending an abstract idea.[45] Hauerwas's telling point is that this process engages the whole creature in company with others and before the cross, rather than the intellect alone in contemplative isolation and before our democratic idols. One can no more relate the history of God without making some general identifications, however, than one can write a human biography without ascribing some typical traits. Properly understood, saying "Jesus is Lord" is synonymous with saying "God is love." *Agape* itself "rejoices in the truth" (1 Cor. 13:6).

Another questionable dualism is evident in Hauerwas's claim (2) about stories. Stories, like principles, can be read (self-)deceptively or enacted (self-)destructively; and even *New Testament* narratives about the Father and the Son are open-ended, requiring free participation by finite "children" for their full significance (e.g., Matt. 5:44–45; Eph. 5:1–2; and cf. Matt. 23:37–39). Although irreducibly Christocentric, the Christian story is not fixed, nor is it told exclusively by God, nor is it infallible, in so far as it is mediated by fallen creatures. One does not have to be deaf to others' stories, furthermore, or to other genres within one's own tradition, to be a faithful (re-)teller of scriptural wisdom. However unintentionally, Hauerwas leaves the impression that efforts to find common ground with other religions or constructively to employ nonconfessional arts and sciences (including the language of "rights") is apostasy. In a highly situationalist and secular age, his caveats help keep the church true to itself, but one does not have to be John Rawls to want to balance particularity and universality, or Pelagius to want to validate a measure of human freedom as responsive to divine grace.[46]

Perhaps the most troubling division set up by Hauerwas is that in (3), between love and justice. The division trades, I fear, on a distressing habit of treating perverse or indulgent versions of love as though they were the genuine articles. There are many false coins of "love" in circulation, but the task is to spot and reject them, not to devalue the treasury altogether. I have already said a good deal about love and justice above, so I will only protest here that *truly agapic* love, a love genuinely rooted in God's holiness, has priority in Christian ethics, not some manipulative or sentimental sham. Love never falls below justice, never gives less than is due, but if history has taught us anything it is that a reciprocal "justice"

---

[45] I elaborate this observation in chap. 1, associating it with the primacy of biblical theology over Hellenistic philosophy.

[46] I too have warned against undermining biblical faith by accommodating it too closely to secular reason. See Jackson, "To Bedlam and Part Way Back" and "*Prima Caritas, Inde Jus:* Why Augustinians Shouldn't Baptize John Rawls," *Journal for Peace and Justice Studies* 8, no. 2 (1997): 49–62. Yet the limits of secular reason stem largely from its misunderstanding of the meaning of love.

without love is itself volatile and destructive. To speak only of what has been earned or contracted for is to forget that we all require unconditional nurture and forgiveness. The neglect of care and mercy leads at best to dishonest social philosophy, at worst to corrosive hatred and endless vendetta.

With great rhetorical force, Hauerwas claims that "the black man [in the United States] discovered that there is no greater enemy to his people than the white liberal's attempt at loving reconciliation, for such reconciliation comes without destroying the structural racism of our society."[47] But one might hold up the Truth and Reconciliation Commission's work in South Africa as a useful contrast. As Hauerwas knows, the Commission is a courageous and highly practical effort to attend to *love, justice, and truth simultaneously*. It does not deny or ignore the structural racism of apartheid, but rather challenges its legacy out of a faith that refuses any fundamental divide between charity and veracity. To set these two at odds is to risk a cynicism in which forgiveness must always be based on dishonesty and reconciliation on connivance. Hauerwas avoids cynicism when he goes on to say, "my argument is that love, even in interpersonal relations, that is embodied without justice is sentimental and destructive rather than realistic and upbuilding."[48] This is a marked departure from his more oppositional language, however, and is quite compatible with strong *agape*.

We are left, in the end, with this thesis from Hauerwas:

> Even if love is freed from its sentimental perversions, it is still not an adequate principle, policy, or summary metaphor to capture the thrust of the Gospel for the Christian's moral behavior. Love is dependent on our prior perceptions of the truth of reality that can finally be approached only through the richness of the language and stories which form what we know. The Christian is thus better advised to resist the temptation to reduce the Gospel to a single formula or summary image for the moral life.[49]

Two comments are in order. First, Hauerwas himself comes close to announcing a single principle "to capture the thrust of the Gospel": the priority of truth, rather than the priority of love. Jesus does say, "I am the way, and the truth, and the life" (John 14:6), but he also summarizes the law and the prophets with the two love commands of Matthew 22 and fulfills the law and the prophets with the final love command of John

---

[47] Hauerwas, "Love's Not All You Need," p. 230.

[48] Ibid., p. 231. See also Hauerwas and Charles Pinches, *Christians among the Virtues* (Notre Dame: University of Notre Dame Press, 1997), pp. 85–88, where the "true love" whose name is "God" makes "forgiveness, reconciliation, and restoration" possible beyond the "either/or of blindness or revenge."

[49] Ibid., pp. 231–32.

15:12. Can there be any better testimony to the harmony of *veritas* and *caritas* than this convergence? Is it not because God so loved the world that we have the Suffering Servant about whom we share gospel truths (cf. John 3:16)? Second, to reiterate, the priority of love is not a monism that "reduces the Gospel to a single formula." Strong *agape* neither wallows in tolerant "sincerity" nor venerates "general utility."[50] There are many virtues, acts, and effects required by Scripture; and to call (human) charity a necessary condition for Christian morality is not to say it is sufficient.[51] It is slightly more accurate to think of *agape* as a "summary image" for the moral life, yet this in no way threatens the richness of the Gospel stories. The stories themselves witness to the one true God whose essential nature is love; as von Balthasar notes, "love is not just *one* of the divine attributes, any more than man's answering love is *one* of the Virtues."[52]

Let me return now to Hays and his three objections to love and its priority:

4. "At least four major New Testament witnesses—Mark, Acts, Hebrews, and Revelation—resist any attempt to synthesize their moral visions by employing love as a focal image."[53]

5. "[Love] is not really an image; rather it is an interpretation of an image."[54]

6. "The term ['love'] has become debased in popular culture; it has lost its power of discrimination, having become a cover for all manner of vapid self-indulgence."[55]

Concerning (4), I grant the descriptive exegetical point: the word "love" does not often appear in the four texts he lists. As Hays himself points out, however, Mark 12:28–34 itself describes love of God and neighbor

[50] Hauerwas writes, "Great immoralities are not the result of evil intentions, but [of] a love gone crazy with its attempt to encompass all mankind within its purview" (ibid., p. 235). This is a useful critique of a utilitarianism that treats human welfare as an aggregate sum, but the Gospels themselves call for something very like the "craziness" Hauerwas alludes to. The difference is that, in Scripture, one is called to love all persons, like Christ, where they are and one at a time. Tribalism is just as much a temptation, Desmond Tutu and others remind us, as false "universalism."

[51] With Charles Pinches, Hauerwas has recently written: "We affirm the centrality of charity, but contrary to a good bit of recent theological opinion, we believe that charity cannot stand alone." See *Christians among the Virtues*, p. xv. I am not sure whose "theological opinion" Pinches and Hauerwas are objecting to, but it cannot be that of the strong agapist.

[52] von Balthasar, *Love Alone*, p. 49.

[53] Hays, *The Moral Vision of the New Testament*, p. 202.

[54] Ibid.

[55] Ibid.

as having significant primacy: "There is no other commandment greater than these" (12:31). Moreover, the signal emphasis on love in so many other places in Scripture seems to justify giving it general pride of place as an ethical focus. "Words from the *agape* family occur 341 times," William Klassen notes, "and are found in every book of the NT."[56] The very heart of ethical monotheism, in both biblical *Testaments*, is expressed by the equation of God with a holy love and by the correlative commandment to love as God does (see pages 14–15 above). This observation means little without a concrete context in which love takes practical form, but the same can be said of any biblical virtue or symbol.

Hays would have us employ "community, cross, and new creation" as regulative images in doing Christian ethics, and I find this strategy highly edifying. The three focal images do not preclude our triangulating on a single subject, however, any more than speaking of God as "Father, Son, and Holy Spirit" prevents us from calling God a "Trinity" (a triune Person). If we lose sight of the indicative unity of God's personality, on the other hand, we will also fail to see the imperative unity of human virtues. One of Hays's paramount concerns is to "speak meaningfully about the unity of New Testament ethics,"[57] but his metaphorical means tend to thwart his moral end. He sometimes juxtaposes analyses from his three focal points without integrating them or harmonizing their tensions; yet when he does reconcile the three images, it is by giving the cross exclusive authority. I myself have highlighted the importance of openness to self-sacrifice in Christlike love. But Christian feminists come into their own when they insist that an occlusive or uncritical emphasis on crucifixion may be disruptive, not just of secular society between women and men but also of the kingdom of God. The unqualified extolling of self-sacrifice and/or nonresistance may encourage masochism on the part of women and perpetuate misogyny on the part of men, the feminist case

---

[56] Klassen, "Love (NT and Early Jewish Literature)," in *The Anchor Bible Dictionary* (New York: Doubleday, 1992), vol. 4, p. 384. Klassen concludes that the double commandment that results from associating Deuteronomy 6:5 and Leviticus 19:18b probably did not originate with Jesus himself (pp. 385–86). This conclusion meshes well with an emphasis on Jesus' final commandment in John 13:34 as supplanting self-love as a standard in Matthew 22:39. Klassen also makes an important point relevant to my response to Hays: "Interpreters of Jesus are appropriately united in seeing the command to love one's enemy as a normative summary of the attitudes and action of Jesus, even though the words 'neighbor' and 'love' are not current [i.e., common] terms of Jesus. He thinks in concrete terms" (p. 386). Hays, like Hauerwas, understandably wants to focus on the concrete and historical, but this does not preclude normative summary. There is a Fourth Gospel in addition to the Synoptics, and even the Synoptics generate general ideals out of personal encounters with God (see my chap. 1).

[57] Hays, *The Moral Vision of the New Testament*, p. 204.

runs, hence we need criteria to help us discern when and how such *kenosis* is appropriate.[58]

These criteria may be found, I believe, in the logic of agapic love. *Agape*'s willing of the good for the whole person, as well as for the wider community, means that self-respect, voluntariness, and social constructiveness are all relevant factors. Concerns for community and new creation themselves must move us to refuse to go to the cross at times. If self-denial would be despairing or coerced or destructive, then *agape* itself must rule it out. Hays notes that Saint Paul does not recommend suffering for its own sake,[59] and his discussion of Paul's ambivalent yet (for its time) impressive endorsement of male-female equality is nuanced.[60] One wants to hear more, however, about the principled limits (if any) Hays himself would place on suffering and service, especially for those without social power. What are the proper means and ends of action for those who wish sincerely to be obedient to God? Hay's commitment to pacifism is clear, but I am not sure how he squares his conviction that "love [in 1 Corinthians 13] does not mean uncritical acceptance"[61] with the utter nonresistance to evil literally enjoined in Matthew 5:39.[62]

This brings us to objection (5). Hays maintains that "the content of the word 'love' is given *fully and exclusively* in the death of Jesus on the cross; apart from this specific narrative image, the term has no meaning."[63] That is an overstatement. Christ's cross is the most profound revelation of God's love for creatures, but it is not the only revelation. As the self-giving logic of *agape* writ large, the cross has singular (in the sense of unsurpassable) power and authority, but it is not the sole temporal enactment of divine love. Dining with tax collectors, feeding the five thousand, forgiving the woman caught in adultery, healing the sick, giving sight to the blind, enabling the lame to walk, suffering little children to approach, challenging the scribes and Pharisees, even driving the moneychangers from the temple—as Hays well knows, all of these are potent images of Jesus' love for God and the world. Jesus' raising of Lazarus from the dead, although it lacks the soteriological import of his own crucifixion, is a striking manifestation of charity: love both lifts up and goes under, both gives life and surrenders it. Kenotic self-surrender is a defining fea-

---

[58] I do not mean to suggest that Hays is unaware of the feminist misgivings I describe; see, for example, his respectful but critical discussion of Elisabeth Schüssler Fiorenza in ibid., pp. 266–82.

[59] Ibid., p. 31.

[60] Ibid., esp. pp. 55–56 and 65.

[61] Hays, *First Corinthians: Interpretation* (Louisville: John Knox, 1997), p. 232.

[62] I discuss Christian just war theory and pacifism in chap. 3, and I return in that context to a dialogue with Hays's position concerning the use of violent means to resist evil.

[63] Hays, *The Moral Vision of the New Testament*, p. 202; emphasis mine.

ture of Christ's identity, a prototype that all who would follow him are called to emulate (Mark 8:34–35), but contagious joy (John 15:11) and righteous indignation (Mark 11:15–19) are also morally salient.

Although his Passion is in basic respects the consummation of Jesus' life and teaching—the watermark of his obedience to God and service to humanity—it need not overwhelm the rest of the gospel. Because it is indispensable to the Father's redemptive purpose carried out by the Son, the cross is not to be understood as some horrible calamity or freak accident. But neither is it all we know of divinity. The Son of God, the biblical canon attests, is both vital life and slain death, the model of joy who walks on water as well as the man of sorrows who stoops to rescue those in despair. It would be a grave mistake to think that openness to self-sacrifice is either tangential to Jesus' character or optional for his followers. The need and vulnerability of human beings, together with their sinfulness, make unreciprocated giving essential for both Christ and Christians. Yet it would also be shortsighted to ignore incarnate love's capacity for fellowship and even prudence. In short, all three features of interpersonal *agape*, not merely willing sacrifice, are crucial for a complete Christocentric ethics.[64]

Let this be said a thousand times: Christian love suffers for the truth and embraces martyrdom when necessary. Christ movingly resists the temptation to let God's cup pass from him and avoid the cross, but not all invitations to drink from the grail of death and self-denial are from God. Jesus wisely escapes would-be murderers on a number of occasions (e.g., Matt. 12:14–15; John 11:53–54). Moreover, he commends Mary for anointing him with costly nard (John 12:1–8), an act that must seem self-indulgent to pure utilitarians even as Judas finds it wasteful. The

---

[64] In "The Ethics of Self-Sacrifice," *First Things* (March 1999), John Milbank mounts a powerful critique of disinterested self-giving. In spite of numerous insights, however, Milbank fails to distinguish sufficiently between self-sacrifice as a necessary means to various ends (including conviviality and joyful sharing with God and others) and self-sacrifice as an end in itself. To celebrate self-sacrifice as *the* good, desirable for its own sake, is indeed masochistic, as Milbank suggests; even as to treat death as the precondition for ethics is nihilistic. But given the neediness and vulnerability of human beings in this life, forms of unreciprocated service are often necessary. Milbank notes the occasional need for unilateral service, but he tends to limit this to extraordinary or fallen circumstances, to be fully repaired or redeemed in heaven. In reality, however, self-sacrifice is not called for by calamity and sin alone; it is also required by human finitude as such. Even the Christ child is born in want. Death does not make ethics possible, but human needs and potentials do; Adam and Eve would not have been self-sufficient even if they had not fallen into mortality. As perceptive and well-written as "The Ethics of Self-Sacrifice" is, what it presents as a critique of the liberal state and its anonymous utilitarianism is actually an assault on the dependency of creatures, as well as on the cross of Christ. In time, Christlike love does take the form of openness to self-sacrifice (cf. John 15:13–15), even if in an afterlife this willingness can be set aside.

challenge is to discern and then act on God's will—"not my will, but yours, be done" (Luke 22:42)—without ordaining in advance what precise form this obedience must take. Some means (e.g., murder, rape) will be forever ruled out as hateful by the end of God's love, while other means (e.g., forgiveness, service) will be regularly ruled in as hopeful. But self-sacrifice is not an end in itself. If talk of "the priority of love" risks becoming overly abstract and permissive, Hays's accent on the cross risks becoming overly concrete and preemptive.

As for Hays's objection (6), again his point is well taken, but only to a degree. "Love" has been bowdlerized in many quarters, as has "freedom," but why let such a splendid moral term be appropriated by mass culture? As Martin Luther King, Jr., wrote: "When I speak of love I am not speaking of some sentimental and weak response. I am speaking of that force which all of the great religions have seen as the supreme unifying principle of life."[65] Instead of quitting the field and leaving it to the enemy, I would rather try to win back a standard that (for all its tatters) can still inspire our best moral allegiances. Hence this book. If relativism is the besetting theoretical malaise of our time, to shift the metaphor, then the Christian antidote must begin with the resounding declarations that "God is love" (1 John 4:8) and "the God of love and peace will be with you" (2 Cor. 13:11). This witness stands the best chance of making clear that the unity of *New Testament* ethics stems from the coherence of the divine Personality rather than the abstraction of deontological rules or the objectivity of utilitarian values.

"Love," one might say, is both a proper name and an ethical concept. "Love" is God's proper name, in the sense that it is the most univocal identification we can make of God; and it is an ethical concept, in the sense that it entails various habits and behaviors as normative for human beings. The cross, on the other hand, is more like God's earthly garment than God's proper name. (It makes sense to say that the Persons of the Trinity "eternally love" one another, but it is nonsense to say that they "eternally go to the cross" for one another.) If we reject the priority of love and multiply moral symbols or criteria without explaining how they might be integrated into a single moral identity (divine or human), then we risk reinforcing relativism rather than combating it. Hays stresses that the Pauline "eschatological reservation" forbids us to see even the servant community as the kingdom fully come,[66] and he even notes elsewhere that "Paul insists that there is nothing to be gained by self-sacrifice where

---

[65] King, "A Time to Break Silence," in *I Have a Dream: Writings and Speeches That Changed the World*, ed. by James M. Washington (San Francisco: HarperSanFrancisco, 1992), p. 150.

[66] Hays, *The Moral Vision of the New Testament*, p. 25.

love is absent."[67] Like Mark (on his interpretation), however, Hays would apparently have Christians use "the cross" as the "controlling symbol" and "single fundamental norm" that gives shape to "community" and "new creation."[68] Thus self-abnegation in a more or less fixed cruciform pattern becomes, de facto, the singular Christian measure.

Why, in contrast, do I put love rather than cross first? More precisely, why do I see openness to sacrifice as a feature of *agape* but actual sacrifice as neither its lone nor its trumping idiom? One reason is that love is the more holistic concept; it has ready implications for the motives of agents (no hatred), the forms of actions (nothing less than justice), and the consequences of actions (palpable benefits must outweigh harms), whereas self-sacrifice tends to reduce to a deontological rule of behavior. In his elaboration of "taking up the cross" in the Gospel of Mark, Hays himself notes: "Mark focuses . . . on simple external obedience rather than on motivation or the intention of the heart. There is no visible concern with the problem of *how* it is possible to obey."[69] As a reflection of unswerving trust in God, this is impressive; but such an elevation of self-sacrifice is likely to be inattentive to both character traits and communal consequences. Love surrenders its legitimate interests only when this can be done consensually and constructively, to repeat; if the motive is self-loathing or the end result is chaos, love is not present. Neither good will nor social utility alone makes for virtue, but narrowing moral vision to a single form of action is also incompatible with strong *agape*. I talk a good deal about suffering and sacrifice in chapter 1, and I contend in chapter 4 that the willingness to give forgiveness, although a mini-crucifixion, should be unconditional. But a preoccupation with the cross as the unique epitome of Christian virtue leaves us with a truncated ethics, insensitive to context. Although far from a dour rule-monger, Hays hazards such truncation in his relentless exhortation to walk the *Via Dolorosa*.[70]

A second reason for love's priority is that when we affirm with John that "God is love" (1 John 4:8) and with Paul that "the God of love and peace will be with you" (2 Cor. 13:11), we can better remind ourselves that the life of charity is participation in the holiness of a personal God, and commanded as such. Because God has the narrative coherence of a person, it is possible to know God via stories, parables, and even direct encounters. Hays is correct to emphasize the story of the crucifixion as deeply revelatory of God's nature. But Christians declare "God is love," rather than "God is cross," precisely because God is a living Person

---

[67] Hays, *First Corinthians*, p. 226.

[68] Cf. Hays, *The Moral Vision of the New Testament*, pp. 80 and 84.

[69] Ibid., p. 83.

[70] Friend that he is, Dr. Hays will forgive me for the playful suspicion that his being raised a Boston Red Sox fan is not irrelevant here.

rather than any one object or any past act, however ideal and reproducible. By foregrounding John's definitive affirmation, Jesus' endorsement of (proper) self-love (Matt. 22:39), Jesus' closing command to "abide in my love" (John 15:9), together with Paul's own putting of charity first (1 Cor. 13:13), we are better able to keep Christian virtue from lapsing into a cramped resentment or world-hatred.

Heaven knows that inordinate zeal to be self-immolating is not the chief vice of our time. But why not say that the three focal images of "community, cross, and new creation" triangulate on charity as God's essence, thereby illustrating how the ethical monotheism of the Bible can help rectify contemporary relativism? Of all the virtues, agapic love most opens itself to the reality of others to address them as they are. *Agape* is internally complex, to be sure, but so is the Trinity. It is precisely this diversity within unity—the balancing of unconditional commitment, equal regard, and passionate service—that permits a lithe yet resolute following after God, as opposed to a desperate and chaotic pursuit of happiness. Since you are creatures of the Most High, the *New Testament* counsels, you must "pursue love and strive for the spiritual gifts" (1 Cor. 14:1).

First Corinthians 13:4–8 is often thought of Saint Paul's "panegyric" on *agape*:

> Love is patient; love is kind; love is not envious or boastful or arrogant or rude. It does not insist on its own way; it is not irritable or resentful; it does not rejoice in wrongdoing, but rejoices in the truth. It bears all things, believes all things, hopes all things, endures all things. Love never ends.

Paul culminates chapter 13 by calling *agape* "the greatest of these," more indispensable even than faith and hope. Hays warns against the sentimentality that easily results from lifting these and the preceding lines out of context and treating them as "a hymn or an independently composed oration on love," but Hays himself writes that the purpose of the chapter "is to portray love as the sine qua non of the Christian life and to insist that love must govern the exercise of all the gifts of the Spirit."[71] In the Corinthian setting, "gifts" refers most immediately to speaking in tongues, prophesying, and other charismatic practices. It is legitimate to add, even so, that a Christian ultimately sees the whole of existence as a gift of the Spirit to be governed by love.[72] The challenge is to discern what, specifically, this means.

In sum, one need not apologize for praising love above all. When properly understood, love's priority cannot be pressed into the service of

---

[71] Hays, *First Corinthians*, p. 221.
[72] Hays himself makes this "hermeneutical transfer"; see ibid., pp. 231–32.

a reductionism that would make moral propositions deductively certain and moral persons sublimely self-sufficient, but it can be a crucial aid in countering an errant "pluralism" that would make moral claims utterly relativistic and moral persons psychologically fragmented. The detaching of charity from certainty and self-sufficiency—as well as from procedural justice (chapter 1), personal immortality (chapter 2), in-principle pacifism (chapter 3), endless vengeance (chaper 4), and both pure autonomy and crude vitalism (chapter 5)—amounts to a disconsoling doctrine in many ways. Love's embracing forms of self-sacrifice may even seem close to masochism. I conclude, nonetheless, that love has its own brand of optimism. Love serves the authentic needs of others even unto death, but it also joyfully affirms the goods of life; to put charity first is to enter into a fellowship with the Creator of life (theonomy) that is the foundation of all other virtues. Perhaps charity is a "useless passion" (Sartre), an unrequited longing for a nonexistent God in an absurd world; perhaps "love" is now but a smokescreen for "vapid self-indulgence" (Hays), a hopelessly romantic notion in a debased culture. But the superlative charisma of a Goodness larger and more "personal" than ourselves, for whom we constantly pine and whom we occasionally intuit, suggests otherwise. The strong agapist holds, at any rate, that even amid ambiguity and suffering we can be touched by Love and, however haltingly, love in return.

ONE

Christlike Love and Reciprocal Justice

Mercy is above this scept'red sway;
It is enthroned in the hearts of kings,
It is an attribute of God Himself,
And earthly power doth then show likest God's
When mercy seasons justice.
—William Shakespeare[1]

Human justice is only a very imperfect
semblance of divine justice.
—Søren Kierkegaard[2]

OBSTACLES TO A CHRISTIAN THEORY OF JUSTICE

To the extent that Christlike love transcends reciprocity, it is distinct from justice (defined as *suum cuique*), but it is not opposed to it. The ideal of giving to everyone according to past achievement was part of biblical prophecy at least as early as it was debated in Greco-Roman philosophy;[3] and when equal regard is seen as ingredient in charity, some definitions of justice make it internal to the virtue of love itself. Yet agapic love is most characteristically productive rather than distributive of worth, emotionally engaged rather than objectively aloof. Love is deeply concerned with fair distribution, even aligning itself at times with nonpreferential maxims like Bentham's "each is to count as one and no more than one," but this is only a fraction of the story. As commonly understood, justice distributes a range of goods (food, money, honor) according to various objective criteria (contract, merit), whereas charity

---

[1] Shakespeare, *The Merchant of Venice*, spoken by Portia, act IV, scene i, lines 192–96. All Shakespeare quotations are from *The Complete Signet Classic Shakespeare*, ed. by Slyvan Barnet (New York: Harcourt Brace Jovanovich, 1972).

[2] Kierkegaard, "Strengthening in the Inner Being," in *Eighteen Upbuilding Discourses*, ed. and trans. by Howard V. and Edna H. Hong (Princeton: Princeton University Press, 1990), p. 89.

[3] Roughly two hundred years before Plato wrote *The Republic*, Jeremiah quoted God as saying: "I the LORD test the mind and search the heart, to give to all according to their ways, according to the fruit of their doings" (Jer. 17:10). In spite of Jeremiah's frequent pleas that sinners be shown no mercy by God (e.g., 18:23), however, God goes beyond what is historically owed to Israel in continually sustaining a covenant. Steadfast love endures alongside strict justice (cf. 9:24 and 31:3).

produces values (primarily love itself; cf. Heb. 10:24) in part according to no appraisive criterion at all.

Although epistemic realists rightly affirm the intrinsic worth of some human goods (e.g., freedom from pain), the final goodness of the world depends upon love's going beyond the just distribution of what is antecedently judged valuable.[4] As crucial as "realism" is, it is not enough. We all rely on the kindness of strangers to nurture us, more or less gratuitously, into personhood. Not everyone shares the same interests *of* the self (contingent preferences and activities), but everyone has defining interests *in* the self (basic needs, including the need for a secure sense of identity).[5] The latter are only met by a care that exceeds narrow conceptions of reciprocal justice.[6]

Reciprocal justice includes both distributive and retributive questions. In this chapter, I concentrate on the general obstacles to a Christian theory of justice, fully aware that these bear on matters of both payment and punishment (cf. chapter 4). The obstacles occur, most fundamentally, because charity is prior to philosophy as the quest for *theoria*.[7] The

---

[4] One might think of justice as occupied with the parceling out of impersonal objects or abstract rights, and then contrast this with love's concern to promote personal sympathy and interpersonal community. This contrast can be misleading, however. A neglected issue of social justice is the basis on which virtues (including justice itself) are distributed: who has been allowed to become whom, so to speak. It remains the case, nonetheless, that modern accounts of justice distinguish it from agapic love. Justice is a largely retrospective virtue, for instance, focusing on what others have done or who they have been; while agapic love is more prospective, attentive to who others are or have been but emphasizing what they might become (e.g., more loving).

[5] See Richard Fern's "Two Kinds of Self-Interest" (unpublished manuscript).

[6] For a feminist critique of "the distributive paradigm" of justice—"the morally proper distribution of social benefits and burdens among society's members"—see Young, *Justice and the Politics of Difference*, esp. chap. 1. Young finds two problems with the distributive paradigm: "First, it tends to ignore, at the same time that it often presupposes, the institutional context that determines material distributions. Second, when extended to nonmaterial goods and resources, the logic of distribution misrepresents them" (p. 18). The misrepresentation comes when nonmaterial social goods, such as opportunity and self-respect, are depicted "as though they were static things, instead of a function of social relations and processes" (p. 16). Young makes it clear that justice "is not identical with the good life as such," but the good life, for her, is comprised of two "universalist" values: roughly, self-development or self-expression, on the one hand, and self-determination, on the other (p. 37). Thus what I am identifying as the cornerstone of Christian social ethics (*agape*) differs from the "communicative ethics" Young defends. She begins with the quest for self-fulfillment, such that domination and oppression are the prime evils (p. 16); strong *agape* begins with unconditional love for God and the neighbor, such that pride and self-satisfaction are the original sins.

[7] In Greek, *theoria* literally means viewing or contemplation. James K. Feibleman and Max Black define theory as "the hypothetical universal aspect of anything. For Plato, a contemplated truth. For Aristotle, pure knowledge as opposed to the practical. . . . systematically organized knowledge of relatively high generality." See Dagobert D. Runes, ed., *Dictionary of Philosophy* (Littlefield, Adams, 1963), p. 317.

problem is how to communicate distinctively Christian contents, including motives, emotions, precepts, and principles, in a form that bears on *theoria* (i.e., classical political philosophy), edifies (or at least persuades) one's peers, and yet remains faithful to Scripture. The task is to reconcile two evolving (perhaps incommensurable) traditions: (1) one originating in Hebrew Scripture, realized in Jesus Christ, interpreted by Saint Paul, defended yet transmuted by Saint Augustine, and branching into Thomist, Reformed, and other theological variations and (2) the other originating in Pythagoras, realized in Socrates, interpreted by Plato and Aristotle, defended yet transmuted by the Enlightenment, and now branching into distinctively modernist and postmodernist philosophical schools.

Compare the Hebrew prophets' use of the terms *mishpat* and *tsedaqah*, usually translated "justice" or "righteous judgment," with Western liberals' understanding of these English words. Are the prophets and the liberals even talking about the same thing? For Amos, as for the biblical writers generally, it is unjust to fail to assist the poor, regardless of whether we are directly responsible for their condition. For many bourgeois liberals, our response to poverty is a matter of neither justice nor injustice, as long as we have not cheated or otherwise abused others. Philanthropy is a possibility, of course, but we are under no *positive* obligation. This disagreement is not readily reducible to lack of information on either side. One wonders if it is possible, even in principle, to adjudicate the dispute in terms acceptable to both parties.[8] Let me discuss three problems in particular.

The Personality Problem

The Judeo-Christian conviction that justice is personal is an insuperable obstacle to *theoria*, as traditionally understood. Within the Christian tradition, justice is what Charles Taylor has called a "subject-referring" term,[9] and this in two senses. First, justice cannot be understood objectively by finite persons; a proper appreciation of it presupposes experiencing it in a certain way. Second, justice makes reference to the Incarnation; in Christ, justice itself became a human subject, and the life and death of

---

[8] Consider a more recent example. It is perhaps all too clear that a major reason for the emotional opposition to the Catholic pastoral, *Economic Justice for All* (Washington, D.C.: United States Catholic Conference, 1986), is that American business has a fundamentally nonbiblical paradigm of economic justice. In a sense, businesspersons were quite rightly outraged by the pastoral's pronouncing the U.S. economy "unjust," for they could in most cases plausibly deny transactional wrongdoing. Not having positively cheated anybody, they felt hurt and misunderstood. The bishops should have made more clear that they were calling business to a higher *and different* standard than currently prevails.

[9] Taylor, "Self-Interpreting Animals," in *Human Agency and Language*, vol. 1 of *Philosophical Papers* (Cambridge: Cambridge University Press, 1985).

this subject are decisive for apprehending justice in its fullest form. Any "theoretical" account of justice that neglects these facts will, by Christian standards, be hopelessly skewed. Therefore, a ready appropriation of philosophical motifs (whether Platonic or Aristotelian or Kantian) destroys a Christian account of justice and the love on which it trades. Speaking literally, *justice is something about which Christians can have no theoria*, a "Christian theory of justice" being virtually a contradiction in terms. Christian justice, however, need not embrace irrational forms of fideism. I have elsewhere criticized Christian doctrine divorced from a realistic understanding of truth.[10] Christian justice is no more reducible to extreme pragmatism than to orthodox Platonism, no more to be equated with a performative utterance alone or a grammatical rule alone than with an Abstract Idea.

Ever since Socrates, Western philosophy has tended to treat justice as a common noun, and this is the source of one of its major differences from Hebrew-Christian Scripture. In the middle dialogues, Socrates believes justice to be a unified reality about which one can intelligibly ask, "What is it?" "Justice" is a substantive term subject to, or at least investigated in terms of, discursive definition. In *The Republic*, Socrates brings his interlocutors to grant that the just polis cannot finally be captured in speech and that the desire for justice cannot be fully realized on earth (bk. IX, 592b). This realization makes possible a critique of all existing political institutions, but the irony of an entire dialogue dedicated to an impossible political ideal is not usually thought to extend, here, to the existence of the forms themselves.[11] In at least one major strand of Christianity (the Pauline or Reformed), however, justice is not first an abstract entity but a person; the word "justice" is not so much a common as a *proper* noun.

Saint Paul speaks of righteousness (*dikaiosune*, the same word used by Plato), but given that God is the source and object of this righteousness, the primary question is "*Who* is justice?" rather than "*What* is justice?" The former query invites a story rather than a definition, poetry rather than theory, and finally imitation rather than contemplation. Given the dynamism of God's personal identity, predicative uses of the verb "to be" are inadequate for theological purposes. One may well say that "God is love" or "God is just and merciful," but such formulations come only in and through detailed narratives of God's actions and passions: God's leading Israel out of bondage in Egypt, God's revealing Holiness in the life, death, and resurrection of Jesus Christ. This means that Judeo-Christian

---

[10] See, for example, my "Against Grammar," *Religious Studies Review* 11, no. 3 (July 1985): 240–45.

[11] Cf. Alan Bloom's discussion of these points in his "Interpretive Essay," accompanying his translation of *The Republic of Plato* (New York: Basic, 1991), esp. pp. 409–15.

references to justice tend to be fluid and metaphorical—"Let justice roll down like waters, and righteousness like an ever-flowing stream" (Amos) or, "The kingdom of heaven is like . . ." (Jesus)—rather than abstract and literal—"Justice is doing one's own thing [*to ta heautou prattein*]" (Plato). Justice as righteousness has the narrative unity and pathos of a loving personality (or perhaps of a society of such persons) rather than the solidity of a physical object, or even the immutability of a Platonic form. One can have abstract theories about inanimate things or general predicates, but not about virtuous persons. A loving subject, whether human or divine, is reliable, but he or she is not definable precisely because not necessitated by objective circumstances. To "know" God is to trust a person rather than to cognize a fact. So we must be made to see, feel, taste, and smell Goodness as He freely interacts with us, as in the Gospel narratives.[12] The search for a theory here is Pharisaical.

If, as Heidegger, Derrida, and others contend, the entire Western philosophical tradition—from Plato's emphasis on "giving an account" to Rawls's emphasis on "reflective equilibrium"—is logocentric, it must be judged incomplete by Christian standards. Traditional philosophical theories should be compared with the more personalist, auditory accounts of Saint Paul in which "participation/imitation" and "call" are central motifs. Paul clearly believed that the heart of righteousness was not autonomy or rational contemplation, but the transformation of individuals by (and to) the self-sacrificial life of Jesus Christ. One does not become just by contemplating a logical necessity, much less a deeply entrenched custom, but by relating to a Personality whose constancy is a matter of free choice. Richard Hays has pointed out that in Saint Paul's writings, justice (*dikaiosune*) is centrally a matter of God's gracious self-communication. The Greek phrases in Paul usually translated "the righteousness of God" and "faith in Jesus Christ" often indicate a subjective rather than an objective genitive. This implies that the justification God gives to believers is God's very own Spirit and is made possible by the faithfulness of (not merely faith in) God's only begotten Son. Paul even employs olfactory images to describe Christian virtue, saying of believers, "we are the aroma of Christ to God" (2 Cor. 2:15).[13] In short, a strict, legalistic justice based on contract or merit falls short of God's spontaneous *agape*.

[12] Edith Wyschogrod makes a related point about writing the lives of saints: "the sequential structure of hagiography is such that the story's denouement is not a theory built up from events that serve as the theory's supports but a coming to fruition of a life by way of the story's time-tied events." See her *Saints and Postmodernism: Revisioning Moral Philosophy* (Chicago: University of Chicago Press, 1990), p. 9.

[13] See Hays, "Christology and Ethics in Galatians: The Law of Christ," *Catholic Biblical Quarterly* 49, no. 2 (April 1987): 269–90. The multifacetedness of the terms *mishpat* and *tsedaqah* also makes the Aristotelian division of justice into distributive, rectificatory, and retributive somewhat problematic, since other English synonyms for these Hebrew words

This is not to say that God, and therefore ethics, are arbitrary. It does suggest, however, that God's own holiness is the key to integrating questions of character, action, and consequence into a coherent picture of biblical justice. Because the character of God is the governing factor in each case, no talk of reciprocal action or utilitarian end alone is sufficient; yet the steadfastness of God's personal care (*ḥésed*) guarantees that there is no contradiction between these. As Abraham Heschel observes:

> There is [in God] no dichotomy of pathos and ethos, of motive and norm. They do not exist side by side, opposing each other; they involve and presuppose each other. It is because God is the source of justice that His pathos is ethical; and it is because God is absolutely personal—devoid of anything impersonal—that this ethos is full of pathos.[14]

God's choice of Israel as covenant partner and the attendant gift of the Torah (and eventually the Son) are expressions of God's very being and independent of any merit on Israel's part. But the choice and the gifts make justice possible rather than suborning injustice. Few lines could be more alien to Judeo-Christian sensibilities than Aristotle's claim that "justice is essentially something human."[15]

Where does this leave the relation between love and justice? Again, if justice is understood as biblical righteousness, it is virtually synonymous with *agape*. If justice dictates *merely* keeping contingent contracts or as giving no less (*but no more*) than is deserved (pure appraisive rationality), however, then *agape* is incompatible with it. For *agape* bestows value beyond what is required by minimal rightness (e.g., in forgiving offenses). Why not define justice prophetically, then, as a personal righteousness that attends to the real needs and latent capacities of others, often regardless of merit? I decline to do so in order to highlight the difference between biblical theology and modern philosophy. I prefer to speak of love "preceding and transforming" justice to accent three points: (1) *agape* undergirds modern, a.k.a. "naturalist," conceptions of justice in

---

include "straightness," "firmness," "vindication," "deliverance," and "truth." Still, Elizabeth Achtemeier has argued that there are three basic senses of justice in the *Old Testament*: individuals are called just or righteous if they have fulfilled the demands of a relationship, been deprived of their right in a relationship, or had righteousness imputed to them by God's grace. See Achtemeier, "Righteousness in the OT," in *The Interpreter's Dictionary of the Bible*, ed. by G. A. Buttrick (Nashville: Abingdon, 1962), vol. 4, pp. 80–85. In all three cases, it is not abstract rules but concrete relationships that are key, the relationships being between people and God or between people and other people. The paradigmatic relation is God's choice of Israel for covenant and as the object of steadfast love (*ḥésed*).

[14] Heschel, *The Prophets*, vol. II (New York: Harper and Row, 1975), p. 5.

[15] Aristotle, *The Nicomachean Ethics*, trans. by David Ross, with revisions by J. L. Ackrill and J. O. Urmson (Oxford: Oxford University Press, 1980), bk. V, chap. 9, [1137a30], p. 132.

that it nurtures individuals and groups into the capacity for self-conscious interests that distributive and retributive principles then adjudicate; (2) *agape* affirms the importance of giving people their due, thus it never falls below what justice (as *suum cuique*) requires; yet (3) *agape* occasionally transcends justice so understood, thereby displaying the leavening priority of the good to the right (*tsedaqah* to *mishpat*).[16] Love most characteristically empowers others to realize their potential for personal care and thus to reflect the Image of God, but love transcends modern justice both when this helps bring individuals to fuller personhood (e.g., parents sacrificing for their children) and when this sustains the well-being of those no longer personal agents (e.g., children attending to their senile parents).[17] It is possible to a degree to formulate abstract principles of "justice," but the persona of righteousness is only conveyed via stories, poems, and parables.[18]

The Orality Problem

Closely related to the "personality problem," there is a second difficulty for any *theory* of justice claiming to be faithful to biblically based Christianity: what I call the "orality problem." Many of the narratives of the early church, conditioned by their oral composition and transmission,

[16] See Paul Ramsey, *War and the Christian Conscience* (Durham: Duke University Press, 1961), p. 178.

[17] On love transcending justice, see Emil Brunner, *Justice and the Social Order*, trans. by Mary Hottinger (London and Redhill: Lutterworth, 1945), esp. pp. 114–18. Brunner equates Christian love with a personal I-Thou relation, while justice is "impersonal and realistic": "It knows no 'thou'; it knows only the intellectual value, the intellectual thing—the dignity of man" (p. 116). Strong *agape* wants relation with other persons, but it should be highlighted that it also extends care to those who are not yet or no longer persons, in the technical sense of autonomous agents. In order to nurture human beings into the capacity for personal relations, as well as to sustain those who are not capable of these relations, love ministers to the very young and the very old alike. In this sense, *agape* can be said to engage "impersonal" needs and potentials (see my chap. 5).

[18] Nicholas Wolterstorff has suggested in conversation that, in addition to love transforming justice, there is a complementary possibility of justice checking and transforming love—as when those who are involuntarily cast into avoidable suffering (e.g., South African apartheid) reject "charity" as tainted. These individuals rightly see themselves as wronged and therefore as not owing gratitude to those (e.g., the white Afrikaners) who offer partially to relieve their plights. The morally injured parties should demand justice rather than accept philanthropy, even as the fact of their oppression ought to move others to remedy injustice rather than to see themselves as supererogators addressing misfortune. Love never falls below justice, and blind or patronizing "love" perverts justice, but Wolterstorff's point is that some deformations of love can be corrected only through appeals to justice. Love is a centripetal moral force, drawing others closer to oneself; while justice is centrifugal, respecting and at times even enhancing the distance between persons. Some people are victims, not merely fellow sufferers, and the language of "(in)justice" reminds us of this. For more on the misfortune/injustice distinction, see Judith Shklar, *The Faces of Injustice* (New Haven: Yale University Press, 1990).

cannot readily be replaced by philosophical formulas. As in all oral traditions, locative and existential uses of "to be" predominate over copulative forms; thus much of the Scriptures are closer syntactically to the epic poetry of Homer and Hesiod than to the theorizing of Plato and Aristotle.[19] Socrates' conviction that *dikaiosune* refers finally to a single reality beyond the flux of human history and convention—beyond the traditional mores referred to by Homer and Hesiod with *dike*—is partially paralleled in Judeo-Christian monotheism. Saint Paul does use *dikaiosune* in referring to justification by faith, but for Paul justice is primarily a person or a relation to a person, not a general principle or idea.[20] The best way to appreciate a person is via enacted stories shared with others, rather than via memorized formulas that can be rehearsed alone. The difference between oral and written communication, at least in ancient times, was that the spoken word required two or more people to be present to each other, while the written did not.

Plato wrote dialogues between real or imagined interlocutors, while Saint Paul wrote epistles to the early Christian churches, but there is a key difference between them. In *The Republic*, Plato construes justice both psychologically and politically, as the state of a well-ordered soul and the condition of a well-governed city. But, to repeat, in neither case is harmony a function of relating to something personal. Quite generally for Plato—with the important exception of those mystical passages largely ignored by later philosophers (e.g., *Timaeus* 28a–30c and *Theaetetus* 176a)—justice is a matter of rational truth but is not itself a personality. The apprehension of justice may require dialectical interchange with others, according to Plato, but justice itself is a static form.[21] For Christianity, in contrast, both the apprehension and the practice of justice require a per-

---

[19] For discussion of some of the issues in comparative justices raised here, see Eric A. Havelock, *The Greek Concept of Justice* (Cambridge, Mass.: Harvard University Press, 1978) and Alasdair MacIntyre, *Whose Justice? Which Rationality?* (Notre Dame: University of Notre Dame Press, 1988). I am especially indebted to Havelock.

[20] John Donahue has characterized the overall biblical conception of justice as "fidelity to the demands of a relationship." This implies not just individual moral uprightness or supposed blamelessness but something more holistic, encompassing right relations to God, self, and others. It certainly exceeds modern notions of "justice" as based on the fulfilling of explicit contractual obligations or rewarding merit/punishing demerit. As I note below, biblical "justice" effectively equals what I call "charity." See Donahue, "Biblical Perspectives on Justice," in *The Faith That Does Justice*, ed. by John C. Haughey (New York: Paulist, 1977), pp. 68–112. See also P. J. Achtemeier, "Righteousness in the NT," in *The Interpreter's Dictionary of the Bible*, vol. 4, pp. 91–99.

[21] One need not question Socrates' piety before the gods or his pity for the benightedness of his fellow Athenians to observe that he had a notoriously difficult time explaining why a philosopher aware of the forms ought to consent to become a king. If the immaterial forms are the really real, the only knowable things because the only unchanging things, then concern with the embodied world of needy people would seem to be a temptation to slip back into ignorance. See *The Republic*, bk. VII, esp. 519b–520e.

sonal relation to a personal Deity, as well as to (all) other people. For Christianity, that is, both knowing and doing justice call for a "conversation" between persons rather than an internal monologue. God's character is partially intelligible, but not by way of deductive demonstration or even intellectual intuition; faith is required and is more a matter of willed obedience than rational insight. Correlatively, commandments such as "Love one another" are not premised on the desert of the neighbor but on the holiness of God, a God who speaks to His people. Biblical justice is not a principle of reciprocity or keeping contracts but a personal righteousness or keeping covenant with the Creator and creation. In the *New Testament*, love and justice coalesce sufficiently that no simple contrast between them is tenable.

The orality of much of the early Christian tradition is not simply a difference in form compared to speculative philosophy. The difference extends to content. It is not just that Christ and the early church employed metaphors and parables to depict justice, whereas today philosophers of religion and political theologians have (with the help of John Rawls et al.) purified the faith by translating these *Vorstellungen* into speculative terms. Theological journals are full of efforts to turn justice into a *Begriff*, but when justice is defined speculatively, God and faith are usually no longer present. To depersonalize justice is to depersonalize one's relation to justice, even as to write about justice, without also speaking to or for or as the just, is to write justice off. There are "writing prophets" in the Hebrew Bible, usually postexilic, and no contemporary author of books can consistently vilify the pen. But, as Søren Kierkegaard reminds us, religious faith is not an esoteric doctrine but an existential communication. A personal relation is only possible with what is itself personal, and a moral tradition that would survive cannot do so without verbal witness and preaching, followed by corporate action. Justice may well require the transcendence of limited perspectives and private preferences, but such self-overcoming does not abandon but fulfills the personal. One becomes morally articulate only in relation to other people, and the articulateness itself is an interpersonal practice of word and deed.

The Perversity Problem

A third and final obstacle to a Christian theory of justice grows out of human perversity. In Christian Scripture as well as the Augustinian theological tradition, faith involves the cognitive apprehension of truths about God, but qua justification (*dikaiosune*) it is more centrally a matter of passionate *willing* than detached intellection. Biblical justice is most fundamentally obedience to God's commands, conformity of the whole person to God's righteous will. In turn, injustice is not primarily a matter of ignorance or weakness of will (i.e., being overcome by the passions), as it is for Plato, but of perversity of will. In stubborn disobedience to God and cruel refusal to relate to fellow creatures, the individual knowingly chooses evil and thereby becomes disordered and unfree. (Satan knows many of the truths known by Christ, but the one is rebellious unto damnation while the other is obedient unto resurrection.) Perversity of will is theoretically opaque. As much as Plato and Aristotle worry about an *akrasia* that knows the good, wants to do it, yet cannot bring itself to act accordingly, neither could make sense of perversity as *witting* malevolence and alienation. Neither allowed for what Saint Paul refers to as "bondage to sin" and Augustine describes as *incurvatus in se*: knowing rejection of the common good.[22] Pace Plato and Aristotle, perversion is remedied, in turn, not by more information but by a conversion of heart and soul. According to Christian faith, sin is overcome only by another's gracious self-sacrifice: forgiveness as the costly bestowal of worth on the guilty that outruns appraisive rationality.[23]

DEFINING LOVE'S PRIORITY: OBJECTIONS IN THE NAME OF "JUSTICE"

We return to the question of definition. The more "doing justice" is associated with faithfully imitating divine goodness and creatively meeting human needs, for example, the less the phrase will carry its preeminent modern connotation of keeping contracts or rewarding merit. The more one identifies "justice" with biblical "righteousness"—with a prophetic *tsedaqah* that cares unselfishly for widows and orphans or a Pauline *dikaiosune* that accepts martyrdom—the more "love" and "justice" will tend to coalesce without remainder.[24] A return to etymological origins can sometimes be illuminating, but in this instance it risks blinding us to our current condition. The danger is that such an extreme reformation of our moral vocabulary will seem merely to change the subject. It is better, I think, to note how the word "justice" is now standardly used and then

[22] I am indebted here to Alasdair MacIntyre's discussion of Platonic and Augustinian conceptions of reason and will in *Whose Justice? Which Rationality?* esp. chap. 9.

[23] The category of "sin" remains either unavailable or highly problematic to any account of virtue that equates it with theoretical knowledge, as well as to any theory of justice that emphasizes contemplation (*ratio*, *nous*). Thomism *appears* the notable exception, but Thomas's discussion of original justice, the infused theological virtues, the Beatific Vision, and so forth would make little sense to Aristotle. If stripped of these elements, Thomism would make little sense to Augustine either.

[24] "The Gospel makes no distinction between the love of our neighbor and justice," Simone Weil insists; "we have invented the distinction between justice and charity." See Weil, *Waiting for God*, trans. by Emma Craufurd (New York: Harper and Row, 1951), p. 139.

to contrast it with the more ancient and more comprehensive ideals of faith, hope, and especially love. Again, "justly" rewarding all individuals according to their behavior is as old as Hebrew Scripture, but it does not exhaust the meaning of steadfast love (human or divine). I do not directly equate justice and love,[25] then, but neither do I set them at one another's throats. I do not give up on justice, so to speak, but I do let love govern it. Even as political ethics cannot be founded on narrow justice alone, with charity relegated to the private, so mercy is central not merely to self-perfection but to social viability and finally to religious faith.

Love without justice or a love that lapses into injustice is less than loving, but a justice without love or that does not aspire to love becomes less than just. Literature and the arts are replete with accounts of the destructive consequences of trying to live by strict justice alone. Shakespeare's *The Merchant of Venice*, Chekov's *Ivan Ivanov*, and Hugo's *Les Misérables* come to mind. Hugo's character Javert is a striking example of the ugliness of the unmerciful. When Javert, the embodiment of just punishment, is forgiven by Jean Valjean, he can no longer make sense of his world and commits suicide. For Javert, love and justice represent an either/or; to be spared by Valjean is to lose his identity as the Law and in effect to be slain. This may seem like an instance where mercy brings harm and thus that Valjean does wrong in forgiving, but surely the problem is in Javert not Valjean. Javert's "integrity" is based on a narrow principle of quid pro quo and a dogmatic conception of the legitimacy of positive law; his refusal of pity and unwillingness to acknowledge the need for charity in interpreting legal statutes cannot be consistently lived out. The fact that Javert takes his own life illustrates the limits of justice, the untenability of a life based solely on the *lex talionis*. Without mercy, *summum jus, summa injuria*.

The relation between love and justice is akin, on this reading, to that between subjectivity and objectivity. Because idiosyncratic feelings and commitments, contingent wants and needs, are partially constitutive of personal identity, a detached objectivity that attempts to bracket these

---

[25] Paul Tillich is right to insist that love not be equated with a leniency or quietism that amounts to "injustice, covered by sentimentality." Love must not fall below justice by failing to give others their due, including on occasion condign punishment. Tillich is also persuasive when he writes: "The relation of love to justice cannot be understood in terms of an addition to justice which does not change its character." Love leavens what we think of as fair distribution, the economy of rights and duties, and so on. I believe Tillich goes too far, nonetheless, when he virtually identifies love with justice: "justice is just because of the love that is implicit in it." One can distinguish, at any rate, between the appraisive rationality and reciprocity associated with modern justice and the emotional identification and self-sacrifice called for by agapic love. See Tillich, *Love, Power, and Justice* (Oxford: Oxford University Press, 1954), pp. 14, 13, and 15.

factors out is not enough to grasp the truth about moral agents. There is an irreducibly subjective coloration to individual experience that can only be apprehended (if at all) via imaginative empathy rather than rational abstraction. In fact, pure objectivity falsifies when the subject is either another person or oneself.[26] To try to grasp a concrete life by taking up a perspective outside its messy particulars—to move from the first person to the third person—is to omit or distort the felt inwardness involved. (As though a neutral report like "Someone in this room is in pain" constitutes fuller awareness of that pain than caring attentively for Helen's broken leg.) Similarly, to try to attend morally to individuals by treating them as interchangeable ciphers in the calculus of modern justice is to miss their unique worth. A capacity for critical distance on oneself and others, the ability to see oneself and every other person as "one and no more than one," is no doubt *a part* of moral intelligence. But abstract equality alone leads notoriously to injustice, for it licenses us to treat persons and their projects as means to the end of social utility. We sacrifice the individual in the name of an anonymous general welfare.[27] (As though by eliminating the suffering Helen we solve the practical problem and can triumphantly announce that "no one in this room is in pain.")

There are risks in maintaining that love is prior to and sustaining of justice, without itself being reducible to justice. I have already noted the danger that love will seem merely optional, and one way to escape this danger is to distinguish between "duties of charity" (based on need or potential) and "duties of justice" (based on merit or contract).[28] Both sets of duties are moral requirements in the broadest sense, but the latter are dependent on the former in that if human needs are not met and human potentials not cultivated (in love), there can be no persons deserving of rewards or contracting for goods (in justice). *Persons only come to be persons, and continue to act like persons, because they have been shown a care that outstrips standard modern conceptions of justice.* Beyond the concern that love will seem optional, however, there is the fear that promoting the priority of love will actually subvert justice.

There are four basic critiques of agapic love commonly grouped under the rubric "justice"; they are often interrelated and at least two are ancient, but each has been elaborated with renewed vigor of late:

[26] See Thomas Nagel, "The Limits of Objectivity," in *The Tanner Lectures on Human Values*, vol. 1, ed. by S. McMurrin (Salt Lake City: University of Utah Press, 1980); and *The View From Nowhere* (Oxford: Oxford University Press, 1986).

[27] See Bernard Williams, "A Critique of Utilitarianism," in *Utilitarianism: For and Against*, ed. by J.J.C. Smart and Bernard Williams (Cambridge: Cambridge University Press, 1973).

[28] See Allen Buchanan, "Justice and Charity," *Ethics* 97, no. 3 (April 1987): 558–75.

The Meritarian Critique

The more we emphasize equal regard for human sanctity and serving the welfare of others as a duty of charity, some argue, the more we threaten efficient evaluation and the dignity rights that correlate with duties of justice.[29] Need and merit can conflict, in short, and giving primacy to the former can mean that love falls below giving others their individual due.[30] If Nietzsche is correct, selfless love is little more than disguised or repressed hatred of the weak for the strong. The desire to "edify" or "serve" or "commune with" the healthy is but the will to objectify them for one's own vengeful or anarchic purposes, while the will to "pity" the sick stunts one's own (and their) moral growth.[31] Christian charity thwarts the heroic virtues (e.g., courage in battle, contempt for weakness) in favor of a decadent egalitarianism, undercutting those hierarchies of power and authority that make for real cultural achievement. Freud too doubts what Nietzsche calls "the value of the 'unegoistic'."[32] Freud argues that to love humanity in general is to slight those genuinely "worthy" or close to us (e.g., family and friends) who rightly claim our special loyalty.[33]

The Naturalist Critique

In addition to faulting *agape* as unjust, Freud also contends that it requires inordinate repression of natural needs and instincts and thus inevitably makes people petulant and unhappy. *Eros* and ego do not get their due when *agape* is extolled as the highest virtue, and this makes for malaise in a civilization and maladjustment in an individual. The attempt to be universally benevolent may seem to safeguard one against the loss of a particular loved object, but such "aim-inhibited" love finally calls for too massive a self-denial, if not self-delusion. The psychic toll is too high, and this leads in turn to social friction. More recently, the philosopher Susan Wolf has expressed powerful naturalistic sentiments in maintaining that "moral perfection, in the sense of moral saintliness, does not constitute a model of personal well-being toward which it would be particularly rational or good or desirable for a human being to strive."[34] We wrongly

---

[29] See Okin, *Justice, Gender, and the Family.*

[30] Robert Nozick raises challenges even to John Rawls's *A Theory of Justice* along these lines. See Nozick, *Anarchy, State, and Utopia* (New York: Basic, 1974).

[31] See, for example, "The AntiChrist" and "Thus Spoke Zarathustra," both in *The Portable Nietzsche*, ed. and trans. by Walter Kaufmann (New York: Viking, 1954).

[32] Nietzsche, *The Genealogy of Morals*, preface, sec. 5, p. 455.

[33] Freud, *Civilization and Its Discontents*, pp. 56–57. Juan Segundo discusses Freud's view of neighbor-love in *Evolution and Guilt*, vol. 5 of *A Theology for Artisans of a New Humanity* (Maryknoll: Orbis, 1974), esp. p. 18.

[34] Wolf, "Moral Saints," *Journal of Philosophy* 79, no. 8 (August 1982): 419.

impede the development of basic human potentials (e.g., the aesthetic), she believes, if we rigorously demand that love and/or justice overrule erotic desire. Sainthood is personally and socially impoverishing.

The Liberal Critique

We may once again look to Freud for a third criticism of *agape*: "When once the Apostle Paul had posited universal love between men as the foundation of his Christian community, extreme intolerance on the part of Christendom towards those who remained outside it became the inevitable consequence."[35] In general, the secular liberal argues, Christian love generates a self-righteousness that foments dogmatism and aggression. The theological virtues frequently move those who think they have them to extirpate those who supposedly do not. Although believers may feel commissioned to "save" others, the fact that this salvation may come in spite of others' actual preferences means that agapists often end up "loving" others to death (as in the Inquisition). Hence it is no surprise that "bourgeois liberals" like Richard Rorty want to distance all talk of "true virtue" as inclining us to "bash each other's heads in" for the sake of dominant goods (natural or supernatural) about which we can get no popular agreement.[36]

However much they may differ among themselves, the meritarians, naturalists, and liberals to whom I refer all agree that the world would be a more just or noble or satisfying place if we read Christian charity and universal benevolence off the list of virtues and constructed our moral selves around the notions of autonomy and self-fulfillment, if not robust self-assertion. In trying to love the neighbor with all our heart, mind, and strength—which may well mean self-sacrificially, as with Christ—we set an ideal either undesirable or impossible or both. It is better, the (post-)modernist consensus runs, to cultivate a prudent attention to one's own wants and needs and to leave social ethics on a largely procedural basis, defining justice in contractual terms. This way we avoid both self-pity and overweening pride. Although the price is personal alienation in the face of our radical freedom and polite disinterest in the private fortunes of others, it is a price worth paying because of the public peace it provides.

It is a troubling prospect that the connection between Christian love and human misery (including that associated with political violence) is *internal*, not an historical contingency that may be guarded against but a psychological and moral given that undermines Christian reflection to the

[35] Freud, *Civilization and Its Discontents*, p. 61.
[36] Rorty, "Postmodernist Bourgeois Liberalism," *Journal of Philosophy* 80, no. 10 (October 1983): 583–89.

extent that this appeals to *agape*. But what may the strong agapist say in response?

It is evident that the first and third objections lodged above tend to cancel each other out. Nietzsche's lament is that Christian charity is too inclusive and egalitarian—in a word, too "liberal"—to give free rein to the will to power and hence the rule of the dominant few. Rorty, on the other hand, fears that unless religion is privatized the theological virtues will make one *il*liberal, disposed to squelch public dissent and overly fond of moral hierarchies and priestcraft.[37] Nietzsche considered Protestantism the worst form of Christianity, Roman Catholicism's decline into an even more decadent (because more Pauline) form of religiosity. Rorty, in contrast, takes Protestant anti-authoritarianism and anti-nomianism to the extreme. God is dead for Nietzsche and Rorty, as well as for Freud, but whereas Nietzsche would have the "overman" spurn Christian love in order to be pitiless and cruel,[38] Rorty (following Judith Shklar) would have the bourgeois democrat be *un*-Christian precisely to avoid cruelty.[39]

Meritarian and liberal criticisms of Christian love work to negate each other, not by directly demonstrating each other's falsity but rather by highlighting the merely partial character of each other's truth. *Agape* can indeed slip into a consoling light-mindedness that shuns strong evaluations and the vulnerability of individual ties, especially sexual ones; *agape* may even degenerate into an intolerant hubris that draws invidious distinctions between "the saved" (us) and "the damned" (them). But these are vestigial forms of the virtue. "We have just enough religion to make us hate," wrote Swift, "but not enough to make us love one another."[40]

The Feminist Critique

A final objection (or set of objections) to charity and its priority stems from feminism's concern with women's health and well-being. Feminist

---

[37] See Rorty, "Religion as Conversation Stopper," chap. 11 of *Philosophy and Social Hope* (London: Penguin, 1999). For a slightly more favorable reading of the relation between religion and liberal democracy, see Rorty's "Pragmatism as Romantic Polytheism," in *The Revival of Pragmatism: New Essays on Social Thought, Law, and Culture*, ed. by Morris Dickstein (Durham and London: Duke University Press, 1998). There Rorty grants that "a Christianity that was merely ethical . . . might have sloughed-off exclusionism by viewing Jesus as one incarnation of the divine among others. The celebration of an ethics of love would then have taken its place within the relatively tolerant polytheism of the Roman Empire" (p. 26).

[38] On the importance of not allowing "morbid softening and moralization" to make one ashamed of cruelty, see *The Genealogy of Morals*, second essay, sec. 7, p. 503.

[39] See Shklar, *Ordinary Vices* (Cambridge, Mass.: Harvard University Press, 1984); and Rorty, *Contingency, Irony, and Solidarity*.

[40] Jonathan Swift, quoted in Howard Mumford Jones, *Violence and Reason* (New York: Atheneum, 1969), p. 35.

critiques of *agape* are not univocal, and they often overlap significantly with meritarian, naturalist, or liberal sentiments. But these critiques remain distinctive in being grounded in the analysis of gender relations. In this section, I outline two separate criticisms of *agape* commonly called "feminist."

The principal target of the first criticism is the traditional division of labor in which women are expected to bear the brunt of caring for spouses, the young, the sick, the disabled, the elderly, and the like without adequate acknowledgment or compensation. Within the family, the designation of the husband as breadwinner and head-of-household and the wife as domestic-nurturer and helpmeet leads inevitably to the male being more valued than the female. He has the chief authority and power by virtue of his income and social role, while she plays second fiddle. Within the wider polis, in turn, this hierarchy is reproduced and expanded. When young girls are socialized to want (and have) few life options beyond such "loving" occupations as homemaking, childrearing, nursing, elementary school teaching, and so on, and when these occupations are either unpaid or poorly paid, adult women are denied what John Rawls calls "the social bases of self-respect."[41] Either women are relegated to a private identity largely outside the public (i.e., male) spheres in which the really important economic, political, and cultural decisions are made, or they are marginalized as second-rate participants in these spheres by virtue of their lack of wages and public responsibilities.[42] Either way, women lack standing and prestige in relation to men.

The traditional division of labor, in effect, *forces* girls and women to be strong agapists. In thus evacuating charity of its voluntariness, the traditional division stunts the moral character of females, leaving them undeveloped as conscientious agents who may choose whether and how to give of themselves. When virtue is compelled, many feminists point out, it ceases to be virtue. Even when a range of career options exists for women, those who choose stereotypically "masculine" roles outside the home are often stigmatized or made to feel guilty for neglecting their families, while those who follow stereotypically "feminine" pursuits inside the home must accept their banishment from or competitive disadvantage within the corridors of power: the market, city hall, the academy, the military, and so on. (It is notoriously hard to become the CEO of a company, the mayor of a city, the chair of a university department, or the commander of a division of soldiers while also serving as wife and mother.) Either way, women are unfairly burdened relative to men, who

---

[41] See Rawls, *Political Liberalism* (New York: Columbia University Press, 1993), p. 180ff.

[42] On these topics, see Okin, *Justice, Gender, and the Family,* and Jean Bethke Elshtain, *Public Man, Private Woman* (Princeton: Princeton University Press, 1981).

are not presumed to be the primary or stay-at-home caregivers and hence are not freighted with such wrenching trade-offs.

A central feminist insight is that love, like justice, is almost always (construed as) gendered, that is, understood differently depending on rights and responsibilities assigned on the basis of sex. Women are expected to love differently from men—more passionately, more self-sacrificially, less impartially, less publicly—although this is not usually admitted. Even as most contemporary theories of justice ignore gender differences, especially within the family, by assuming that their basic subjects are autonomous males heading traditional households,[43] so most theories of love neglect gender by glossing over the disparate burdens that love places upon males and females. Men, like women, are usually enjoined to "love" their neighbors, of course, but men are given much more liberty also to love social causes, abstract ideas, money, power, and themselves. Men, we may say, are not so frequently compelled to choose between the various loves (interpersonal bonds of affection or good will) and social justice (public reciprocity and fair competition).[44]

When female self-effacement carries a religious sanction, it is especially dangerous. We should have real misgivings about the nineteenth-century enthusiasm of Estelle M. Hurll, for instance, when she writes:

> The noblest mother is the most unselfish; she regards her child as a sacred charge, only temporarily committed to her keeping. Her care is to nurture and train him for his part in life; this is the object of her constant endeavor. . . . What is true of all motherhood finds a supreme illustration in the character of the Virgin Mary. . . . Her highest joy was to present [Jesus] to the world for the fulfillment of his calling.[45]

This passage so completely humbles mother to child, so directly identifies motherly love with "constant" service to a son and his mission, that it readily appears a feminist's worst nightmare: an ideal of unselfishness become a divine prescription for female oppression.[46]

One possible remedy for the gender bias described above is to ensure greater sexual equality, as well as more personal freedom, with respect to love's demands. Encourage fathers to share alike in parenting chores, so they too can know the joys and sorrows of "mothering"; allow mothers paid maternity leaves, so they need not surrender their jobs in the mar-

---

[43] See Okin, *Justice, Gender, and the Family*, pp. 8–9; see also Kittay, *Love's Labor*, pp. 75–99.

[44] Compare Okin, *Justice, Gender, and the Family*, p. 13.

[45] Hurll, *The Madonna in Art* (Boston: L. C. Page, 1897), p. 182.

[46] See also Carin Rubenstein, *The Sacrificial Mother: Escaping the Trap of Self-Denial* (New York: Hyperion, 1998).

ketplace; hold deadbeat dads financially responsible for their progeny, so single mothers will not have to go it alone; draft women into the military, so they too can struggle to love their enemies while publicly resisting armed aggression; and so on. A second form of feminist critique takes a different tack, however, and maintains that *agape*'s call to universal good will and self-sacrifice for the sake of anonymous others, even enemies, is immoral (or at least undesirable) in and of itself. The contention here is that the traditional virtue of charity is actually a vice, regardless of whether it is freely embraced and regardless of whether it is required uniformly of men and women.[47] The readiness to demote or displace one's own projects leaves *anyone* aesthetically uncultivated and/or morally spent, even masochistic.

This objection has obvious affinities with the meritarian and naturalist criticisms raised above, but it factors in the question of gender: while the practice of *agape* leaves everyone worse off, the argument runs, its destructive impact is particularly profound on women. The problem is not that *agape* exacts self-sacrifice but that it does so for constituencies distant from "natural" maternal affection. Here, if you will, the usual critique of the unjust family crucible is turned on its head. Rather than faulting charity for the *depth* of self-denial required *uniquely* of women, this feminist perspective indicts the *scope and motivation* of self-denial while granting that a form of such denial is *characteristic* of most women. Whether because of nature or nurture, women tend to be more emotionally invested in their immediate social contexts than men, the story goes, so the insistence that they blind themselves to special relations and act out of unconditional love is more of an assault on them than on men. When women (especially mothers) are expected to serve the interests of their kin by radically subordinating their own well-being, they may be disadvantaged economically, politically, and culturally; but when women (mothers or not) are expected to distance family ties and dispassionately serve the interests of strangers, they are impoverished in absolute terms. In the latter case, women are made to conform to an alien, "masculine" norm of impersonal benevolence/universal love.[48]

---

[47] See, for instance, Wolf, "Moral Saints."

[48] On "universal love" as an "illusion," see Noddings, *Caring*, p. 90; on "masculine" ideals as tragically lacking concreteness, see pp. 94–103 and 128–31. A key contrast is between those who accent a common ideal of justice to be aspired to by both men and women and those who detect different modes of moral reasoning in men and women taken as groups. For her part, Okin believes that "the distinction between an ethic of justice [associated with men] and an ethic of care [associated with women] has been overdrawn" (see *Justice, Gender, and the Family*, p. 15).

Let me now reply at some length to the four critiques of *agape* just rehearsed.

Response to the Meritarian Critique

Jesus responds to merit-based misgivings with his parable of the vineyard:

> "For the kingdom of heaven is like a landowner who went out early in the morning to hire laborers for his vineyard. After agreeing with the laborers for the usual daily wage, he sent them into his vineyard. When he went out about nine o'clock, he saw others standing idle in the marketplace; and he said to them, 'You also go into the vineyard, and I will pay you whatever is right.' So they went. When he went out again about noon and about three o'clock, he did the same. And about five o'clock he went out and found others standing around; and he said to them, 'Why are you standing here idle all day?' They said to him, 'Because no one has hired us.' He said to them, 'You also go into the vineyard.' When evening came, the owner of the vineyard said to his manager, 'Call the laborers and give them their pay, beginning with the last and then going to the first.' When those hired about five o'clock came, each of them received the usual daily wage. Now when the first came, they thought they would receive more; but each of them also received the usual daily wage. And when they received it, they grumbled against the landowner, saying, 'These last worked only one hour, and you have made them equal to us who have borne the burden of the day and the scorching heat.' But he replied to one of them, 'Friend, I am doing you no wrong; did you not agree with me for the usual daily wage? Take what belongs to you and go; I choose to give to this last the same as I give to you. Am I not allowed to do what I choose with what belongs to me? Or are you envious because I am generous?' So the last will be first, and the first will be last." (Matt. 20:1–16)

The point of this story would seem to be that when the landowner pays those who worked briefly the same amount as those who labored long, he is being loving but not unjust. Out of generosity, he freely pays everyone "the usual daily wage," but he does not give less than the early-comers agreed to. He attends to need without violating merit. This pattern is typical of a charity that sometimes rises above, but never falls below, justice.

The parable itself is typical of Jesus' way of reversing his auditors' expectations, especially about their own worthiness as a reliable guide to moral living. The lines take on particular power if one thinks of Jesus as the "wage" offered uniformly by God to a diverse and traditionally unequal world: Jew and Greek, slave and free, male and female (cf. Gal. 3:28). At the evening of history, the free Jewish man is "paid" the same as the enslaved Greek woman: the Son's generous sacrifice on the cross. The kicker is that being paid in this way incurs the debt of Imitation of Jesus' kenotic mildness, a duty not reducible to strict justice.

A strong *agape* that would imitate Christ embraces the reflexive normativity of basic personal care. It assumes that the capacity for care entails the call to give it to others in fundamental need (a duty of charity), and that the need for a minimal level of care entails the right to receive it from others when you can't provide it for yourself (a welfare right). (The principles of self-help and subsidiarity are quite compatible with strong *agape* thus understood.) Strong *agape* values human beings as valuers, taking the capacity for having ends as itself an end to be enhanced by society. The standard for such enhancement is not benign neglect or even Kantian respect but rather the Imitation of God. The dynamics of care in full Imitation of Christ's self-sacrificial love excel the usual language of "duties" of justice and "rights" of dignity. Once more, "justice" and "dignity" now typically refer to some form of achievement or excellence, whereas "charity" and "welfare" focus on lack and potency. When confronting human need, terms like "redemption" and "liberation" are more suitable to characterize the extension of aid than "respect" and "reward." But short of costly acts of altruism that liberate others for profound (even revolutionary) personal growth, a decent level of basic concern is due to all. This concern addresses need and potential in order to make merit possible; it does not subvert merit as such.

The meritarian indicts *agape* in part out of the false assumption that love is a limited resource—a fixed quantity of undifferentiated psychic energy, with family, friends, strangers, enemies, and finally oneself all competing to receive the largest portion. Saint Paul was acutely aware that personal loyalties can conflict, and Jesus himself counsels "hating" father, mother, wife, children, sisters, brothers, and one's own life as a precondition for following him (Luke 14:26). Yet the issue in all cases is not one of quantity of love but of priority among loves. If the priority of *agape* is not decidedly embraced, then special relations will tear one apart; if love of God and neighbor takes precedence, however, then the other relations may find their proper place. It is from the vantage of the cross, after all, that Christ endorses both maternal and filial affection: "Woman, here is your son," he says to his mother (John 19:26), and, "Here is your mother," to the beloved disciple (John 19:27). Love is not a zero-sum game, with someone's gain inevitably entailing another's loss.

More specifically, there is nothing inherent in Christian love that rules out relations based on merit (e.g., friendship), even as there is nothing that requires intolerance of those who do not share a Christian worldview. Charity's point is rather that preferential relations are relativized: one loves spouse, friends, fellow citizens, et al. first of all as neighbors. In fact, as Kierkegaard emphasizes, *agape* makes special associations more stable, less subject to the vicissitudes of time, place, and personal bent because preceded by a commitment to God that transforms the associations into matters of conscience.[49] A conscientious commitment to the principle "You shall love" can constitute, moreover, an exceptionally heroic morality, a saintliness equal in emotional and volitional rigor to anything envisioned by Nietzsche.

Meritarians such as Freud find Christian charity unjust or deluded only because they fail to recognize that love is both appreciative and productive of worth; it both "appraises" and "bestows" value, to use Irving Singer's terms. Singer observes that "love creates a new value, one that is not reducible to the individual or objective value that something may also have. This further type of valuing [opposed to appraisal] I call bestowal. . . . Here it makes no sense to speak of verifiability. . . . For now it is the valuing alone that *makes* the value."[50] Singer sometimes overemphasizes the gratuitousness of love and underemphasizes the way in which being loved objectively improves the beloved. But bestowal is surely a key *part* of what *agape* entails. What to a strict meritarian looks unjust is in fact one of love's greatest mysteries: the gift of worthiness not based solely on another's utility. As Singer points out, "Freud . . . failed to understand how love exceeds appraisive modes of valuation."[51]

By biblical lights, the Image of God resident in every human being is an ontological reality that, however dimmed by sin, calls for honor and protection. So agapic love is for human beings in themselves, not merely for God. Yet the radically unconditional and service-oriented love commanded in the Gospels is best seen as an "Urduty"—a form of "righteousness" that is (largely) unrelated to any present contingent state or any past personal performance. Part of the meaning of the "sanctity" of human life is that its worth is beyond exchange or quantification, that is, beyond the ordinary interest-based "rights" and "duties" associated with modern justice. The only state-related question charity asks of another is "Is this creature capable of receiving Christlike love?" not "Has this creature somehow earned such love?" And the only state-related question charity asks of itself is "Am I capable of giving Christlike love?" not "Will I be praised or rewarded for such love?"

[49] Kierkegaard, *Works of Love*, trans. by Howard V. and Edna H. Hong (New York: Harper and Row, 1962), pp. 140–45.

[50] Singer, *The Nature of Love*, vol. 1, p. 5; and see also pp. 10–13.

[51] Singer, *The Nature of Love*, vol. 3, *The Modern World*, p. 157. Singer makes the salient point most explicitly: "Within itself, love includes appraisiveness as well as the bestowing of value. To neglect either is to misconstrue both" (p. 396). Singer also criticizes Freud for his assumption "that the quantity of love must be limited in accordance with his economic theory [of psychic energies]" (p. 153).

There may indeed be tensions between reverence for sanctity and re-spect for dignity (see chapter 5 on abortion), but the two are finally inseparable. A psychological behaviorism, à la B. F. Skinner, that would go "beyond freedom and dignity" actually fails to achieve either and thus is a prescription for injustice. Strong *agape*, on the other hand, would transcend mere freedom and dignity by showing their dependence on charity. By demonstrating that freedom and dignity alone are inconceiv-able, that attention to the sanctity of human needs and potentials is the sine qua non of ethics, strong *agape* in fact provides the surest safeguard for justice.

Response to the Naturalist Critique

Against the naturalist, the agapist maintains that love of neighbor is never a sign of slavish frailty or world-hatred. A case can be made that, for the early Socrates, only the moral virtues are of real worth, and many a Plato-nist has suggested that natural human needs and abilities are finally insig-nificant.[52] Biblical Christianity is not simply "Platonism for the masses," however, since it does not denegrate temporal goods as such but rather subordinates them to the call to obedience to God and service of neigh-bors. Christian theocentricity may *seem* to parallel Socrates' early view, but acknowledging the primacy of God is not the same as granting sole reality or worth to God. To treat nonmoral goods as, at best, instrumen-tally useful is actually to depart from a biblical view in which creation is originally good in all of its parts and partially redeemed through commu-nal acts of eating and drinking. In healing the sick and feeding the hun-gry, Jesus affirms the goodness of all facets of incarnate life, even while he calls for radical love and restoration of that life. God and *agape* are the highest goods, for him, but not the only goods; and only a Gnostic Christ longs for death or the thwarting of embodied existence. The

---

[52] Gregory Vlastos noted, in a 1979 public lecture at Yale, that there are four classes of goods mentioned in the early Platonic dialogues: (1) material goods such as life, health, bodily vigor, good looks, and material wealth; (2) social goods such as noble birth, prestige, political power, and military success; (3) nonmoral intellectual goods such as mental abili-ties and practical skills; and (4) moral goods such as the virtues of justice, temperance, courage, piety, and wisdom. The early Socrates typically maintains that only moral goods are intrinsically valuable, as in this passage from *Euthydemus*, 281d2–e1:

In sum, then, it looks as though this is to be our position concerning all of those things which we first said were good [classes 1, 2, and 3]: it is not in their nature to be good in and of themselves, but this is how it is, it seems: if guided by ignorance they are more evil than their contraries, since they are then more able to serve their evil guide; while if wisdom leads them they are greater goods, though of themselves nei-ther they nor their contraries are worth anything at all. (Vlastos translation)

agapic imitator of Christ simply believes that to live without *agape* is itself a frustration of our highest human potential.

As suggested in my introduction, the priority of *agape* may be interpreted in a weak and a strong sense. For the "weak agapist," charity surpasses its rivals in worth and obligatoriness, so it is always to be chosen in cases of moral conflict. But charity remains one good among many: greater than but qualitatively similar to others. For the "strong agapist," on the other hand, *agape* is a metavalue; it not only outdistances but also undergirds all other forms of human excellence. For strong agapists, charity is a necessary condition for personal fulfillment across the range of human capacities; without *agape*, no good (moral or nonmoral) may be properly enjoyed. Thus it is neither right nor, in a sense, possible to sacrifice love for lesser goods. Without love, supposed virtues are but glittering vices and putative pleasures bitter dregs. There is this much unity to the moral life.

However *agape* is interpreted, one must distinguish between the ideal (strong or weak) and the unhappy consequences of trying yet failing to live up to it. Many naturalists, including Nietzsche at times, object not so much to genuine love of neighbor as to the mendacity and peevishness that result from halfhearted attempts to embody it. A certain hardheadedness about human limitations is surely appropriate. Yet even if neighbor-love were humanly impossible—or, less dramatically, even if only a few were able to realize it—the *ideal* of universal benevolence could still remain intact. Unless one embraces a priori a strong principle of "ought implies can," which begs the central question, there is no contradiction between the agapist's claim that we should love one another unconditionally and the naturalist's claim that this is for most of us just too taxing to be practical.

Of course, not all naturalistic objections to *agape* can be reduced to the issue of practicality. Christianity assumes that everyone, with God's help, is capable of *agape*; but some "strong naturalists," including Susan Wolf and Nietzsche at other times, fault the ideal as such. They contend that *agape* is impoverishing and therefore undesirable, not merely that it is too tough. In this instance, perhaps the most telling rebuttal (applicable to both strong naturalists and many liberals) is to turn the tables and ask why we should imagine neighbor-love to be such a threat to personal development and/or the public weal. We continue to find modern versions of individualism and contractarianism plausible, and thus to find *agape* worrisome, because our central values of autonomy and justice still largely presuppose a model of the self as detached will. Moral maturity is frequently defined in terms of objectivity toward others and the ability to keep contingent promises to them. Because we *rhetorically* value self-determination (if not self-sufficiency) so highly, we find it hard to picture an active and engaged charity that does not render the giver unduly encumbered or the receiver unduly dependent. I do not minimize the importance of personal freedom and social tolerance, but the defenders of a more relational view of the self—a view in which interpersonal care and mutual assistance are emphasized—have become increasingly persuasive.[53] The more such defenders can harmonize the best of naturalism (and liberalism) with their own communitarian concerns, the more adequate will be our conception of private and public virtue. And the more adequate is our conception of such virtue, I believe, the more compelling will be the case for Christian charity.

Again, *agape* seems a threat to peace of mind or political freedom only (or at least particularly) when we embrace an overly atomistic anthropology. For its part, the Christian church accounts a relationship to God through Christ to make possible nonoppressive relationships to other people, as well as to oneself. If persons are thought of as essentially separate beings most fully human in making rational choices independently of social context, then being deeply committed to or influenced by others (much less the Holy Other) must seem suspiciously heteronomous, even inherently violating. Yet the church believes self-giving love is worth the effort, an indispensable good. As the early Juan Segundo eloquently says:

> To love means to lose our autonomy and to become dependent on another. And this dependence may end up one day as disillusionment and heartbreak, leaving us empty inside. All love is a gamble, wherein we risk the best and deepest part of ourself.
>
> There are no guarantees in this world to cover the gamble. We either accept or reject love. For this very reason every act of love is more than an act of good will; it is an act of trust, an act of faith. It is an act of faith launched into the air, without any precise name or clear content. It is a belief that love is worthwhile, which defies fate and blind indifference to the importance of self-giving.
>
> The point is that *we* [Christians] know that this trust is well placed. We know that it is placed in good hands: i.e., that there is Someone who has responded with a yes and that this gesture is not lost in a void. We are those

---

[53] See, inter alia, the essays by Carol Gilligan and Martha Nussbaum in *Reconstructing Individualism: Autonomy, Individuality, and the Self in Western Thought*, ed. by Thomas C. Heller, Morton Sosna, and David E. Wellbery (Stanford: Stanford University Press, 1986); and Charles Taylor's *Sources of the Self: The Making of the Modern Identity* (Cambridge, Mass.: Harvard University Press, 1989). I am particularly indebted to Gilligan in what I say here.

who "have believed in love," as Saint John says, because we know the name of him who is the origin and object of all love.[54]

Although Saint Paul is the great champion of "Christian liberty," he enjoins above all else a love that "bears one another's burdens" (Gal. 6:2). The virtue of *agape* may not obviate all recourse to violence in defending the common good (see chapter 3), but it does avoid the twin vices of injustice and insensitivity. As what Charles Taylor calls a "moral source,"[55] *agape* is both self-empowering and self-limiting precisely because it forges and sustains personal relations. It empowers people to act (even in the political sphere) by evoking a commitment to serve and protect the neighbor, but this same commitment also limits individuals in the motives and means they may employ (especially in the political sphere). Just war checks on violence, for instance, are an enduring Christian response to naturalists and liberals on how love "transforms" justice. Such checks grow out of love itself and its rootedness in that human community that would be the kingdom of God.

Response to the Liberal Critique

The secular liberal begins by equating *agape* with an overly Platonic vision of love, only then to fault it as impersonal and potentially abusive. When understood as intense concern for an abstract ideal the individual representatives of which are ultimately dispensable, *agape* must indeed seem prone to oppression. Respecting the particularity of finite people will matter far less than promoting the *summum bonum* (e.g., God's will) in which they participate. Individuals will be, at best, interchangeable, and anyone may be sacrificed for the greater good which is the true source of value. Both Augustine and Aquinas seem to lend support to this view of charity, Augustine claiming that only God is to be "enjoyed" for His own sake, thus that human beings are to be "used" for the sake of something higher, and Aquinas contending that "God is the principal object of charity, while our neighbor is loved out of charity for God's sake."[56] But such scenarios unnecessarily impoverish (or risk impoverishing) love of others. A plurality of ends is possible, even if one end has metapriority; to love another human being passionately and for her own sake need not be to elevate her (idolatrously) to the highest good, even

---

[54] Segundo, *A Theology for Artisans of a New Humanity*, vol. 1, *The Community Called Church* (Maryknoll: Orbis, 1973), p. 57.

[55] Taylor, *Sources of the Self*, esp. chap. 4.

[56] See Augustine, *On Christian Teaching* [396/7, with a fourth book added in 426/7], trans. by R.P.H. Green (Oxford: Oxford University Press, 1997), bk. I, chap. 22, pp. 16–17; and Aquinas, *Summa Theologiae*, vol. 3, II-II, Q. 23, art. 5, *ad* 1, p. 1267.

as to love God as *summum bonum* need not be to reduce people (cruelly) to means only.[57]

The genius of true love is its attention to personal detail; such love *is* a respecter of persons, in all their uniqueness. While Platonic love ignores or transcends the particular in order to love the pure form, thereby making more personal kinds of love impossible,[58] *agape* attends to and even accents the particular, thereby enhancing individual commitments. The agapist is not unegoistic because she would lose all personal identity (including her own) in the white light of infinity, but rather because she judges all human lives to be sacred and (with God's help) treats them accordingly. Love of neighbor is preceded by and grounded in, but not negated by, love of God. In response to secular liberals, then, the agapist notes that love honors the consciences of others (within the widest possible limits) precisely because they are fellow creatures made in the Image of God: free beings with shared needs and potentials, yet fallible beings marred by the same Fall that touches everyone.

Love's "unegotism" applies to intellect, will, and emotion. This much was evident to Saint Paul. If faith in God makes for confidence in the ability to love the neighbor—for "it is no longer I who live, but it is Christ who lives in me" (Gal. 2:20)—it also makes for humility in the face of personal ignorance, culpability, and sloth. In spite of his comments on "predestination" and "election," Paul was a universalist with respect to human depravity: "all, both Jews and Greeks, are under the power of sin" (Rom. 3:9). As a result, restraint and mutual forbearance are crucial elements in his social ethics. "Do not repay anyone evil for evil, but take thought for what is noble in the sight of all. If it is possible, so far as it depends on you, live peaceably with all. Beloved, never avenge yourselves, but leave room for the wrath of God" (Rom. 12:17–19). Paul does insist that his gospel message alone is to be preached (Gal. 1:6–9), and in closing his first letter to the Corinthians, he writes: "Let anyone be accursed who has no love for the Lord" (1 Cor. 16:22). So bourgeois liberals have a point when they worry about Christian intolerance: obviously, religion has been and may yet be a "conversation stopper" (Rorty) or even an Inquisitor that replaces conversation with torture. The much more dominant theme in Paul, however, is that of these famous lines: "Love is patient; love is kind. . . . It does not insist on its own way; it is not irritable or resentful. . . . It bears all things, believes all things, hopes all things, endures all things" (1 Cor. 13:4–7). The paramount measure of charity was for Paul (following Jesus) the patient willingness to suffer redemptively for others, rather than the insistence on

---

[57] I discuss these matters at more length in *Love Disconsoled*, esp. chap. 3.
[58] Cf. Singer, *The Nature of Love*, vol. 1, p. 84.

converting them to a particular creed or form of life. This willingness contains the seeds of its own political restraint—respect and tolerance being political expressions, rather than antitheses, of *agape*.

Response to the Feminist Critique

The feminist arguments briefly adumbrated above help us recognize two basic truths. The first is that *agape*, including whatever sacrifice this may entail, is not the exclusive vocation of women. When women alone are called on to be caring and self-sacrificial, this inevitably becomes a vehicle employed by men to victimize and subordinate them. Thus the secular philosopher Eva Feder Kittay calls for "a more equitable distribution of dependency work," the latter defined as "caring for those who are inevitably dependent."[59] Feminist theologians, in turn, need only note that, as commanded by God, *agape* is the métier of all Christians. The "You shall" of the two love commands is not gender-specific, however often it may be interpreted as such. The precise form self-giving obedience may take will depend on context, and, as groups, men and women may tend to live out their responsibilities in different registers.[60] But there is no simple moral division of labor whereby men are the defenders of (public) justice, say, and women are the practitioners of (private) charity. Justice may weigh competing claims and powers, and love extend nurturing care, but neither is the specialty of one sex only. As Kittay concludes, "there is nothing inherently gendered about the work of care."[61]

The second truth highlighted by various feminists is that *agape* is not to be identified uniquely or unqualifiedly with sacrifice.[62] To be sure, Jesus goes to death on the cross, out of obedience to God and for the sake of others. And I have emphasized that there is finally no circumvention of the cross for Christ's disciples. Human need, as well as human sin, will always mean that there is ample call for self-surrender, in the form of service and mercy. Patriarchy can produce false needs, unhealthy dependencies, but not all vulnerabilities can be placed under these rubrics; so any critique of self-sacrifice that would repudiate it altogether fails to appreciate the ineliminable lacks that come with human finitude.[63] As I

---

[59] Kittay, *Love's Labor*, pp. xiv and ix.

[60] Should women be drafted for military combat? Should men be biologically altered so that they too can carry a fetus and give birth? How precisely to balance sexual difference with political freedom and equality is, to put it mildly, still being negotiated in Western society.

[61] Kittay, *Love's Labor*, p. xiii.

[62] See, in addition to Andolsen and many others, Rubenstein, *The Sacrificial Mother*.

[63] In *Beyond God the Father*, Mary Daly criticizes sacrificial love, service, humility, and related ideals as tending to reinforce victimization of the oppressed, particularly women; see

have also noted, however, Jesus' own love sometimes takes other forms than self-sacrifice (e.g., feeding the five thousand). As a male Messiah, Jesus Christ is unacceptable to some feminists, but there are lessons for those who would still imitate him: Jesus himself flees danger when his hour has not yet come, Jesus withdraws from the multitude for the quiet of solitude, and Jesus freely consents to his Passion rather than having it compelled upon him by force. Hence the definition of *agape* in my introduction reflects two things: (1) that sacrifice is not the whole of *agape*—one must also speak of unconditional willing of the good and of equal regard, and (2) that openness to sacrifice is itself premised on its being both constructive and consensual. Masochism and profligacy are not virtues, Christian or otherwise, and even God's grace does not coerce individuals to do good.

Speaking more critically, I do not think that self-love, *eros*, friendship, or autonomy can have the central place, at least within Christian ethics, that some feminists suggest.[64] The second love command requires one to love one's neighbor "as oneself" (Matt. 22:39), and this may seem to make self-love foundational for the moral life. But Jesus' final commandment is to "love one another . . . as I have loved you" (John 13:34; see also 15:12),[65] which significantly displaces *amor sui* as a criterion. It would appear that, toward the end of his life, Jesus became convinced that human beings do not normally know how to love themselves. They are so liable to distraction, fear, and malice that they require a concrete model outside themselves, one based on supernatural inspiration rather than on natural inclination. It is not the case, then, that Jesus simply

---

Beyond God the Father: Toward a Philosophy of Women's Liberation (Boston: Beacon, 1973), esp. pp. 77, 100–102, 105, and 162. Her accent falls on dignity, justice, freedom, and the like, although she also offers a moving description of what she calls "genuine love" (p. 128). She rightly wants to resist "love cut off from power and justice" (p. 127), love that falls below justice, but one wants to hear more about the ways in which love must sometimes rise above a narrow justice, as in generosity to strangers and forgiveness of enemies (see my chap. 4). In *Gyn/Ecology: The Metaethics of Radical Feminism* (Boston: Beacon, 1978), Daly rejects self-sacrifice even more emphatically; see pp. 2 and 374–78.

[64] See, for instance, Andolsen, "*Agape* in Feminist Ethics," and Christine E. Gudorf, *Body, Sex, and Pleasure* (Cleveland: Pilgrim, 1994). For a defense of the distinctive necessity of *agape* over and above all forms of preferential love, including *eros*, see my *Love Disconsoled*, esp. chap. 3; see also Colin Grant's "For the Love of God: *Agape*," *Journal of Religious Ethics* 24, no. 1 (spring 1996), together with responses by Carter Heyward, Edward Vacek, and Gene Outka.

[65] Some commentators have seen the Johannine "one another" as referring to fellow Christians only and thus as a retreat from the universal scope of neighbor-love called for elsewhere in the Gospels. For arguments against this view, see my "The Gospels and Christian Ethics," in *The Cambridge Companion to Christian Ethics*, ed. by Robin Gill (Cambridge: Cambridge University Press, 2001).

replaces Socrates' Delphic "Know Thyself" with his own Judaic "Love Thyself." The worm at the heart of human nature goes deeper than that. If Jesus could begin with proper self-love, or even with the injunction to it, there would be no need for a Messiah and no need for persons to imitate that Messiah's going to the cross.

Sometimes the best way to achieve a goal is not to value it too highly and not to aim at it too directly. Rather like a Zen archer, one must sometimes look away from the target and shut one's eyes before letting the arrow fly. Jesus encourages his (would-be) followers to "not worry about tomorrow" (Matt. 6:34), in fact, to "deny themselves and take up their cross daily and follow me" (Luke 9:23). By forgetting about their own self-interest, disciples are able to open themselves to others; moreover, this very self-denial facilitates true self-possession. "For those who want to save their life will lose it, and those who lose their life for my sake will save it" (Luke 9:24). Proper self-love is one of the blooms on the rose of the Christian life, to change the metaphor, and it is not to be villified. But self-love is not the root, much less the soil, from which Christianity grows. The root is *agape*, defined as love of God and neighbor, and the soil is God's grace revealed in Jesus Christ and in the ministry of the Holy Spirit.

Friendship may stand as the ideal consummation of Christian love in heaven, but it too is not the paradigmatic form that *agape* takes in this life. Healthy and amicable persons do not just happen; they must be "built up," to use the Pauline phrase. We all depend on the kindness of strangers—initially our parents and/or their surrogates—to be fed, materially and spiritually. If we do not receive an unconditional and unearned care early on, we never grow into responsible agents. Moreover, God does not originally meet us as a buddy, but rather as a righteous Creator, Judge, and Redeemer. God loves us first (1 John 4:10), and while we are still sinners (Rom. 5:8), so there can be no question of beginning with our spontaneous knowledge of or affinity for the Holy.

This is not to say that self-love or friendship are illegitimate human ends; it is to say, rather, that they are impossible Christian beginnings. The command of Matthew 22 is to love *all* neighbors, not merely those who, like friends, share our interests or who, like friends, return our affection. Agapic love is not mere abstract benevolence—it wants concrete human relations and offers a practical hand of support and fellowship—but it does not presuppose or require mutuality, the way that a preferential love like friendship does. If *agape* did insist on reciprocation or fellow feeling, it would cease to be akin to *ḥésed*, the steadfast love of Yahweh.[66]

---

[66] On these matters, see Søren Kierkegaard, *Works of Love*, esp. part one, chap. II; and Gene Outka, *Agape: An Ethical Analysis* (New Haven: Yale University Press, 1972), esp. pp. 34–44. See also my *Love Disconsoled*, chap. 3.

Autonomy fails as a touchstone for Christian ethics for many of the same reasons. Andolsen, Daly, and other feminists are quite right to extol such virtues as honesty, courage, and creativity and to reject all forms of heteronomy, for both men and women. Understood as either the external coercion of action and belief or the internal alienation from one's authentic self, heteronomy is destructive of persons. But autonomy (defined as self-governance or even self-assertion) is not the only alternative to heteronomy (defined as self-stunting or even self-loss). Scripture suggests that when we try to begin morally with human autonomy, our own good and powerful will, we end up with either overweening pride or crippling despair. Either we think that we are capable of always doing the right thing, of saving our own souls, of reforming the entire world, and the like, all on our own steam. Or we think that we are hopeless wretches caught, without recourse, in a futile and guilty universe. The latter is, no doubt, a truer picture of our lived reality, but it forgets the good news of the gospel: that we are not alone, neither left to our own devices nor simply at the mercy of blind nature or fallen human beings.

To believe in autonomy as first virtue is to believe that the natural man or woman is enough for righteousness and/or salvation. In contrast, Jesus implies that all people are sinful (John 8:7), and he even downplays, if not denies, his own goodness: "Why do you call me good? No one is good but God alone" (Luke 18:19). For his part, Saint Paul subscribed to a (fundamentally Stoic) version of natural law, holding that all of creation testifies to the nature of God and that what God's law requires is "written on [the] hearts" even of Gentiles (Rom. 1:18–20; 2:14–15). But Paul also believed that many—indeed, all—human beings, although "without excuse" (Rom. 1:20), turn away from the available knowledge of God and His will. "All, both Jews and Greeks, are under the power of sin" (Rom. 3:9), and sin both manifests and occasions the most dreadful fate of all, divine abandonment. What Paul says about the ungodly applies, or could apply, finally to everyone: "since they did not see fit to acknowledge God, God gave them up to a debased mind and to things that should not be done" (Rom. 1:28). The basic reason for divine wrath is idolatry, worshiping and serving the creature rather than the Creator (Rom. 1:25), with individual instances of immorality being not so much the causes of God's punishment as its effects. Left to themselves, that is, human beings become perverse, unable to control themselves or respect others: "full of envy, murder, strife, deceit, craftiness . . . foolish, faithless, heartless, ruthless" (Rom. 1:29–31).

Self-reliance and appeals to natural law are not the only paths to glory, however, according to Paul and the *New Testament* generally. In fact, they are not paths at all. We need not and cannot begin with human efforts to reach up to God, or with human efforts to reach out to the neighbor, or even with human efforts to reach deep within ourselves (for

authenticity or androgyny or whatever). The Fall has seen to that, for
Adam, Eve, and all their descendants. But, mirabile dictu, God has gra-
ciously reached down to us. The Incarnate Son who died on the cross
represents God's forgiving and empowering us from above, independently of any insight or merit on our part.

Some feminists have argued that women, especially in a male-chauvinist culture, are much more likely than men to experience "sin" as tim-
idity, sloth, and self-denigration, and thus that calls to autonomy and
self-assertion have an essential place for females that they do not have for
males. Testosterone-filled men are prone to aggression and abuse of others,
the argument runs, so they need to be reined in with strong principles of
tolerance, humility, sacrifice, mercy, and the like. But tyrannized women
need, in contrast, to be spurred on to a sense of their own value and
power, so rallying cries of self-affirmation, gender solidarity, righteous
indignation, even violent retaliation are appropriate. It should be no surprise that Judeo-Christian Scripture fails to recognize this, since that
Scripture is written largely (if not exclusively) by men who frequently aim
to keep women down. The "original sin" of "man" may be pride, but,
Mary Daly contends, that of woman is the "internalization of blame and
guilt" that is enforced by sexist conditioning in a patriarchal society.[67]

These are plausible contentions, in some respects, and I myself would
defend the moral uses of anger and violent force in some unjust social
situations (see chapter 3). We must avoid what Daly has called "seduction by spiritualization," in which "love/concern for the oppressed . . .
easily translates into love for oppression as the only morally acceptable
state."[68] But the biblical response, here again, is that love of God and
neighbor is not essentially gendered. Sin may take on a different patina in
the lived experiences of most women and men, such that it makes sense
to speak of characteristically "feminine" and "masculine" forms of sin.
This diction risks an unfortunate stereotyping, however, and, in any
event, sin remains *au fond* a willed and knowing separation from God:
"before God in despair not to will to be oneself or in despair to will to be
oneself," to use Kierkegaard's phrase.[69] Disordered selfhood, before God,

---

[67] Daly, *Beyond God the Father*, p. 49. Despite her antipathy to sexual stereotyping, Daly's
repeated and pejorative use in *Beyond* of phrases like "phallic morality" and "the phallic
mentality" (e.g., p. 121), not to mention "the mad world of phallic categories" (p. 126),
inevitably (if unintentionally) associates evil with maleness. There is, no doubt, a problem
with "phallocentric power" (p. 122), defined as the monopoly of authority by men, but the
phallus as such is innocent. In *Gyn/Ecology*, "male" has more or less candidly become a
term of derision. For a similarly unfortunate use of language, see Beverly Harrison's *Our
Right to Choose* (Boston: Beacon, 1983), in which "masculinist" invariably means bad and
"feminist" good (e.g., p. 103).

[68] Daly, *Pure Lust*, pp. 326–27.

[69] Søren Kierkegaard (Anti-Climacus), *The Sickness Unto Death*, trans. by Howard and
Edna Hong (Princeton: Princeton University Press, 1980), p. 96.

is something of which both men and women are guilty; the tendency to draw invidious contrasts between "us" and "them," "mine" and "yours," "I" and "it," is not merely a consequence of "phallic morality."[70] Human sin is universal, and its remedy continues to be faith, hope, and love—especially love. Even though women have been more often victimized throughout history—we must not flich from or deny the disparity of guilt—the primacy of charity remains in place for all creatures who share God's Image. History itself suggests that nothing short of agapic love can sustain the weak and needy and lead to reconciliation with God and other people. Without unconditional nurture, children cannot mature into adults; and without forgiveness, adults cannot escape bitterness and vendetta. If Jesus did not found his kingdom on autonomy and self-assertion when his fellow Jews were under the oppressive thumb of imperial Rome, would he tell women today anything different from what he told his disciples in the first century?[71]

The essential biblical remedy for alienation and tyranny is not autonomy but theonomy, being ruled by God's grace. A version of autonomy may be a valid principle when specifying the limits of earthly authorities, political and ecclesiastical,[72] and these limits may cogently be applied to the traditional androcentric family to make it more egalitarian. But when autonomy is made a metavalue or the wellspring of all duty, for either men or women, it is incompatible with Christian ethics. Participating in and being used by the holiness of God is the key Christian ideal. And such theonomy can be consented to without violating one's integrity, male or female, because God is more intimate to both sexes than they are to themselves. Indeed, it is in patiently waiting on God that women can learn how *not* to wait unjustly or idolatrously on men. Through the life, death, and resurrection of Jesus Christ, God has made a way where before there was no way, including a way out of sexism. It is with *this*

---

[70] Cf. Daly, *Beyond God the Father*, p. 67 and passim.

[71] And why should a male Master have authority? There is no question but that predominantly masculine symbols for God and teachers of faith have impoverished the spiritual life of both women and men, thus that new "models of God" and new "models of church" are called for. Jesus' pointing beyond himself to the transcendent Source of all goodness, together with his association with women and an attendant relativization of gender differences, would seem to make his own sex irrelevant. But this is not to say, of course, that it has not been seen as relevant by generations of male theologians. *Some* role models—heroes and heroines—would seem to be indispensable for moral and religious education. For a now classic critique of taking Jesus (or virtually anyone else) as a model, nevertheless, see *Beyond God the Father*, chap. 3, "Beyond Christolatry."

[72] "Initially standing for a political conception in Greek thought, the term ['autonomy'] came to be used in religious controversies during the Reformation; but its main use in early modern times was in political discussions. Kant seems to have been the first to assign broader significance to it, using it in his theoretical as well as his practical philosophy." See J. B. Schneewind, *The Invention of Autonomy* (Cambridge: Cambridge University Press, 1998), p. 3, n. 2.

liberation in mind that Christian feminists may say a genuinely healing word to both halves of the world's population.

To repeat, if men or women look first or chiefly to their own free wills, there is no escaping either self-righteousness or the sense that the world is full of chaos and dilemma. "Discovery of the self's potential"[73] is an important by-product of relation to God, and heaven knows that females (like males) require praise and encouragement throughout their lifetimes. Anorexia, starving oneself of both spiritual and material sustenance as an irrational form of self-punishment, continues to plague a shocking number of girls and young women. But it is precisely the moral valorization of autonomy, the assumption that one can or should make the world perfect by one's own efforts, that lies at the root of anorexia. This terrible affliction is not due to lack of (female) autonomy but rather to insistence on autonomy run amok: "Because I cannot change the world or myself alone, I do not deserve to eat."[74] In contrast, relation to God reveals two things: (1) even the best human self is inconstant and corrupt in comparison to true holiness, yet (2) the prescription for healing human misery is a joyful letting go of preoccupation with self in favor of trusting reliance on God.

"Man would like to be an egoist and cannot," Simone Weil observes,[75] and in this case the word "man" should be read as inclusive of all humanity. If men and women are converted to look first to God's grace, rather than their own volition, it is possible to trust that, however bleak a soul or situation may appear, God provides a sustainable faith, hope, and love. Properly understood, these virtues are not enemies of self-actualization; to think that the Creator would intentionally stunt creatures is to make God schizophrenic. What these Christian virtues do imply, however, is that we need not do evil that good might come (cf. Rom. 3:8–9), that perseverance is possible even in the worst of cases. More specifically, Christ's obedience on the cross symbolizes for Christians the fact that the corrective for sin, as well as want, is innocent self-giving instead of either vengeful self-assertion or resigned self-destruction. As I explain in chapter 3, this is not a prescription for nonresistance to evil, for mere acquies-

[73] Daly, *Beyond God the Father*, p. 66. Professor Daly recommends "conscious participation in the *living* God" (p. 96), a spirituality in which both men and women are open to transcendence, the power of Being. I am not as optimistic as she is, however, that calls for "female autonomy" and "the free and independent woman" (p. 85) will serve this purpose. Given the history of misogyny, her emphasis on female pride and self-affirmation, "the promise in ourselves" (p. 158), is understandable. But die-hard supernaturalists like myself can only urge, respectfully, that the priority is God's.

[74] I rely here on the ground-breaking work of Peggy Claude Pierre, documented in the ABC News *20/20* presentation entitled "The Hunger Inside" (December 2, 1994).

[75] Weil, *Gravity and Grace*, trans. by Emma Craufurd (London and New York: Ark Paperbacks, 1987), p. 53.

cence in social injustice, but it is a radical distancing of all worldly or egocentric starting points for ethics.

Secular feminists such as Eva Feder Kittay actually support a chastened view of agapic love in contrast to the more agonistic accounts of justice associated with autonomy and capitalist society. Kittay is wary of acquiescing to "the 'feminine' virtues of self-effacing self-sacrifice," but she insists that our usual conceptions of mutuality, often emphasized by feminists, are "inapplicable" in some cases of care.[76] As important as it is to cultivate responsible individuals, male and female, "no one escapes dependency in a lifetime, and many must care for dependents in the course of a life."[77] Indeed, "there are moments when we are not 'inter' dependent. We are simply dependent and *cannot* reciprocate."[78] Kittay's aim is not to deny all human interdependence, but rather "to find a knife sharp enough to cut through the fiction of our independence."[79] Her skepticism about self-sufficiency and the unencumbered will resonates well with strong *agape*. What divides Kittay from the biblical witness, nevertheless, is that the latter would highlight human beings' dependence on God, as well as on one another, with the former having priority.

This is not to say that, according to Scripture, genuine caring is not possible for non-Christians. Kittay's own example of raising a disabled daughter demonstrates that there can be profound love without a conscious embracing of the rituals and creeds of the Christian church. Still, a Christian will see the providence of God active, anonymously, in these impressive lives. Kittay's entirely convincing thesis is that a just society must recognize and nurture its nurturers—for example, by so structuring political and economic opportunities that caregivers ("dependency workers" who are still usually female) are not unfairly disadvantaged. A biblical strong agapist will contend that the indispensable support here comes from God's prevenient grace. This is not mere metaphysical overlay: confessing before and giving gratitude to God will condition the whole of one's moral life. Still, there are deep affinities among such charitable "laborers" as Eva Feder Kittay, the Dalai Lama, Martin Luther King, Jr., and Dorothy Day.

PROPHETIC LIBERALISM

As noted, social liberals often worry that calls to agapic love will lead to political despotism. In the name of caring for human needs and cultivat-

[76] Kittay, *Love's Labor*, p. 180.
[77] Ibid., p. xiii.
[78] Ibid., p. 180.
[79] Ibid., p. xiii.

ing human potentials, they fear, an intrusive and omnicompetent state or church will emerge. This fear is reasonable in light of sixteenth- and seventeenth-century conflicts, but it is not ultimately telling against strong *agape*. Such *agape* keeps its account of the good life, as well as the good society, liberal because it respects freedom of conscience as an intrinsic rather than merely an instrumental good. Unlike many secular defenses of liberalism, prophetic liberalism is motivated by neither moral skepticism, nor fear of retaliation, nor even longing for temporal peace and prosperity. Instead of focusing on these negative or "thin" elements, prophetic liberalism is founded on a positive willing of the good for others as fellow creatures of God. Liberty and tolerance remain central values precisely because they grow out of a prior commitment to love of God and neighbor. Manipulation and dogmatism are rejected, that is, not because one has no substantive moral opinion or because one fears one will be an outsider but because one deeply empathizes with those who are already outsiders.

Strong *agape* is distinctive because it rejects what Amy Gutmann critically characterizes as the great impasse between freedom and virtue,[80] as well as the related impasse between reason and charity. Sincere goodness cannot be compelled, so virtue without freedom is empty; but meaningful choice must aim at an end judged worthy, so freedom without virtue is blind. One cannot claim that education for rational choice is somehow "neutral" and thus entirely separable from controversial pedagogy in moral goodness, any more than one can aspire to produce a just (i.e., procedurally fair) society without investing in just (i.e., virtuous) citizens.[81] Both rationality and morality presuppose nonrelative standards that are realized only with practical wisdom. Differing conceptions of human flourishing may, within limits, be equally valid, and love of the loves of others sets severe restrictions on what may be imposed on those who depart from majority opinion. But bare freedom of choice is insufficient for both love and justice. If we cannot specify a range of human needs to be met and potentials to be cultivated—needs and potentials shared by all undamaged human lives[82]—then "love of neighbor" is simply an

---

[80] Amy Gutmann, "Undemocratic Education," in *Liberalism and the Moral Life*, ed. by Nancy L. Rosenblum (Cambridge, Mass.: Harvard University Press, 1989), pp. 77–78.

[81] Cf. Hauerwas and Pinches, *Christians among the Virtues*, p. 149.

[82] Martha Nussbaum endorses the idea that, in seeking a basis for "claims of justice," we ought to "begin with the human being: with the capacities and needs that join all humans across barriers of gender and class and race and nation." See her "Human Capabilities, Female Human Beings," in *Women, Culture, and Development*, ed. by Martha Nussbaum and Jonathan Glover (Oxford: Clarendon, 1995), pp. 61–62. Nussbaum sometimes neglects the language of "need" in favor of "capability," and a theist would begin most basically with God's grace, but Nussbaum's universalism resonates well with aspects of Chris-

empty incantation from a bygone era. And if promises do not bind and the integrity of the weak need not be respected as such, then "social justice" is exactly as irrelevant as the Athenians told the Melians it was in 416 B.C.E.

If substantial accounts of both love and justice are seen as vapid, however, then liberal democracy has lost touch with its moral inspiration. The resultant "liberalism" will tend to make unconstrained liberty the primary if not the sole good, while "the prophetic" will look back to an *agape* in which such liberty (*liberum arbitrium*) is internal to but not exhaustive of true virtue (*libertas*). *Libertas*, as the spontaneous and joyful disposition to do the good, encompasses but outstrips autonomy, as absence of external restraint. *Libertas*, "the freedom of a Christian" in Paul's and Luther's sense, is most fully realized in a love of all neighbors sensitive to needs as well as deserts. This egalitarianism is a natural ally of classical liberal democracy: everyone counts because everyone shares the *Imago Dei*.

One way to underscore the priority of liberal charity relative to recent theories of bourgeois justice is to point out that in social ethics, as in market economics, production precedes distribution. The fair distribution of benefits and burdens arises as an issue only when individual persons have been produced who are capable of being benefited and burdened. Persons to whom something can be due are partially made rather than fully found. They are made, moreover, only in company with others who extend them personal care. It is an achievement to be a member of the body politic capable of being owed (or owing) something. We neglect at our peril the social processes—educational, ritual, moral—by which our healthy members are generated.

The language of "production" is admittedly disconcerting when applied to persons. But the satiric point of the analogy is to undermine the hegemony of the abstract conceptions of social relations that often prevail in Western political and economic contexts. The maturation of dependent human beings into persons with free and meaningful lives is the necessary condition for activities in which distributive (and retributive) justice matters. The cultivation of subjectivity is chronologically and lexically prior to the celebration of objectivity. Indeed, the only way to rein in the excesses of supply-side economics and its accent on the profit motive is by insisting upon solidarity ethics and its openness to self-sacrifice. (It may be that people today must make money, but the reverse proposition is not the case.) People get to be people and continue to act like people only when they are extended care *by* others and are schooled in

tian charity. For more on where Nussbaum and strong *agape* part ways, see my *Love Disconsoled*, esp. chap. 7.

how to extend it *to* others. Any society that fails to appreciate and act on these facts will inevitably find itself chaotic, confused, and unjust.

As important as personal liberty is, one cannot make sense of private choices, much less public cooperation, without reference to the community that grounds those choices. In American society, a number of intermediate affiliations (such as family and church or synagogue) stand between the individual and the state, supporting and checking both; but frequently our theoretical (mis)understanding of ourselves blinds us to this fact. Perusal of a calendar from a recent local newspaper highlights both the strength and the weakness of our social arrangements. Among some eighty groups listed were:

MOTHERS OF TWINS ASSOCIATION
LESBIAN RAP GROUP
SCIENCE OF THE MIND STUDY GROUP
TRAUMATIC BRAIN INJURY SUPPORT GROUP
ADULT CHILDREN OF ALCOHOLICS COUNSELING GROUP
MEN'S CONSCIOUSNESS RAISING GROUP
COURSE IN MIRACLES SUPPORT GROUP
APPLE COMPUTER USERS' GROUP
À LA CARTE TRAVEL CLUB
OVEREATERS ANONYMOUS
TAIZÉ PRAYER COMMUNITY

Evidently we need each other. Americans, supposedly so individualistic, form clubs, committees, panels, and alliances without limit. Such associations, independent of the federal government yet part of public life, are indispensable schools of moral experience and safeguards of political and economic liberty. In these elective communities, much of the business of living gets worked out. The danger, nevertheless, is that we will lose sight of people very *un*like ourselves. If we recognize only those with whom we have an explicit affinity, we cease to practice love of neighbor. The neighbor is not someone chosen but someone found and cultivated. Other than God, the self is its own nearest neighbor, and even self-love cannot wait on delight.

Strong *agape* does not amount, then, to a prescription for a highly intrusive and paternalistic state. Prophetic liberalism holds that civil society must not only respect but also engender virtue. Thus the typically adversarial language of "rights" and "duties" of justice must be transformed by (although not necessarily replaced with) that of "the call to charity" and "the good of cooperation." Character will be formed collectively one way or another, so a neutral public philosophy is a chimera. But there are severe limits on what the coercive power of the state may do. Here I rely on William Galston over Gutmann in affirming that "the civic standpoint does not warrant the conclusion that the state must (or may) structure public education to foster in children skeptical reflection on ways of life inherited from parents or local communities." As Galston observes, "legitimate intrusive state powers . . . are limited by their own inner logic. In a liberal state, interventions that cannot be justified on this basis cannot be justified at all."[83] Physical force is used only to protect civic competence, thus the public sphere is normally conversational and persuasive rather than dogmatic and coercive.

Civic competence includes not just self-direction (the "rational liberty" of Locke as reconstructed by Rogers Smith, or the "self-reliance" of Emerson as defended by George Kateb) but personal care (for Christians, the "love of neighbor" embodied most fully in Jesus Christ). To think that Christ is the Incarnation of virtue is not to insist that authoritative or exclusive appeal be made to him in school textbooks, but neither does affirming liberalism mean that substantive moral claims must be eliminated from public domains in the name of "toleration" or "fairness." In civic forums (including presidential debates, Supreme Court decisions, state laws, and church sermons), there is an ineliminable place for the prophetic language of "love." Harold J. Berman, Woodruff Professor of Law at Emory University, goes so far as to contend that "law, understood in a Christian perspective, is a process of creating conditions in which sacrificial love, the kind of love personified by Jesus Christ, can take root in society and grow."[84] A pluralistic society will honor a wide range of religious traditions, but the idiom of "charity" and "personal care" can be embraced more or less nondenominationally. As Alexander Pope observed,

> In Faith and Hope the world will disagree,
> But all Mankind's concern is charity:
> All must be false that thwart this One great End
> And all of God, that bless Mankind or mend.[85]

In any case, thick biography and sociology, rather than thin "theory," is the sine qua non. In public school curricula, true pluralism could mean assigning works on Moses, Christ, Buddha, Krishna, Muhammed, and Mary Baker Eddy—as well as Sappho, Cicero, Napoleon, Marx, Freud,

---

[83] William A. Galston, *Liberal Purposes: Goods, Virtues, and Diversity in the Liberal State* (Cambridge: Cambridge University Press, 1991), pp. 253, 255. Chapter 11 of Galston's book, from which these quotes are taken, also appears in *Liberalism and the Moral Life*.

[84] Berman, *Faith and Order: The Reconciliation of Law and Religion* (Atlanta: Scholars, 1993), p. 313.

[85] Pope, "An Essay on Man," epistle III, lines 307–10, in *Alexander Pope: Selected Poetry and Prose*, ed. by William K. Wimsatt (New York: Holt, Rinehart and Winston, 1972), p. 220.

and Susan B. Anthony. Prophetic liberals would tell stories and live lives of quality, then let the cultural chips fall where they may, confident that even amid abiding disagreements, substantive truth claims about human well-being can be elaborated, defended, and jointly acted upon. Open dialogue aimed at insight into universal needs and aptitudes—shared regardless of race, gender, class, faith, or ethnicity—will itself be partially constitutive of the common good.[86]

Only basic assaults on the capacity for care warrant coercive governmental intrusion, but this should not imply either the moral indifference of the state or the privatization or trivialization of religion. The state will inevitably engage in forms of moral pedagogy, and the church is free to argue its case (within wide limits) in the domain of public discourse.[87] Faith's true raison d'être is the worship of God, not the balance of temporal powers, but part of worship will be "speaking truth to power."[88] And this is to be welcomed. "Civic tolerance of deep differences is perfectly compatible with unswerving belief in the correctness of one's own way of life. It rests on the conviction that the pursuit of the better course should (and in many cases must) result from persuasion rather than coercion."[89] The church's success in a liberal context depends on whether religion is seen to promote inwardness and openness rather than docility and oppression. "Diminished inwardness" does indeed make for "disdain for rights," as Kateb notes.[90] But I believe that Kateb is overly optimistic about the ability of a secular version of "democratic individuality" to discern the limits of interest-based rights and to rein in the misanthropy that often results from the Nietzschean refusal of rights altogether. If civic virtue entails charity and vice versa, then, as Galston allows, "In some measure, religion and liberal politics need each other."[91]

[86] Cf. Martha Nussbaum's "Non-Relative Virtues: An Aristotelian Approach," in *The Quality of Life*, ed. by Martha C. Nussbaum and Amartya Sen (Oxford: Clarenden, 1993). In "Feminist Internationalism: In Defense of Universal Values," an address given at Emory University on September 28, 1998, Nussbaum focused on ten "central human capabilities": life, bodily health, bodily integrity, senses-imagination-thought, emotions, practical reason, affiliation, relation to other species, play, and control over one's environment.

[87] See my "Love in a Liberal Society: A Reply to Weithman," *Journal of Religious Ethics* 22, no. 1 (spring 1994): 29–38.

[88] Stephen L. Carter's *The Culture of Disbelief: How American Law and Politics Trivialize Religious Devotion* (New York: Basic, 1993), is a superb critique of treating religion as a private hobby, although he sometimes approaches religion too completely as a form of political resistance (e.g., pp. 134–35). For criticisms of a "bourgeois masculinist" conception of the public sphere that "requires a sharp separation between civil society and the state," see Nancy Fraser, "Rethinking the Public Sphere: A Contribution to the Critique of Actually Existing Democracy," *Social Text: Theory/Culture/Ideology* 25/26 (1990): 62ff.

[89] Galston, *Liberal Purposes*, p. 253.

[90] George Kateb, "Democratic Individuality and the Meaning of Rights," in *Liberalism and the Moral Life*, p. 201.

[91] Galston, *Liberal Purposes*, p. 279.

Religion and liberal politics need each other, but Christian love retains its priority; it is no mere handmaiden to democracy. As participation in the life of God, strong *agape* surpasses appraisive rationality as well as bourgeois efficiency. Christlike love is neither describable by abstract theory nor directly identifiable with any finite human action or institution. It can be narratively related and personally imitated, however, in private and in public. Civic *agape* need not be statist, for it remains an open question to what extent government ought to be the instrument of care. The state is not the church, but strong *agape* dictates a nonpragmatic variety of liberalism: "liberalism-as-morally-perfectionist."[92]

Our civilization may be known by its self-images, and central to those images is what we think we owe one another. The most distinctive biblical contribution to social ethics is that we owe one another love. Being in the debt of love is one dimension of human sanctity: it is not a regrettable necessity, but rather a divine gift, that we need and must care for each other. The Greek basis of ethics is a dignity grounded in teleological rationality (realized intellect), while the Kantian basis is a dignity found in personal autonomy (good will). The biblical basis of sanctity, in contrast, is the passive potential for charity (the ability to give and/or receive love). This potential constitutes the Image of God, and although it is in no way antithetical to the dignity associated with contemplation and choice, it precedes these as their necessary condition. As I define them here, "dignity" is an achievement in time, "sanctity" an essence from eternity, but a prophetic liberalism attends to both.[93]

CONCLUSION

Athens after Pericles poisoned its greatest philosopher, even as Jerusalem under Pilate crucified its greatest prophet. These facts continue to symbolize the problematic relation between moral revolutionaries and political justice. Pure democracy tends to silence philosophy, but political philosophy itself frequently murders love. Even after the dawn of political

[92] Cf. ibid., p. 98. Civic *agape* is a version of what John Rawls calls "comprehensive liberalism"; see his *Political Liberalism* (New York: Columbia University Press, 1993), p. xxvii. For a further elaboration and defense of liberalism-as-morally-perfectionist, see Jackson, "The Return of the Prodigal?"

[93] Some theologians, especially Roman Catholics, speak of "the personal dignity and inviolability" of humanity, often referring thereby to the intrinsic capacity to give and receive charity. See, for instance, John Paul II, *The Splendor of Truth* [*Veritatis Splendor*] (Washington, D.C.: United States Catholic Conference, 1993), p. 137. I usually prefer to reserve "sanctity" for this purpose, to flag what is distinctive about a Christian anthropology and ethic. For more details, see chap. 5 below and my "A House Divided, Again: 'Sanctity' vs. 'Dignity' in the Induced Death Debates," in *In Defense of Human Dignity*, ed. by Robert Kraynak (Notre Dame: University of Notre Dame Press, 2002).

liberalism, charity has often been made to give way to reciprocity or pro-
ceduralism. Nevertheless, I have defended in this chapter a preeminent
place for love in a good society, as well as a good soul, a place prior to
both philosophy (the quest for theoretical truth) and pure democracy
(the denial of moral truth in favor of public convention). The virtuous
society, unthreatened by the diversity of its members, requires neither
veils of ignorance nor bread and circuses but rather philiaphile citizens.
Such citizens are the sort of moral revolutionaries who, if welcomed,
would make for political stability in a free state. They seldom are welcomed.

There is a prophetic value more basic than autonomy and still more
meta than reciprocal justice: personal care, or what the Christian tradition calls "charity." Without the cultivation of care for and by individuals
within a community, private choice and public cooperation become un-
imaginable. Without attention to objects worthy of desire and to people
due solidarity, both personal happiness and equal regard for others (cor-
nerstones of liberalism itself) vanish, or never emerge. Thus culture and
politics, ethics and ethos, must be more integrated than any purely pragmatic vision of justice allows.[94] We must recognize human dependency as
well as freedom, nurture love as well as fairness. There is no way, in short,
to avoid uttering and embodying ("performing") substantive truth claims
about the meaning of life and the ends of society.[95]

For many, the meaning of life is provided by *eros*, while the central end
of society is justice. Among philosophers, *eros* is often defined as a preferential love that is emotionally invested in particular individuals judged
beautiful or otherwise advantageous, while modern justice is frequently
contrasted with *eros* and characterized as an impartial adjudication of universal rights and contractual obligations.[96] I can summarize this chapter
by saying that *agape* offers moral resources that transcend this dichotomy.
Indeed, *agape* may be seen as something like a marriage of classical *eros*
and modern justice. Like *eros*, *agape* is passionately concerned with concrete individuals; unlike *eros*, however, *agape* does not premise its commitment on the perceived (and mutable) excellences of these individuals.
Agapic love attends to others for their own sakes but is constant and

[94] For an heroic attempt to combine prophetic Christian thought with American pragmatism, see Cornel West, *The Cornel West Reader* (New York: Civitas, 1999). West's is a
powerful prophetic voice, but I am less optimistic than he is that liberal democracy can be
defended on the basis of a pragmatic epistemology (or anti-epistemology).

[95] Cf. Robert Bellah et al., *The Good Society* (New York: Alfred Knopf, 1991).

[96] See Martha Nussbaum, *Love's Knowledge: Essays on Philosophy and Literature* (Oxford:
Oxford University Press, 1990), esp. chaps. 3, 11, 13, and 14. In "Steerforth's Arm,"
Nussbaum eloquently describes the marriage, in Dickens's *David Copperfield*, of Agnes (the
personification of moral judgment) and David (the personification of erotic love). Although
she does not use the term, the resulting picture is very close to my account of *agape* presented below.

unconditional. Like justice, *agape* entails an equal regard for others; unlike justice, however, *agape* does not premise this regard on the even-handed appraisal of rational agents and their agency. *Agape* sometimes gives more than is due according to reciprocal calculation, but never less. If *eros* is prejudiced in favor of a select few, while justice is neutral and inclusive, then *agape* may be said to synthesize both by being "prejudiced in favor of everybody."

There is a sublime excessiveness to charity manifest in words as diverse as Jesus' Sermon on the Mount, Lincoln's Second Inaugural Address, and Etty Hillesum's letters from the concentration camp at Westerbork. The same sublimity is also apparent in the relevant lives, even unto death. Their charity is indiscriminate, yet it affirms particular individuals, even enemies; it is egalitarian, yet it inspires an extraordinary saintliness in some; it is indomitable, yet it is "made perfect in weakness" (2 Cor. 12:9). Such exemplary figures illustrate that *agape* is not opposed to justice or *eros* as such, any more than to friendship or aesthetic enjoyment: Lincoln aspired to "charity for all," yet he directed a costly Civil War to emancipate the slaves and preserve the Union; Hillesum relished physical pleasures, yet she managed to forgive her Nazi tormentors; and Jesus had close friends, yet he died to ransom the entire world from sin. *Agape* is almost paradoxically expansive, but it is not antithetical to other human goods; it supports other virtues and values, but it also transcends and governs them, forever reminding us that we all live by an unmerited grace in both our private and our public lives. Because of its chronological priority (loving care is the first thing we must receive as infants), its axiological priority (without care individuals do not mature into responsible persons), its lexical priority (without care we have no substantive access to other human goods), and its priority of itself (care's agenda is to make others caring), agapic love is rightly deemed the first virtue in all contexts.[97]

---

[97] Portions of this chapter first appeared in Jackson, "Liberalism and *Agape*: The Priority of Charity to Democracy and Philosophy," *Annual of the Society of Christian Ethics* (1993): 47–72.

TWO
Is God Just?

Let him who glories glory in this, that he
understands and knows me, that I am the LORD
who practice steadfast love, justice, and righteousness
in the earth; for in these things I delight,
says the LORD.
—Jeremiah 9:24

Is creation . . . botched?
—Gustavo Gutiérrez[1]

It would be troubling indeed for most believers if God, the paradigmatic Person, were not just. Yet three influential philosophers of religion—Marilyn Adams, Thomas Morris, and William Alston—have recently argued for this conclusion or for theses that directly entail it. In the name of divine transcendence or necessary goodness or holy indeviance, they deny that God can have obligations of right to creatures. I try to say in this chapter why this view is mistaken. My counterclaim is that, far from God's essential nature precluding justice, God is just precisely *because* essentially loving. God's justice is kenotic, my Athanasian line runs: God suffers Himself to be bound to us morally, for our good.

Discussion of God's character may seem out of place in a book dedicated centrally to love of neighbor and social justice—why the transcendental reference?—but Christianity typically ties human values to divine grace. God's moral nature empowers humanity's own, according to the strong agapist, so if God is not just or loving, neither are we. Correlatively, the better we understand God's nature, the more we open ourselves to it, the more we will both approximate God's righteousness and fulfill our own potential as God's creatures. In short, this chapter is not merely about God; it is also about us as Images of God and how we are to live as such, in eternity as well as in time.

---

[1] Gutiérrez, *On Job: God-Talk and the Suffering of the Innocent*, trans. by Matthew J. O'Connell (Maryknoll: Orbis, 1987), p. 71.

THREE ARGUMENTS AGAINST GOD'S JUSTICE
Adams and the God of the Gap

In "The Problem of Hell: A Problem of Evil for Christians," Marilyn Adams contends that God is neither just nor unjust—at least not with respect to human beings. There is too big an "ontological gap" between creatures and their Creator to use the language of "justice" or "injustice" in describing their relation. God and humanity are "incommensurable,"[2] and this translates, for Adams, into divine antinomianism:

> Created persons have *no rights* against God, because God has *no obligations* to creatures: in particular, God has no obligation to be good to us; no obligation not to ruin us whether by depriving our lives of positive meaning, by producing or allowing the deterioration or disintegration of our personalities, by destroying our bodies, or by annihilating us.[3]

God has no duty to care for finite persons, evidently, nor even an obligation not cruelly to torment them. God's nonjustice is not a matter of *contingently* avoiding all ensnaring relations with humans, like a hermit who flees from the world in order not to be morally responsible to or for anyone. It is (onto)logically *impossible*, Adams thinks, for God to bind Himself in justice to finite persons such that He has a duty to relate to them in any particular way whatsoever. Following Anselm and Duns Scotus, she affirms that "God is not the kind of thing that could be obligated to creatures in any way"; and she does not flinch from the logical implication that "God will not be *unjust* to created persons no matter what He does."[4]

Adams rejects divine obligation (and with it divine justice) not because she fears that God may in fact be cruel or creation botched but because she believes that God's love for creatures infinitely transcends anything that can properly be called obligatory.[5] Moreover, talk of "divine obligation" might seem to imply that God needs or is beholden to creatures, an impious thought to many.[6] For Adams, God's charity is so sublime and

---

[2] Marilyn Adams, "The Problem of Hell: A Problem of Evil for Christians," in *Reasoned Faith*, ed. by Eleonore Stump (Ithaca: Cornell University Press, 1993), p. 308.

[3] Ibid., p. 324.

[4] Ibid., p. 308.

[5] Her attitude of absolute trust is akin to Abraham's unquestioning willingness to sacrifice Isaac in Genesis 22, rather than to Abraham's "Far be it from thee . . . to slay the righteous with the wicked" speech, addressed to God in protest of His plan to destroy Sodom and Gomorrah, in Genesis 18.

[6] There is arguably a difference between needing another and being obligated to that other, between dependency and duty. If there is such a distinction, however, it is often blurred. Kierkegaard's pseudonym Johannes Climacus expresses the relevant sentiments

gratuitous that we denigrate the Deity (and inordinately elevate ourselves) by speaking in terms of "rights and duties," "claims and counterclaims," or "justice." I have considerable sympathy for this disinclination to use the language of "rights" with respect to God and His relation to the world. The primary moral attribute of the biblical God is steadfast love (*ḥésed*, *agape*), a willing of the good for all creation, that vastly outstrips the contractual balances of power that individuals living in a secular culture tend to identify with justice. If an agapic attitude of voluntary service is to be at the heart of a Christian's attitude toward the neighbor, she rightly downplays any talk of "rights and duties" that amounts to prudential self-assertion. Nevertheless, Adams is mistaken in her categorical denial of the existence of divine obligations. The biblical tradition's reference to "the justice and mercy of God" is not to be abandoned but rather rehabilitated in nuanced opposition to common secular parlance. "Shall not the judge of all the earth deal justly?" (Gen. 18:25).[7]

In the spirit of Adams, I grant that the God of Genesis has no *original* obligations to anyone or anything, inasmuch as He might not have created the world of finite persons and objects to begin with, and this without diminishing His goodness. God would still have been omnipotent, omniscient, and innocent of any wrongdoing had He never brought the universe into being. But both the Gospels and the personal experiences of many religious believers suggest that kenotic obligations for God are not only possible but actual. In a divinely reflexive *Akedah*, God has *voluntarily* bound Himself in obligation to creatures—by making promises to them, for instance. Indeed, the free self-limitation of omnipotence for humanity's sake is at the very heart of the pathos of Christian Scripture.

Consider two basic facts: (1) Scripture is replete with instances of divine "promises" in which God is represented as binding Himself (e.g., His promise to Abraham concerning the fatherhood of Isaac, His pledge

---

thusly: "God needs no man. It would otherwise be a highly embarrassing thing to be a creator, if the result was that the creator came to depend upon the creature. On the contrary, God may require everything of every human being, everything and for nothing. For every human being is an unprofitable servant." Observe how the denial of divine need is translated into the assertion of divine right, the power to obligate creatures without reason or reciprocity. This notion may be, in some respects, an admirable expression of humility, but it threatens to make God a martinet—a cruel and cavalier Force rather than a kind and kenotic Father. The quoted lines certainly seem blind to the long-suffering God of Scripture who enters into a covenant with His people. (On whether Kierkegaard himself endorsed Climacus's troubling view, see my *Love Disconsoled*, chap. 6.)

[7] This Bible translation is from *Tanakh* (Philadelphia: Jewish Publication Society, 5746/ 1985), as cited by Jon D. Levenson, *The Death and Resurrection of the Beloved Son* (New Haven and London: Yale University Press, 1993), p. 129. Levenson offers a helpful discussion of Genesis 18 and 22 as they bear on the varying forms of Abraham's submissive relation to God.

to Noah concerning the nonrepetition of the flood, His covenant with Israel concerning the survival of the nation). Sometimes the commitment is a hypothetical one, and sometimes the prophetic "promise" is rather more like a threat (cf. Amos and Hosea), but in both cases obligations of justice seem freely incurred. In the absence of any place for divine obligation, these biblical passages must be given a heavily metaphorical or analogical reading, in which it is only *as if* God has bound Himself to keep His word.[8] Yet this leaves God in the awkward position of being incapable of a number of performative utterances usually thought to be central to moral agency, as well as to biblical narrative. One does not have to be a biblical literalist to feel that it is a strained exegetical approach which evacuates the gospel in particular of its character as narrated promise.[9]

(2) As important as it is to protect charity against the corrosive effects of modern contract theory by insisting that love rises above the demands of secular justice,[10] love can never fall below such justice into unfairness or arbitrariness and remain love. Adams's suggestion that God will not be unjust whatever He does is motivated by the desire to protect God's majesty and sovereignty, but it risks making Him seem capricious. The God who became incarnate in Jesus Christ has indeed promised not to be cavalier or cruel, I would contend, out of a charitable concession to human doubt and frailty. Covenantal love, which at base is unconditional, may nevertheless employ explicit contract as a means of expressing and furthering the good of the other. In *New Testament* terms, Love has nailed Himself to the cross of justice. God's binding Himself to obligation does not mean that He ceases to act out of love; it is not as though God could be a reluctant Kantian doing his duty out of respect for the moral law alone, all the while fighting an inclination to be abusive or self-indulgent. Self-giving love remains the (or at least a) divine motive, but it is now a love that has committed itself in justice to behave in a certain way. A God who cannot do this seems a mere abstraction.

For the sake of fallen persons, Love has surrendered some of its spontaneity—some of its infinite room to maneuver—and given creatures a genuine claim against the Deity. Subsequent to the divine promise, then,

---

[8] Professor Adams has taken this "as if" position verbally. William Alston has defended it in print in "Some Suggestions for Divine Command Theorists," in *Divine Nature and Human Language: Essays in Philosophical Theology* (Ithaca and London: Cornell University Press, 1989), p. 265. I discuss Alston below, but for a more detailed critique of his claim that God can make no promises or covenants, see Eleonore Stump, "God's Obligations," in *Philosophical Perspectives, 6, Ethics, 1992,* ed. by James E. Tomberlin (Atascadero, Calif.: Ridgeview, 1992).

[9] See in this respect, Ronald Thiemann, *Revelation and Theology: The Gospel as Narrated Promise* (Notre Dame: University of Notre Dame Press, 1985).

[10] See my "Liberalism and *Agape*" and "To Bedlam and Part Way Back."

God's duty and humanity's rights are real rather than merely apparent. Subjunctively to echo Jonah, we "would do well to be angry" were God to break a promise; but, of course, She never does. At times, we (like Jonah) think God unjust, but this is only because we fail to understand the precise nature of God's promises and/or the precise form of God's fidelity to them. This, at any rate, is what the Bible would have individuals believe. It is one thing to say that God will not break Her promises; it is another to say that She cannot make them. In insisting on the latter, Adams undermines the very pastoral confidence in the Creator that she wants to bolster.

Morris and God's Necessary Goodness

Thomas Morris bases his case against divine obligations on the necessity of God's essential attributes, particularly His goodness, coupled with a libertarian account of freedom. If God is necessarily good, then He cannot but do what is right. But if He cannot but do what is right, then He does not fulfill obligations, since such fulfillment requires freedom and (according to the libertarian) freedom requires the ability to do otherwise. Morris still thinks that what he calls "the duty model" can be adapted to help explain God's goodness. But the point is that God is not *bound by* duty and its rules, even though He acts *in accordance with* duty and its rules:

> We human beings exist in a state of being *bound* by moral duty. In this state we act under obligation, either satisfying or contravening our duties. Because of his distinctive nature, God does not share our ontological status. Specifically, he does not share our relation to moral principles—that of being bound by some of these principles as duties. Nevertheless, God acts *in accordance with* those principles which would express duties for a moral agent in his relevant circumstances. And he does so necessarily.[11]

The motivation behind these lines is the desire to avoid conflict among (1) a libertarian account of freedom, in which true freedom with respect to action X requires the ability to do other than X, (2) a belief in God's necessary goodness, and (3) an explanation of God's goodness in terms of His freely fulfilling his duties. With Morris, however, as with Adams,

[11] Thomas V. Morris, "Duty and Divine Goodness," in *Anselmian Explorations* (Notre Dame: University of Notre Dame Press, 1987), p. 36. This essay also appears in Thomas V. Morris, ed., *The Concept of God* (Oxford: Oxford University Press, 1987). William Rowe shares Morris's fondness for divine determinism; in "The Problem of Divine Perfection and Freedom," in *Reasoned Faith*, p. 226, Rowe writes: "since one cannot be morally obligated to do what one is not free to do, there are no actions God has a moral obligation to perform. At best we can say that God does of necessity those acts he would be morally obligated to do were he free to do them."

"the God of Abraham, Isaac, and Anselm" so transcends obligation as apparently to fall below it. For, as Morris realizes, merely acting in accordance with duty is often seen as defective dutifulness. More on this later.

Alston and the Impossibility of God's Deviance

William Alston has offered a slightly different account of why God can have no obligations, defending "the view that a necessary condition of the truth of 'S ought to do A' is at least the metaphysical possibility that S does not do A." The upshot of this view is that "no moral obligations attach to God, assuming, as we are here, that God is essentially perfectly good."[12] For Alston, unlike Morris, freedom with respect to some action *X* does not require the ability to do otherwise; but *obligation* does require such an ability. If there is no "possibility of deviation"[13] from duty, there is no duty either. So, again, because God *necessarily* does what is right, God cannot be obligated by justice.

The problem with Alston, as with Morris, is that he fails to see that God's essential goodness does not consist in His *necessarily* doing what is right but in His *freely* doing it. With creation and Incarnation, God's goodness participates in the contingency of the world. If this were not so, He could not respond to finite agents as they are. Granted, God would not be God were He not omnibenevolent, so the attribution of goodness to Him is *de dicto* necessary. But if, as seems plausible, freedom is an internal component of the exercise of all virtue (love and justice), then God's *occurrent* goodness cannot be *de re* necessary. If God ceases to be good, then He ceases to exist; but this self-extinction is now a real possibility, I would maintain. The possible death of God is a consequence of His choosing to create beings in need of love and desirous of justice, since the need and the desire may logically be the occasions for divine dereliction. God's death could only be suicide, but for believers in the Judeo-Christian God there seems no denying that He could freely forsake us and thus cease to be. In making His covenant with "Abram" (Genesis 15), it is *God* who symbolically walks between the sacrificial animals cut in two, thereby staking *the divine Life itself* on His voluntary fidelity.[14] And, indeed, the terror of the cross is not merely the painful death of an innocent man but the temptation of a good God to betray Himself, and thus to die despairing.

Talk of "the death of God" may sound impious or absurd—how could an essentially good and necessary Being cease to exist?—but it is neither. My account of divine justice retains the biblical belief that in God good-

---

[12] Alston, "Some Suggestions for Divine Command Theorists," p. 264.
[13] Ibid.
[14] I owe this reference to Andrew P. Cuneo.

ness and power coincide (see, e.g., Psalms 62 and 63). I depart from exponents of divine impassibility, however, in taking God's benevolence to condition His might. To experience God is to feel oneself touched by that perfect Reality that sustains the world, but we must revise our understanding of perfect strength in light of God's kenotic love. Divine power is not a self-sufficient Greek immutability, a detached narcissism, but rather a self-sacrificial creativity. This thesis is arguably as old as Job and theologically self-conscious by the time of Athanasius.[15] The most powerful Christian argument in support of the thesis is the cross, the most decisive revelation of God's will to redeem humanity.

Necessary existence cannot be thought of as a perfection, Anselm notwithstanding,[16] if this precludes God's creating free beings to whom He can relate redemptively; to create and relate morally (including justly) to creatures, an act of *agape*, God must open Himself to the possibility of not being. Again, omnibenevolence qualifies what we may think of as omnipotence. "God is love" (1 John 4:8) is perhaps the one nonequivocal thing we can say about the Deity, and this implies that if all love ceases so does God. An all-powerful Being cannot be brought into or taken out of existence by something else, or by degrees, but it might wink out at once of its own accord. To admit this is to clear the way for worship of God's actual steadfastness, not to thwart or denigrate it.

In claiming that God might cease to exist, I take exception to Spinoza's sentiment that "To be able not to exist is want of power." Spinoza reasons that "since ability to exist is power, it follows that the more reality belongs to the nature of some thing, the more power it will have to exist; and accordingly a being absolutely infinite, or God, has an absolutely infinite power of existence from itself, and on that account absolutely exists."[17] Yet why cannot God's supreme power be construed as the ability to exist or not exist, as He wills? This seems as plausible a conception of self-causation, of having existence as internal to one's essence, as any other. And it is required if we are to do justice to God's charity for

---

[15] See, for example, Athanasius, *"Contra Gentes" and "De Incarnatione,"* ed. and trans. by Robert W. Thomson (Oxford: Clarendon, 1971), pp. 151 and 153: "in his benevolence towards us [God] condescended to come and be made manifest . . . he had pity on our race, and was merciful to our infirmity, and submitted to our corruption, and did not endure the dominion of death." My views are in the spirit of Athanasius, but I radicalize his kenotic theology in suggesting, for example, that God the Father might even die by His own hand.

[16] See the discussion of this point in John H. Hick and Arthur C. McGill, eds., *The Many-Faced Argument: Recent Studies on the Ontological Argument for the Existence of God* (New York: Macmillan, 1967), esp. the essay by Norman Malcolm.

[17] Spinoza, *Ethics*, trans. by Andrew Boyle and revised by G.H.R. Parkinson (London: J. M. Dent, 1989), proposition XI, pp. 10–11.

the world and for the finite beings in it. A necessarily existent Being might open Herself to the possibility of nonexistence, I hold, for the same reason that a timelessly eternal Being might enter time, and a perfectly good Being might suffer temptation: for the salvation of sinners.

What, then, does divine necessity amount to? I would repeat that God's necessary existence implies that He cannot be taken out of existence by something outside Himself, nor can He fade by increments. I would even grant that "God exists necessarily" entails that "God exists" cannot be false, that is, is a necessary truth and thus is true in all possible worlds.[18] But if God freely implodes, so to speak, so do all possible worlds. As properties of intelligible propositions, truth and falsity (both possible and necessary) require a mind;[19] but if God ceases to be, so do all minds (both finite and infinite), thus so do truth and falsity. In this sense, "God exists" is not false in any (or all) possible world(s) even if God ceases to exist. "God does not exist" is not so much a necessary falsehood, although it may be called that, as the refusal of the very idea of truth and falsity. Truth and falsity stand or fall with God Himself, even as do good and evil. Indeed, insisting that "God is just" is a true statement in this world does not imply that "God is unjust" might be a true statement in some other world, for, again, the divine injustice would entail the end of all worlds, the end of all minds, the end of all truth, the end of God Himself. God's justice presupposes that He might *be* unjust, in the limited sense of *fall simultaneously into nonexistence altogether*, but no one could ever *know* this utter nullity from which God freely preserves Himself, and us.

To say that a divine action is free is not to say that it is unreliable. We can be confident of God's goodness without fatalism, for we can trust that God does not fail and will not fail without insisting that God cannot fail. Only a profound pessimist would think that all freedom must tend to corruption or inconstancy; only a misguided Platonist would prefer a dispassionate and unchanging theoretical Deity over the compassionate and faithful biblical God. The first person of the Trinity is not impassible in creating and overseeing the world; and the incarnate Son on the cross experiences dread, an ineliminable accompaniment of temporal freedom, although He does not sin. The Judeo-Christian God is worthy of worship exactly because His fidelity to love neither necessitates Him nor extinguishes others. (Again, divine freedom makes creaturely agency possible,

---

[18] On the elusiveness of necessary truth, especially with reference to God, see Robert M. Adams, "Divine Necessity," in *The Concept of God*. Adams draws on both Leibniz and Quine in an effort to distance necessary truth from mere analyticity.

[19] Cf. ibid., p. 52.

by voluntarily letting it be voluntary.) If God were not relevantly free, then God could not rightly be admired for His goodness or thanked for His gifts (including creation), since God could not be or do otherwise.

I trust my central point is now clear enough: pace Spinoza, the ability not to be is not an *im*perfection but rather the necessary condition for the divine perfections witnessed to in the Bible. Nevertheless, let me summarize my position as strongly as I can, and then I will make a little concession. (1) The biblical God is a just Creator who makes binding promises to creatures; (2) since freedom (partially defined as the ability to do otherwise) is internal to all good and evil, to be just requires the ability to be unjust; (3) to be even *potentially* unjust is, for the God who is essentially good and whose existence follows necessarily from His essence, to be potentially nonexistent; therefore (4) God is potentially nonexistent. This is the case at least after God's voluntary creation of the world. If we want to call God "just," in short, as Scripture seems to demand, then we must grant that He could cease to exist. We could never *know* that He had ceased, however; God's nonexistence is the one existential proposition that no one in heaven or on earth could ever have justified true belief about.

Now for the small concession. I have assumed (with Morris) that a libertarian account of freedom is compelling, but this is far from uncontroversial. Those who find moral freedom compatible with determinism, perhaps defining freedom (with Harry Frankfurt) as roughly the ability to act as you want,[20] will take exception to my four points above. I would uphold these points as crucial to the defense of God's goodness and the rejection of pernicious notions of irresistible grace. (Those who would be comforted by the thought of God predetermining, ineluctably, the bliss of "the elect" should be willing to surrender this abstract consolation for the sake of those who suffer doubt and would be thrown into despair by the idea of a fated damnation.)[21] Still, at a minimum, I can put my main

[20] Frankfurt equates freedom with having your "second-order volitions" conform to your causally efficacious "first-order desires," even if you could not but act on those desires. See Frankfurt, "Freedom of the Will and the Concept of a Person," in *The Importance of What We Care About* (Cambridge: Cambridge University Press, 1988). Yet freedom thereby ceases to be an intrinsic power embodied by all agents and presupposed by habitual virtue, and becomes a matter of personal preference suitably adjusted by external factors (whether liberal therapy or totalitarian tyranny).

[21] Religious versions of compatibilism are vetust, even venerable. The list of theologians who see divine determinism—God's irresistibly moving the will of human beings—as the very essence of freedom and fulfillment, includes Augustine, Aquinas, Luther, and Calvin. We Arminians believe, nevertheless, that one must break with this august camp, on this issue, if humanity is to be morally responsible and the love of God is to be done justice. Even fallen humanity has the freedom to say "Yes" or "No" to the grace essential for faith, or else God is responsible for evil. A God who reprobates some persons irresistibly to hell is

thesis hypothetically: *if* freedom requires the ability to do otherwise, *then* it is better to grant that God could be other than just (even cease to exist) than to deny that She is ever just. For if we gainsay divine justice, we have to reject divine goodness as well: *ex hypothesi*, God's goodness also requires libertarian freedom. This rejection is too high a price to pay. An unfree God is not a just God, and a nonjust God cannot be fully loving either; a fully loving God freely makes kenotic promises to creatures.

Love Embracing Justice: An Instructive Analogy

Let me offer an analogy to help clarify how the God who is Love may nonetheless become freely obliged in justice. Imagine that a woman succeeds in embodying the virtue of neighbor-love in practically everything that she says and does. Her actions are dedicated to the well-being of others, many of them deeply afflicted, and her motives are unselfconsciously beneficent; she is animated by the Holy Spirit and gives little or no thought to "rights" (especially her own) and "duties" (especially other people's). Far from being grudging or one-dimensional, her life is radiant and happy, if occasionally winded. (I think of someone like Mother Teresa of Calcutta, although gender is unimportant; Albert Schweitzer also comes to mind.) Imagine now that this saint begins visiting a secular friend who has inoperable cancer. The friend, touched by the attention, feels loved for the first time in his life. As the pain worsens, nonetheless, the friend fears the loneliness and suffering that are likely to accompany his final days, so he asks for an explicit vow that the woman agree to visit him until the bitter end. "Promise you won't abandon me," he implores.

Might not the woman make such a promise, *out of love and for the friend's sake*, and thus become genuinely duty-bound? The woman might very well have intended to keep up her visits in any case; she may even be a little hurt that the friend needed a formal vow; but once the commitment is made, admittedly as a concession to his fear and mistrust, is it not a real obligation? I think that reasonable persons would concur that it is. I think, moreover, that God's relation to creatures is rather like this: a characteristically voluntary self-sacrifice to meet us where we are.

---

not worthy of worship, and to assert that His sovereignty requires this is impious. Did not Christ die for "all men" (Rom. 5:18; 1 Tim. 2:1–4), and does He not invite them to respond with belief unto salvation (John 3:16–18), although they may not (Matt. 23:37)? Belief is itself an unmerited divine gift, but it may be refused—or else, as Kierkegaard pointed out, we have "fatalism"; see his *Journals and Papers*, vol. 4, ed. and trans. by Howard and Edna Hong (Bloomington: Indiana University Press, 1975), entry 4551, p. 352.

The God of Abraham and Isaac, Mary and Jesus, loves human beings steadfastly and continues to promote their good come what may, but as a response to their finitude and sin, their anxiety and uncertainty, He has given them concrete promises which He is obliged to honor. His motive in making the promises is love; His motive in keeping them is perhaps some combination of love and justice; but God is genuinely bound by His word as a matter of justice. God's making promises is not merely the announcement of His intentions, and God's keeping promises is not merely action in accordance with (rather than out of) principles of duty. Some forms of divine obligation are *close* to impossible: God could not promise to cease to love, for instance, at least not so as to remain in being. But God did not merely induce Abraham to *believe* that Isaac was "the child of promise" or behave *as if* He had given Noah a pledge of never again destroying the earth; rather, the promise and the pledge were literal obligations undertaken by a charity that found its fullest expression in the Incarnation. If justice is, formally, giving each their due, then human beings are now due whatever God has promised to them. It is not too much to say, therefore, that finite persons now have a claim against God—although this is a claim that God has freely given them without antecedent merit on their part. It is not the upshot of a right that creatures might have asserted independently of the divine benevolence. Love precedes justice and often rises above it, but love also sometimes stoops to embrace justice, thereby limiting itself. Divine charity makes kenotic promises, thereby bridging the "ontological gap" made so much of by Adams and her medieval forebears. Would God be God if She did any less?

A "Third Alternative" Rejected

Someone might object that I have neglected a third alternative to a God who does not promise, and thus is not bound, at all and a God who makes promises, and thus is bound, to creatures. What of the possibility of God binding Himself *to Himself*, making promises not *to* creatures but *for* them? Hebrews 6:13–15, for instance, reads: "For when God made a promise to Abraham, since he had no one greater by whom to swear, he swore by himself, saying, 'Surely I will bless you and multiply you.' And thus Abraham, having patiently endured, obtained the promise." Does this not amount to a *tertium quid* between Adams et al. and myself?[22]

No, it does not. This putative third option in fact collapses into my

---

[22] Andrew Cuneo has pressed this line in conversation. His comments motivated much of this section and improved the whole.

own. Although God's swearing "by himself" is a unique *means* to executing an oath, the *end* is still that of promising "*to Abraham.*" It is Abraham who "obtains the promise," not God, thus God becomes obligated to a creature, not merely to Himself. We do speak of "promising ourselves" something, but genuine promising normally requires two parties. This is especially relevant here, for what reason could a loving God have to promise anything only to Himself? God swears by Himself to reassure Abraham that He will *keep* His promise to him—to render the patriarch "fully convinced that God was able to do what he promised," in Saint Paul's words (Rom. 4:21)—rather than to avoid incurring such an obligation.

Adams, Morris, Alston, and my imaginary objector all underestimate the power of divine condescension. Alston in particular helps us see, *malgré lui*, an irony that is typical of God's way with the world. Let us suppose that obligation does presume "the possibility of deviation," even if (pace Morris) freedom does not presume the ability to do otherwise. Let us further suppose, however, that Scripture can here be taken literally and hence that (1) God has in fact obligated Himself and so (2) God is actually characterized by the possibility of deviation. Alstonians will see this as a hard paradox, asking, How could and why should an essentially perfectly good Creator embrace the possibility of Her not being good? Necessary goodness is incompatible with the possibility of doing evil. The defenders of divine justice, in contrast, will see (1) and (2) as a splendid irony, answering, God embraces (possible) deviation kenotically, for the sake of making meaningful promises to creatures. The irony resides in the fact that, in order to be able to promise at all, God must freely empty Himself of His self-sufficiency such that He might break whatever specific promise He makes. The splendor consists in the ineffable humility of this sacrifice of the strong for the weak, a sacrifice that opens purity to the possibility of impurity to redeem the impure.

In sum, God's being bound by duty to creatures and accepting the mantle of (possible) guilt initially seems antithetical to His supreme goodness, but this condescension is actually an instance of God's omnibenevolence trumping His omnipotence—or rather its revolutionizing *our* idea of omnipotence. God chooses tenderness over impassibility, a service to the weak that risks becoming embroiled in their weakness over a sublime detachment that remains essentially aloof. With the Fall of humanity, God drives *Himself* out of the Garden as well. God makes promises for humanity's sake, not His own; He obligates Himself in order to address human fear and mistrust, to meet finite persons where they live. This pattern of sacrifice is familiar from the life of Jesus, who although divine permitted himself to be genuinely tempted and eventually killed.

DIVINE PROMISES AND THE QUESTION OF IMMORTALITY

Apart from the explicit promises to Abraham, Noah, Moses, et al., already mentioned, there are at least two actions of God that carry an *implicit* promise: the creation and the Incarnation. Let me bolster my cumulative case for a just God by examining these in slightly more detail. This will require a digression on first immortality and then the problem of evil, but my subsequent conclusion can be quite brief.

Whether God created the best of all possible worlds,[23] in creating this one and calling it "good," He was in effect guaranteeing that it was worth it, that on balance it is better that this world be than that it not be. Since God might not have made anything at all, this is a promise that He might not have given. But God's having created persons amounts to His having pledged that each of their lives *can* be meaningful taken as a whole, or else God is unjust. In general, if bringing about X is known to be harmful overall or otherwise wrong, then knowingly bringing about Y amounts to an implicit promise that it is not X-ish. Hence God's creating the world implicitly guarantees that it is not harmful overall for Him to have done so.

The standard problem of evil looms large here: What are we to make of those human lives beset by affliction and absurdity through no fault of their own?[24] I doubt that there is any argument in the face of such evil that constitutes a strict theodicy. I am also inclined to endorse Marilyn Adams's heartfelt opinion that even sins "freely" committed do not deserve endless punishment and thus cannot be cited as justifying the traditional conception of a permanent hell. Just punishment is unobjectionable, but even God must make the punishment fit the crime. Sympathy for the horror of some lives, even when that horror is self-inflicted, is an indispensable moral emotion urging one to doubt any doctrine of the perpetual and irreversible damnation of the wicked.[25] Unlike Adams, however, I do not insist that there be a "definitive divine triumph"[26] amounting to universal salvation in a traditional heaven. We may hope for the latter, but we can *only* hope. I suspect (with Barth, von Balthasar, and others) that if there is eternal life for anyone, freely accepted as a good gift of God, then there is eternal life for everyone, similarly accepted. But the goodness of God may be affirmed even if there is an

---

[23] On this question, see Robert M. Adams, "Must God Create the Best?" chap. 4 in *The Virtue of Faith* (New York: Oxford University Press, 1987), pp. 51–64.

[24] Cf. Origen, and Robert Adams's "Existence, Self-interest, and the Problem of Evil," chap. 5 in *The Virtue of Faith*, pp. 65–76.

[25] Adams, "The Problem of Hell," pp. 326–27.

[26] Ibid., p. 325.

afterlife for no one, as the example of Job indicates.[27] Love's priority may be to cultivate persons in this life only; there is that much truth in Stoic Christianity.

To suggest, as Saint Paul does in 1 Corinthians 15:12–34, that Christian charity would be in vain without personal immortality is to risk instrumentalizing the virtue. To be sure, when Paul explores the implications of Christ's Resurrection for believers he is making chiefly a logical point. Because Christ is the "first fruits" (1 Cor. 15:20, 23), the captain of our salvation, to believe in resurrection for him is, more or less explicitly, to affirm and anticipate it in one's own case, according to Paul. "As all die in Adam, so all will be made alive in Christ" (15:22; see also Rom. 6:5). In addition to this Christological observation, however, Paul also offers a more normative judgment. The virtues of faith and hope (and presumably of love) would be futile or pathetic, it seems, if there were no personal immortality: "If for this life only we have hoped in Christ, we are of all people most to be pitied" (1 Cor. 15:19). This claim I find unpersuasive. Taking inspiration from the Johannine teaching that "eternal life" can be experienced here and now through fellowship with Christ (e.g., John 5:24; 11:25–26; 17:3), I have argued elsewhere against Paul's normative insistence that a future raising from the dead is indispensable to Christian moral existence.[28] As communion with God and service of neighbor, agapic love is more intrinsically good, more self-justifying, than that. Put most forcefully, Saint Paul undercuts his own splendid panegyric on love (1 Corinthians 13) when he asks, "If the dead are not raised at all . . . why are we putting ourselves in danger every hour?" (1 Cor. 15:29–30). When he goes on to propose that "if the dead are not raised, 'Let us eat and drink, for tomorrow we die'" (1 Cor. 15:32), he retreats from strong *agape*'s affirmation of this world in spite of evil and fails to treat charity as its own reward and the absence of charity as its own punishment.

The strong agapist's diffidence about immortality is not inspired by the usual philosophical questions about the possibility of resurrection—Is

[27] See my "Must Job Live Forever? A Reply to Aquinas on Providence," *The Thomist* 62, no. 1 (January 1998): 1–39. The first, and arguably the only, clear affirmation of the resurrection of the dead in Hebrew Scripture comes in the apocalyptic book of Daniel, 12:1–2, written circa 167–164 B.C.E. As Hans Küng has observed, "For more than a thousand years, *none* of these Jews [Abraham, Isaac and Jacob, Moses and the Judges, the kings and the prophets, Isaiah, Jeremiah and Ezekiel] *believed in a resurrection of the dead* or in an eternal life in a positive sense of the term, in a 'Christian' heaven. With remarkable consistency they concentrated on the present world, without bothering about what was in any case a dismal, dark, hopeless hereafter [Sheol]." See Küng, *Eternal Life? Life after Death as a Medical, Philosophical, and Theological Problem*, trans. by Edward Quinn (Garden City, N.Y.: Doubleday, 1984), p. 83.

[28] See *Love Disconsoled*, chap. 5.

not consciousness reducible to biological processes? Can personal identity be sustained without bodily continuity? If bodily continuity is required, to what stage of physical life is one resurrected? and the like—but rather by moral misgivings. It is not easy to spell out the metaphysics behind the varying biblical pictures of the afterlife, as I note in more detail below, but this is only one part of the problem. There are three specifically moral reasons to deemphasize eternity as postmortem perdurability: (1) to avoid a cruel denigration of this life and its suffering/joy; (2) to avoid instrumentalizing charity, making it a means to extrinsic ends; and (3) to avoid dogmatism about what can be known with certainty about one's possible afterlife and its relation to God's justice. The agapist asks, Which requires more faith and hope: belief in the reality of God and the primacy of love, even if death is the end of one's individual existence, or dogmatic insistence on personal continuance beyond the grave as a reward for either orthodoxy or orthopraxis? If we would find charity a futile existence without an afterlife, then, again, we are not practicing it for its own sake.

In an eloquent little treatise on immortality, Harry Emerson Fosdick writes:

> When . . . a man of insight demands a life to come, it is not because he seeks outward recompense for a good life here; it is because his goodness here, if it is to be passionate and earnest, must have the eternal chance of getting better. His value lies in what he may become—not in what he has or does or is, but in his possibilities.[29]

Fosdick does not hold that an ethical life would be impossible without firm faith in immortality; he even presumes that love and self-sacrifice would persist in some diminished form. But he nevertheless maintains that "immortality is that affirmation of the eternal worth of character which alone can make reasonable the devotion, aspiration and self-denial which great character requires."[30] Truly *great* virtue requires belief in an afterlife, in his view, not so much because such virtue would be futile without the belief as because it would be impossible. "No man will work hard sewing diamonds on tissue paper,"[31] as he puts it. This is a powerful rejoinder to the "virtue its own reward" argument I have sketched. It shifts our focus from postmortem reward for virtue to present growth in virtue, and it also suggests how God's own righteousness is implicated in our moral prospects. I myself will contend in chapter 5, on abortion, that if one has induced the needs and potentials of another by bringing him into existence as a dependent, then one owes it to that other, as a matter

[29] Fosdick, *The Assurance of Immortality* (New York: Macmillan/Association, 1913/1924), p. 22.
[30] Ibid., p. 31.
[31] Ibid.

of duty, to meet his needs and to cultivate his potentials. If God does not grant an afterlife at least to the souls who aspire to be fully good and thus who want and need immortality, is this not an unjustifiable abortion of the human race?[32] Has not God, by virtue of creating the world, implicitly promised us "an eternal chance of getting better," of fulfilling our "possibilities"?

If it could be shown that God has promised immortality, then God would indeed have bound His goodness and justice to this gift. But I am not sure how to interpret either the act of creation or those biblical passages (e.g., Matt. 8:11–12; 19:28–30) that refer to the "kingdom of heaven" and "eternal life." God does promise never again to destroy the earth by flood (Gen. 9:8–11), but this is not equivalent to promising never-ending-personal-existence to believers. Jesus is presented in the Gospels as believing in the final resurrection of the righteous, as well as the imminent resurrection of himself, but do these passages represent a divine pledge or covenant? Perhaps.[33] In John 6:40, Jesus says: "This is indeed the will of my Father, that all who see the Son and believe in him may have eternal life; and I will raise them up on the last day." In light of several other verses in the Gospel of John, however, immortality can as

---

[32] In his second *Critique*, Kant argues that we must postulate a God who ensures that the human soul is immortal precisely to guarantee that what we ought to do (i.e., become perfect) we can do (i.e., in heaven). Without the practical premise of immortality, all morality falls to the ground, for Kant. The question of whether he held that one must postulate the *existence* of God or merely the *possibility* of God, however, is moot. See Kant, *Critique of Practical Reason* [1788], trans. by Lewis White Beck (Indianapolis: Bobbs-Merrill, 1956), part I, bk. II, chap. II, secs. IV and V, pp. 126–36.

[33] Concerning Christ's own resurrection, A.J.M. Wedderburn writes:

It is true that Jesus is portrayed in the Gospels as foretelling his passion and his resurrection (Mark 8:31, 9:31, 10:34, 14:28, etc.), and one would therefore expect the disciples to be eagerly awaiting the fulfillment of these predictions. However, not all [scholars] are prepared to take these predictions at face value as the very words of the earthly Jesus; many see them, as well as the more detailed predictions of the passion (esp. Mark 10:34 parr.), as prophecies after the event, written with the advantage of hindsight.

Wedderburn elaborates by summarizing the view of some biblical exegetes (e.g., Jürgen Becker) "that, although John the Baptist and Jesus may have known of the belief in the general resurrection of the dead, it played no role in their message(s); for them salvation or judgment concerned the living, and the proclamation of salvation or judgment concerned this world and the present life. The coming of God's reign need not involve a new heaven and a new earth and the attendant resurrection of the dead; it can unfold in this world." See Wedderburn, *Beyond Resurrection* (Peabody, Mass.: Hendrickson, 1999), p. 45. For the variability of postbiblical interpretations of both Christ's and the believer's resurrections, even amid the persistence of corporeal images, see Caroline Walker Bynum's *The Resurrection of the Body in Western Christianity, 200–1336* (New York: Columbia University Press, 1995).

readily be interpreted qualitatively as quantitatively: "eternal life" can be taken as readily to mean an existence permeated by, and imitative of, the loving presence of God here and now as to mean a remote and endless afterlife.[34] Jesus himself accents the immediate reality of "resurrection" when, in response to Martha's confidence that Lazarus "will rise again in the resurrection on the last day," he says: "I *am* the resurrection and the life" (John 11:24–25; emphasis added). Note Jesus' use of the present tense here and elsewhere: "Very truly I tell you, anyone who hears my word and believes him who sent me *has* eternal life, and does not come under judgment, but has passed from death to life" (John 5:24; emphasis added; see also 6:47). Belief in future immortality in heaven does not necessarily exclude current inspiration by the Holy Spirit on earth, but it is not merely the detractors of Christianity that see in the afterlife a temptation to postpone our recognition of God and our practice of both love and justice toward the neighbor. A saint is precisely someone who refuses to let eternity postpone, or even violate, time in this way.

Not all accent on immortality stems from narrow self-concern, of course. Some truly noble individuals see an eternal afterlife as the context in which a just God must remedy *others'* temporal suffering, rather than their own.[35] This is a fine sentiment in many respects, and I will return to the issue it raises in the next section on theodicy. But the point remains that whatever moves us to take present sin and bodily pain and death less than seriously is an un-Christlike "spiritualization" of the kingdom of God. One does not have to hold that resurrection is a legend or wish

---

[34] Inspired by aspects of the Fourth Gospel, Wedderburn would discard entirely the future dimension of immortality; see *Beyond Resurrection*, pp. 91 and 158–63. Against Saint Paul, Nietzsche writes: "What are the 'glad tidings' [of Jesus]? True life, eternal life, has been found—it is not promised, it is here, it is *in you*." "The 'kingdom of heaven' is a state of the heart—not something that is to come 'above the earth' or 'after death.'" See Nietzsche, "The AntiChrist," sec. 29, p. 601, and sec. 34, p. 608. One need not jettison future eschatological hope altogether to find an admirable candor in Wedderburn. And one need not endorse Nietzsche's atheistic will to power to find some truth in his charge that Paul at times replaces the courageous faith of Christ with a dogmatic, even resentful, faith in Christ. See ibid., esp. secs. 39–43, pp. 612–20. In a similar vein, Stephen Mitchell maintains: "The gospel they [the disciples and Paul] preached was not the good news which Jesus proclaimed. Instead of teaching God's presence, they preached 'that Christ died for our sins, in accordance with the Scriptures.' . . . Instead of God's absolute love and forgiveness, they preached a god who condemned most of humankind to eternal damnation and would save only those who believed that Jesus was the Son of God." See Mitchell, *The Gospel According to Jesus* (New York: HarperCollins, 1991), p. 65. Mitchell's reconstructions of Christ's teachings are sometimes highly speculative, even dogmatic, and I am not as convinced as he is that the-kingdom-as-future-event and the-kingdom-as-present-reality constitute an either/or. But, like Nietzsche and Wedderburn, Mitchell identifies unmistakably the moral perils of various Pauline assumptions.

[35] Amy Laura Hall has helped me to appreciate this point more fully.

fulfillment to be wary of an otherworldliness emerging even in Paul. As John Dominic Crossan writes, "When . . . [Paul] says that 'flesh and blood' cannot enter the kingdom of God, a gulf in sensibility opens up between him and Jesus. . . . For Jesus, *anyone* incarnating divine justice on earth was 'flesh and blood' entering the kingdom of God."[36]

There is something irremediably sad about the corruptibility of the flesh, and, although it may be faced with dignity, death itself threatens the oblivion of all our life projects and thus is inherently dreadful.[37] Even for a thoroughly secular soul, it may comfort only a little to think of a legacy left to one's children and one's children's children. For the demise of all future generations, culminating in the final extinction of the species—if not in nuclear war, then when the sun goes nova—would seem to suggest that the whole of humanity comes to naught. Still, we must take care to avoid what might be called "the fallacy of decomposition": as though a quality of the species as a whole, such as its having no meaningful consummation, must also be ascribed to each individual member of the species. Even if the species ends without general resurrection, particular persons might nonetheless find final meaning in love for God and service to their neighbors.

For the Christian, how one reacts to the dreadfulness of death, to the fact that one must do one's own dying, will significantly condition one's relation to God and other people. If one clutches after invulnerability and closes oneself off from risk, this will inevitably lead to sin against God and alienation from others; if, in contrast, one remains open and generous even in the face of threatened extinction, this is all that Christlike love could ask. Even Jesus experiences dread before the prospect of his crucifixion—"remove this cup from me" (Mark 14:36)—and the dark reality of even a painless death makes pining after immortality an understandable human reaction. When belief in immortality becomes a dogmatic denial of death's sting or a utilitarian motive for charity's gifts, however, that belief ceases to be a Christian virtue. Nothing seems further from Jesus' mind than his Resurrection when he says, first, "not what I want,

---

[36] Crossan, *The Birth of Christianity* (San Francisco: HarperSanFrancisco, 1999), p. xxxi.

[37] See Paul Ramsey, "The Indignity of 'Death with Dignity,'" in *On Moral Medicine*, 2nd ed., ed. by Stephen E. Lammers and Allen Verhey (Grand Rapids and Cambridge: Eerdmans, 1998). Rather than seeing death as a natural "part of life," Ramsey sees it as an "indignity" (p. 216), an "enemy" (p. 220) usually to be resisted. For several of his observations about mortality and dread, Ramsey draws on Reinhold Niebuhr, who in turn drew on Søren Kierkegaard. In an appreciative elaboration and critique of Ramsey, Oliver O'Donovan argues that his former teacher fails to give sufficient place to the "evangelical proclamation" of bodily resurrection. See O'Donovan, "Keeping Body and Soul Together," also in *On Moral Medicine*. For his part, Ramsey wishes to avoid being "tempted into endless speculation about an after-life" (p. 218).

but what you [God] want" (Mark 14:36) and, later, "*Eloi, Eloi, lema sabachthani*" (Mark 15:34).

But even a great soul will tend to despair in the absence of immortality, according to Fosdick, because without "some universal consummation that is adequate to explain and justify the strife and suffering of the earth,"[38] the world is horribly unjust. So the question before us may seem simple: Would not a righteous God grant at least to the faithful a personal afterlife in which their suffering is forever redeemed? If one holds, as I do, that justice is applicable to the Deity, then this question cannot be rejected as ill-formed. But our answer to it may be. The challenge for Christians remains the time-honored one of holding Good Friday in dynamic tension with Easter Sunday. Many pious minds see Christ's Resurrection as a vindication by a just God of His obedient Son, the sine qua non of humanity's redemption; but how rare is the heart that can keep from also translating believers' resurrection into an acquittal given *to* God by *Christians*, the sine qua non of *God's* redemption. "Unless both Christ and the elect are raised," the seduction runs, "charity is pointless or unsustainable. But, because we few will surely be rewarded with deathlessness, we can find this troubled life worthwhile."[39] Again, a more admirable impetus for belief in immortality is the thought, not that "we few" will be rewarded, but that all the wretched of this world require and will receive a heavenly compensation for, or healing of, their earthly affliction. It seems best, nonetheless, to uncouple strong *agape* from things largely extrinsic to its purpose and motivation, including future rewards, punishments, and compensations.

More specifically, I would defend two distinct, but related, theses about immortality. My *epistemic* thesis is that we cannot know with certainty

---

[38] Fosdick, *The Assurance of Immortality*, p. 36.

[39] John Calvin writes: "It is not by [Christ's] death, but by his resurrection, that we are said to be begotten again to a living hope (1 Pet. I.3); because, as he, by rising again, became victorious over death, so the victory of our faith consists only in his resurrection. . . . For how could he by dying have freed us from death, if he had yielded to its power? how could he have obtained the victory for us, if he had fallen in the contest?" See Calvin, *Institutes of the Christian Religion*, vol. one, trans. by Henry Beveridge (Grand Rapids: Eerdmans, 1979), bk. II, chap. 16, sec. 13, pp. 446–47. Calvin wisely insists that the word "resurrection" should be seen as a synecdoche: to mention Christ's being raised is also to allude to his death, and vice versa (ibid., p. 447). But one need not deny Christ's Resurrection to doubt, pace Calvin, that his significant victory over death *requires* literally being raised. In "The Ethics of Self-Sacrifice," John Milbank also emphasizes the indispensability of belief in an afterlife for Christian ethics. To claim, however, that resurrection *must* be a reward of virtue, that ethics is *impossible* without personal immortality, is in fact to embroil charity in mixed motives and exchange economies that strip it of its focus on God and the neighbor. If a just God must grant (faithful) creatures an afterlife, then it ceases to be a free and serendipitous gift. With regard to personal immortality, *agape*, in contrast, does not let the left hand know what the right hand is doing.

that there is a postmortem afterlife or even that fidelity to Christ and Christlike love requires us to believe that there is such an afterlife.[40] My *moral* thesis is that it is a betrayal of charity to hold that it must eventuate in a postmortem afterlife.[41] The epistemic thesis is comparatively uninteresting, but some catechistic folks have denied it and excommunicated others on this basis. Epistemic certainty has often bred political and ecclesial tyranny. The moral thesis emphasizes motive and holds that the desire for eternal life ought not to be a major motive for practicing charity—at least when "eternal life" means postmortem perdurability—because then charity is not practiced for its own sake. Personal immortality in a future heaven can remain a "blessed hope" (Titus 2:13), if I may still use that Pauline phrase; but "this *is* eternal life, that they may know you, the only true God, and Jesus Christ whom you have sent" (John 17:3; emphasis added).

THEODICY AND GOD'S OBLIGATIONS

The traditional theodicy question asks: "How is the existence of an all-powerful (omnipotent), all-knowing (omniscient), and all-good (omnibenevolent) God compatible with the reality of evil and suffering in the world?" But there has never been a fully satisfying answer to this query.[42] After all is said and done with respect to the free will defense, the claim that pain and vice somehow glorify God or edify humanity, the argument that evil is privation or illusion, the thesis that all will be made well in the eschaton, and so on, a viable Christian faith will always turn on two things: (1) God's promise that creation is finally good, and (2) His enduring presence with us in the form of the Holy Spirit, sharing our doubt and grief, even when creation seems very bad. To let either one of these

[40] Hans Küng sounds an appropriate note of epistemic humility when he reminds us that the Christian canonical writings "never describe the resurrection of Jesus itself, but only what happened for believing witnesses *after* the resurrection." "The New Testament Easter testimonies . . . are meant to be *not* testimonies to the *resurrection as event* but testimonies to the *risen one as person*." As Küng summarizes, "The new life [of resurrection] remains something for which we can hope, but which is *beyond our vision or imagination*." See Küng, *Eternal Life?* pp. 99, 100, and 109.

[41] Putting these points negatively, I reject both the dogmatic (epistemic) claim to know the details of immortality and the cowardly (moral) claim that charity need guarantee an afterlife.

[42] Stanley Hauerwas argues that theodicy is either "a theological mistake" or at best "a parasitic endeavor"; see his *God, Medicine, and Suffering* (Grand Rapids: Eerdmans, 1990), pp. ix and 39. In the face of evil and innocent suffering, he believes, Christians ought to look for neither consolation nor explanation but rather "a way to go on." The proper response to the problem of evil, that is, is not abstract theory but communal practice (see pp. xi, 49, and 51–53).

themes go, even in the name of enriching ideas of God's justice or our destiny, is to impoverish them instead.

My primary reaction to the problem of evil (natural and moral) is to allow that, whatever God's reason for creating a world where death and suffering exist, God's response to these is an incarnational one. Having created persons vulnerable and liable to sin, God actively addresses their bodily needs and builds up their spiritual potentials, most emphatically by sending His Son to earth. Against those who see God as impassible, however abstractly benevolent, Scripture depicts the heart of God's *agape* as a *kenosis* that accepts both obligation and suffering in the flesh.[43] Indeed, obligation is a form of suffering. Whether there are some temporal tragedies that even God cannot redeem, God takes history and human agency seriously, and so should we. A child's having been deeply abused and stunted by her parents, for instance, cannot simply be "made not to have happened" by a wave of some divine wand. Having created both time and freedom, God does not (indeed cannot) simply override them now as insignificant. God sends His suffering presence among us, and God can bring good out of evil in the sense of offering the Holy Spirit as power for moral reform. But so long as time lasts, the Nazi Holocaust, the killing fields of Cambodia, the rape of Bosnia, the genocide in Rwanda, and the like will be real and horrifying losses. As for what happens in "eternity," we have reasons to hope for the best—but *only* to hope. This hope affirms the justice and mercy of God without presuming to know what specific form this must take in every case.

Are we left, then, with utter agnosticism about God's relation to the world? Not at all. It is often pointed out that the "Augustinian" interpretation of God's love as a sublimely detached benevolence rules out His suffering with creatures;[44] it is not so frequently pointed out that the Plotinian-Augustinian God cannot experience obligation to creatures either. Professors Adams, Morris, and Alston are exceptional in frankly acknowledging that their positions entail the impossibility of a divine duty to creatures. Nevertheless, I believe that an adequate view of God's love will affirm *both divine suffering/sympathy and divine obligation/duty*. This dual affirmation is founded on the nature of the Incarnation. As the fullest revelation of God's *agape*, the Incarnation itself involves both a Passion and a Promise. Indeed, the Promise is implicit in the Passion; so great a suffering, freely accepted, implies that God will be with human beings in and through their worst pain. If God cannot make promises, then He cannot incarnate either.

[43] Cf. Wolterstorff, "Suffering Love," in *Philosophy and the Christian Faith*, ed. by Thomas V. Morris (Notre Dame: University of Notre Dame Press, 1988).

[44] E.g., Wolterstorff, ibid., pp. 212–13 and 223.

The foregoing claim may be rendered more plausible by appealing to a distinction akin to that between God's antecedent and consequent will: a contrast between God's antecedent and consequent love. Before that *kenosis* called creation, one imagines God was rather like the "Augustinian" Deity: simple and impassible, experiencing unabated joy within His own perfect beauty and goodness. At this stage, God's love consisted exclusively in self-love, a reciprocal benevolence for the Persons of the Trinity. Prior to His creation of finite beings, God was arguably without both obligation and suffering. Neither divine duty (narrowly construed) nor divine sympathy (literally construed) existed, for they were not needed. The charity among the three Persons of the Trinity was uninterrupted bliss and sufficient unto itself, hence God possessed that exalted aloofness that Augustine ascribed to the Deity eternally. With creation, in contrast, God binds Himself in justice to creatures as well as opening Himself in compassion to their pain. The creation was not itself motivated by duty or sympathy; God did not owe us existence as a debt of obligation, nor did God take pity on our nonexistence. But having been voluntarily offered, creation opens God to moral claims against Him: the creative Word is a performative utterance, in that sense. The existence of created "otherness" entails an obligation not to violate that creation.

On an "Augustinian" view, as noted, God cannot manifest sympathy or incur a real duty—neither in time nor in eternity—since He is unconditioned and cannot be truly affected by or bound to a reality outside the Godhead.[45] This traditional account fails, however, to appreciate the revolutionary character of both the creation and the Incarnation as love's *kenosis*. For Platonic rationality, the divine is typically something liberated from the human, a matter of attaining timeless order and control by transcending spatio-temporal chaos. Christian faith in effect reverses the Hellenic vision: the divine must descend into the human, a matter of redeeming the flesh incarnationally rather than escaping or denying it noetically. Plato did not despise the body, but (with Aristophanes) he evidently did see sexual longing, the present existence of the sexes themselves, as due to a loss of original unity and thus as something to be overcome. This is quite contrary to the spirit of Genesis 1:26–27, where maleness and femaleness, together, are part of God's original plan, part of what it means to be made in the divine Image. (Even the second, less egalitarian biblical creation story [Gen. 2:4b–3:24] calls woman "a helper

---

[45] I am not centrally concerned here with the exegesis of Augustine, hence I have put "Augustinian" in scare quotes. Augustine does write of the "justice" of God, but it is significant that divine "judgments" are quite "unsearchable" and "inscrutable" to fallen creatures. See *On the Gift of Perseverance* [428 or 429], in *The Nicene and Post-Nicene Fathers*, vol. V, ed. by Philip Schaff (Grand Rapids: Eerdmans, 1971), chaps. 18 and 35, pp. 531 and 539.

fit for [man].") Plato is no dualist and his praise of *eros* is unrivaled, but his ideal is finally one of contemplative self-sufficiency in which the body is forgotten. In contrast, the biblical ideal, however often violated, is relational and corporeal to the core. For Socrates in *The Symposium* the key temptation is to be all too human, aroused to bodily passion by Alcibiades. The great Satanic temptation for Christ in the Gospels (e.g., Matt. 4:1–11), in contrast, is to be, so to speak, merely divine, above human need and fellow feeling.[46]

We might very well ask with the Psalmist, "What is man that Thou art mindful of him?" But it is possible to glimpse the splendor of divine righteousness by contrasting it with the squalor of human sin. The two divine acts of creation and Incarnation represent mysteries infinitely greater than and opposite from the Fall of humanity. Whereas Adam and Eve fell from innocence into guilt and from obedient dependence on God into a would-be self-sufficiency, God "fell" from pure self-love into a love embracing justice for others and from actual self-sufficiency into a willingly suffering relation with others. (As Simone Weil teaches, one moved by grace, unlike by gravity, falls upward.) The Incarnation suggests, in particular, that subsequent to the creation God wills to be with the world in its suffering; and this motive is itself what leads Him to take on obligations well beyond the one implicit in creation itself. The Incarnation is the promise of God's self-sacrificial presence in time so long as time exists, even unto the end of the world. Immanuel ("God with us") is the only distinctively Judeo-Christian response to the problem of evil.[47] This incarnational response is not a philosophical justification for evil;[48] nevertheless, rather like Job we may find the suffering company of a just and loving God enough.

---

[46] Suzanne Lilar comments on the tempted Christ as "anti-Socrates," but she insists that "In the secrecy of the Platonic soul, the flesh itself leads to the divine." See her *Aspects of Love in Western Society*, trans. by Jonathan Griffin (New York: McGraw-Hill, 1965), pp. 84 and 76. The latter insistence seems to me an exaggeration. The body is for Plato a launching pad for the ascent of *eros* to the forms; in Christianity, to put it crudely, the body is more like a landing pad for God's own *agape*.

[47] Compare the scene from Elie Wiesel's *Night* in which the SS hangs a young boy in front of thousands of spectators at Auschwitz:

> "Where is God? Where is He?" someone behind me asked. . . .
> "Where is God now?"
> And I heard a voice within me answer him:
> "Where is He? Here He is—He is hanging here on this
> gallows."

See *Night*, trans. by Stella Rodway (New York: Bantam, 1986), pp. 61–62.

[48] Terrence Tilley writes convincingly about the tendency of theodicy to blind us to, or even legitimate, human evil and suffering. See his *The Evils of Theodicy* (Washington, D.C.: Georgetown University Press, 1991).

CONCLUSION

"Man is by nature mortal in that he was created from nothing"—so says Athanasius in *De Incarnatione*[49]—and in light of this observation, even a firm faith in personal immortality must appreciate it as an utterly gratuitous gift from God. Unlike Athanasius, I do not believe that survival beyond this life is a necessary condition for God making good on either creation's or the Incarnation's implicit pledge. It may be sufficient that, with the help of the Holy Spirit, individuals are able to love here and now. But the question of how God will fulfill His promises is separate from whether He has made any. Marilyn Adams, Thomas Morris, and William Alston hold that it is impossible for God to become obligated to creatures (via promises or any other way); someone might think, in opposition, that God could obligate Himself but has not actually done so;[50] I have embraced the other alternative and characterized divine obligations as both possible and actual. God's goodness is not exhausted by His promise-keeping, but the latter is indispensable to the former, lest both creation and Creator be botched.

Is God just? A biblical faith must answer with a resounding "Yes!" Because God is just, moreover, we may be also. Noting this is nothing more nor less than giving credit where it is due, itself an act of justice.

---

[49] Athanasius, *"Contra Gentes" and "De Incarnatione,"* p. 145.
[50] Julius Moravcsik has defended this thesis in conversation.

THREE
Christian Love and Political Violence

*[God] afflicts in mercy. And in mercy, also, if such a thing
were possible, even wars might be waged by the good.*

*The wise man, they say, will wage just wars. Surely, if he
remembers that he is a human being, he will rather lament the
fact that he is faced with the necessity of waging just wars.*

*But it is a higher glory still to stay war itself with a word, than
to slay men with the sword, and to procure or maintain peace
by peace, not by war.*
—Saint Augustine[1]

Essays on love and violence often become disquisitions on the ethical
uses of adversity. How can love respond effectively to a violent world?
Better, how can we translate our charitable motives into the prevention of conflict and the avoidance of coercive force altogether? These
questions are important, but a liability of approaching matters via such
"hows" of violence control is that it may lead us to assume that we understand what love is, and that its priority is morally unproblematic. Such
an assumption is unwarranted; both love and violence must be interro-
gated, independently and in their interrelation. I want, therefore, to ask
two basic questions in this chapter: How, if at all, may *agape* combat
unjustifiable forms of violence, especially political violence? Does *agape*
itself ever act violently?

Although there is some warrant in common speech for defining all
violence pejoratively, as the *unjust* use of force, such usage is not universal. Moreover, it largely begs the normative question of what Christian
love demands in the political sphere. In my pages, then, "violence" will
mean force deliberately employed by persons so as to cause psychological
or bodily injury, or death; distinctly *political* violence will be such force
used by social groups or their proxies, against either individuals or other
groups, for purposes of public order, power, legitimation, liberation, and
the like. I reserve the term "aggression" for the unjust use of force, *im-*

---

[1] Augustine, "Letters," CXXXVIII, in *The Political Writings of St. Augustine*, ed. by
Henry Paolucci (South Bend: Regnery/Gateway, 1962), pp. 179–80; *The City of God*
[413–425/6], trans. by Henry Bettenson (London and New York: Penguin, 1984), bk.
XIX, chap. 7, pp. 861–62; and "Letters," CCXXIX, p. 183.

moral violence, by both individuals and groups. For a pacifist, of course, "immoral violence" is redundant, but I want to leave room for distinguishing forms of violence that may be justifiable from forms that are not.

The chapter unfolds as follows. First, I examine the relevant views of an in-principle pacifist, a Christian "realist," a just war theorist, and a liberationist: Stanley Hauerwas, Reinhold Niebuhr, Paul Ramsey, and Juan Segundo, respectively. The stage thus being set, I briefly discuss the ancient tension between religious separatism and apology. I then offer a more constructive analysis of moral conflict and how this relates to the Christian commitment to putting charity first among the virtues. A third question, at best only implicit in my second question above, will loom large at this point: To what extent may *agape* be the *cause* rather than the remedy of *culpable* political violence, that is, political aggression? This query cuts to the very heart of Christian social ethics, for while violence is stereotypically seen as the crudest response to the frustration of desires, it appears upon reflection that even our (putatively) best moral aspirations may lead us, at times, into elaborate forms of injustice. Violence, we commonly presume, is a cheap consolation; but, in fact, we seem led to cruelty and intolerance by such "worthy" motives as pursuit of the common good and cultivation of individual righteousness. That *agape* may be a vice is a rather disconsoling thought for religious believers.

In concluding, I defend a species of just war theory inspired, and restrained, by Christian charity. The key to this defense comes in locating a host of traditional contrasts (e.g., judgment/mercy, defense of the innocent/embodiment of forgiveness) *within* love itself, rather than identifying love with one or the other pole exclusively. Such a view of love is not new, but it may provide a helpful approach to the specific debate over *agape* and political violence.

STANLEY HAUERWAS AND THE PEACEABLE KINGDOM

Stanley Hauerwas is an indefatigable exponent of visionary ethics, in the best sense. He is rightly admired for helping to restore the centrality of virtue and imagination in Christian moral reflection; of primary import is who we are and what we can see, rather than which rules to follow or results to generate. Somewhat more controversial is his commitment to pacifism. This commitment springs from an inspiration (Judeo-Christian Scripture) and an exasperation (modern secular society). Because the first is by far the more basic, however, his position represents a eucharistic rather than a tactical nonviolence. It looks first to Christ, only secondarily to consequences.

The redemptive self-sacrifice of Jesus on the cross frees his disciples from the need to use coercion to protect or further their interests, according to Hauerwas. The world at large knows not the reality of God's grace and therefore believes it must employ violence to survive; Christians trust otherwise. Knowing themselves to be creatures of the Most High, in need of and granted forgiveness, Christians are able to relinquish control of their lives and of history for a more "adventurous" vocation, love of God and neighbor.

> Jesus proclaims peace as a real alternative, because he has made it possible to rest—to have the confidence that our lives are in God's hands. . . . We can rest in God because we are no longer driven by the assumption that we must be in control of history, that it is up to us to make things come out right.[2]

At the center of Christian ethics is the Imitation of Christ, which is facilitated by the biblical stories of his life, death, and resurrection. Appropriation of these narratives—recognizing them to be true and forming our lives by them—develops personal virtues and communal traditions which, in turn, allow the church to be a peaceable witness to the world. The church is able to welcome the stranger and generally to live without fear because it has glimpsed the justice and mercy of God's kingdom. Conversely, because they belong to the heavenly city, Christians can never be at home in any earthly state. All states, especially modern secular ones, are founded on powers and resentments foreign to a covenant community, thus the church "stands as a political alternative to every nation, witnessing to the kind of social life possible for those who have been formed by the story of Christ."[3] Christians are "resident aliens,"[4] in whichever culture they live.

Although he speaks of the faith community's necessary "separation" from the world, Hauerwas insists that he is not offering an ethic of withdrawal. "I have no interest in legitimating and/or recommending a withdrawal of Christians or the church from social or political affairs. I simply want them to be there as Christians and as church."[5] Such repeated disclaimers make the point that although the Christian's first institutional loyalty is to the church, he or she nonetheless constructively engages the

---

[2] Hauerwas, *The Peaceable Kingdom* (Notre Dame: University of Notre Dame Press, 1983), p. 87.

[3] Hauerwas, *A Community of Character* (Notre Dame: University of Notre Dame Press, 1981), p. 12.

[4] Hauerwas, *Resident Aliens: Life in the Christian Colony*, coauthored with William Willimon (Nashville: Abingdon, 1989), p. 12.

[5] Hauerwas, *Against the Nations* (Minneapolis: Winston, 1985), p. 1; see also ibid., pp. 7 and 117; *The Peaceable Kingdom*, p. 102; *Resident Aliens*, pp. 42–43; *Christian Existence Today* (Durham: Labyrinth, 1988), pp. 13–15, 96, 183, and 195; and *Dispatches from the Front* (Durham: Duke University Press, 1994), p. 18.

temporal powers. In fact, it is exactly in living faithfully to God and the confessing community that individual Christians best serve their respective states; they inspire by example of their extraordinary solidarity. "[The confessing] church knows that its most credible form of witness (and the most 'effective' thing it can do for the world) is the actual creation of a living, breathing, visible community of faith."[6] This much is clear and cogent.

Less clear, however, is how these claims relate to the evaluation of concrete social institutions designed to restrain aggression, such as armies, police forces, law courts, and prisons. With respect to liberal institutions in particular, Hauerwas displays two tendencies not always distinguished. At times his insistence that the church remain true to its traditions and to the example of Jesus serves to distance liberalism by distancing *all* (secular) political arrangements. The message here is a bracingly prophetic one: all temporal structures and ideologies are of relative and secondary importance, and only if Christians keep this in mind may they contribute significantly (if indirectly) to "the nations."[7] If at times the best way to realize an end is to deflate its perceived importance, Hauerwas reminds us that this applies to good federal government as well as to close personal friendship.

At other times, however, Hauerwas brings liberal institutions under specific and sustained attack, as though he has something better in mind *qua political economy*. Not only is liberalism and its distinctive way of coping with conflict not to be identified with the kingdom, it is not even compatible with striving for the kingdom. Pluralism and the balance of power are not, even now, the norms of a good polity.[8] This is troubling because by jumping back and forth between the general and the particular thesis, between prophecy and partisan politics, he appears to hit and run without accountability. One finds Hauerwas saying simultaneously that the church *is* a social ethic, but that it must also *have* a social ethic; that it *does not need* a particular theory of government, but that it also *has a stake in* a limited state.[9] This leaves the political implications of Christian pacifism unclear and is frustrating for sympathizer and critic alike.

The problem, as Hauerwas realizes, is that responsible political engagement that wishes to avoid withdrawal cannot be purely negative or anachronistic; it must have a consistent vision of what it is for as well as what

[6] Hauerwas, *Resident Aliens*, p. 47.

[7] See Hauerwas, *A Community of Character*, pp. 3 and 83–84.

[8] Cf. Hauerwas, *The Peaceable Kingdom*, p. xxiii, and *Resident Aliens*, pp. 41 and 50.

[9] Hauerwas, *The Peaceable Kingdom*, pp. 111–13. William Werpehowski has suggested to me that the ambivalence here reflects a theoretical unclarity between a metaethical claim ("We don't need theories") and a more straightforward normative claim ("The state is part of God's preserving work, so Christians have a stake in it").

it is against, including how to govern a modern society in which everyone is sinful but not everyone is of the same race, creed, party, or sex. If Hauerwas's point is that the church ought not to subordinate itself to or pattern itself after a violent secularity that rejects robust virtue in the name of "pluralism,"[10] the proper response is that this is precisely what perfectionist versions of liberalism at their best are designed to allow groups to do.[11] If, in contrast, his point is that any version of liberal democracy is unacceptable, even qua theory of statecraft, then he owes it to his readers to elaborate and defend a viable alternative to its various institutions, especially those designed to cope with conflict. In fact, Hauerwas must offer alternatives to *all* political structures (liberal or otherwise) which depend, however secondarily, on force to govern.

Hauerwas's response here, as indicated, is that "the most creative social strategy we [Christians] have to offer is the church. Here we show the world a manner of life the world can never achieve through social coercion or governmental action."[12] This may not be "the sectarian temptation" warned of by James Gustafson,[13] but it does suggest, in some matters, a rather decisive either/or between church and state. Hauerwas does not advocate political withdrawal for its own sake, but what he does advocate partially entails it.

> Christians must withdraw their support from a "civic republicanism" only when that form (as well as any other form) of government and society resorts to violence in order to maintain internal order and external security. At that point and that point alone Christians must withhold their involvement with the state.[14]

Not all politics is based on state killing or coercion, as he notes, so a commitment to nonviolence does not dictate complete abstention from

---

[10] See Hauerwas, *Dispatches from the Front*, p. 25.

[11] Liberalism, like violence, comes in different varieties. Liberalism can degenerate on the side of theory into attempts to be morally empty and on the side of practice into efforts merely to maximize individual desires; but this is neither compatible with Christianity nor what the founding fathers, for all their indebtedness to the Enlightenment, had in mind. Christian ethicists make a fundamental mistake in allowing the manifest faults of pragmatic versions of liberalism to make them altogether anti-liberal. See Hauerwas's discussion of Max Stackhouse and the "Liberal-Puritan synthesis" in *Christian Existence Today*, p. 186, n. 9. A slightly more optimistic analysis of the possibility of political virtue in liberal democracies comes in ibid., pp. 195–96. See also my "The Return of the Prodigal?"

[12] Hauerwas, *Resident Aliens*, p. 83.

[13] Gustafson, "The Sectarian Temptation: Reflections on Theology, the Church, and the University," *Proceedings of the Catholic Theological Society* 40 (1985): 83–94. For Hauerwas's response, see the introduction to *Christian Existence Today*.

[14] Hauerwas, *Christian Existence Today*, p. 15.

political involvement. Yet by the same token nonviolence alone is not an adequate philosophy of government.[15]

Christian agapists may say "Amen" to the desire to preserve religious integrity against the hegemony of worldly politics. But we still need to know a good deal about concrete means and ends. Who should hold public office and on what basis; who may own what and how much or how little; with whom may we associate and under what conditions? More important for present purposes: Who should be imprisoned and for what reasons; how is civic order to be maintained against domestic and foreign threats; and so on? These are not the only questions facing society, but if Christians are not responsible for any of this, then we do have in effect an ethic of withdrawal.

Hauerwas rightly wants to avoid what he calls "the false Niebuhrian dilemma of whether to be in or out of the world, politically responsible or introspectively irresponsible,"[16] but to note that "the church's only concern is *how* to be in the world, in what form, for what purpose" is but to ask the crucial question not yet to answer it.[17] Hauerwas candidly acknowledges that "in some circumstances Christians will find it impossible to participate in government, in aspects of the economy, or in the educational system."[18] An obvious implication of his pacifism is that believers must refrain from participating in the army, police forces, and probably much of electoral politics. Yet one need not measure the meaning of life purely in wordly terms—for example, preservation of life, liberty, and property—to worry about impracticality here. God's creatures are highly vulnerable, and we must ask whether virtuous service of them is always nonviolent. The securing of basic human sanctity and community, not just autonomy and utility, is at stake in dealing with torturers, terrorists, and totalitarians. A citizen may wonder what faithfulness to God, not just the nation-state, demands when an aggressor wages war or an assailant threatens murder. Thus there are several challenges facing eucharistic pacifism, even on its own terms.

[15] Robert Nozick argues in *Anarchy, State, and Utopia* (New York: Basic, 1974) that a state inevitably arises from the need for reliable protection against force, fraud, theft, and so on. And as a necessary condition of its existence, "A state claims a monopoly on deciding who may use force when; it says that only it may decide who may use force and under what conditions; it reserves to itself the sole right to pass on the legitimacy and permissibility of any use of force within its boundaries; furthermore it claims to punish all those who violate its claimed monopoly" (p. 23). If the quoted passage is correct, then pacifists (like anarchists) must judge the state to be intrinsically evil. But see John Howard Yoder's *Christian Witness to the State* (Newton, Kans.: Faith and Life, 1964).

[16] Hauerwas, *Resident Aliens*, p. 43. Whether H. Richard Niebuhr himself was as unnuanced as Hauerwas and Willimon suggest is highly debatable.

[17] Ibid.

[18] Hauerwas, *Christian Existence Today*, p. 15.

As indicated, Hauerwas's version of pacifism does not look first to consequences, so it is far removed from utilitarianism;[19] but talk of "rights" and "duties" is also alien to its interpretation of the Bible, so deontology is not its mode either. The language of "natural rights" has many classical and medieval sources—from Roman law through Thomas Aquinas—and, although it underwent distinctive evolutions within the Reformation as well as the Enlightenment, it is not inevitably tied to individualism or subjectivism in ethics.[20] Hauerwas largely cuts himself off from "rights talk" in political discourse, but this is a mixed blessing. It allows him to escape critiques of in-principle pacifism as a misconstrual of the logic of rights, for example, but it also rules out enlisting analyses of rights (religious or secular, classical or liberal) as support for Christian social reform. Certainly no appeal to the right of self-defense or to the duty to defend others against unjust attack can have a decisive place, but neither can most claims to liberty or equal justice for the downtrodden, since these typically depend on acknowledging powers or balancing countervailing interests in terms of "natural rights." Moreover, if Jesus' injunction "do not resist an evildoer" (Matt. 5:39) is taken nonliterally, so as to permit *nonviolent* resistance, then already a strict obedience to Christ is itself compromised. As Paul Ramsey emphasized, a biblical pacifist must explain, without primary reference to rights or duties of justice, why the line is drawn at nonviolence and not at nonresistance.[21]

Such explanation has been attempted, of course. Some Christian pacifists aver that certain forms of coercion (e.g., economic boycotts) are compatible with respect for other people as free and equal neighbors and thus with the heart of Jesus' teaching. These forms are thought not to include violence, however, because violence (especially when lethal) inevitably treats others as objects only.[22] Apart from the rather odd elevation

---

[19] Hauerwas calls utilitarianism "a form of Christianity gone mad"; see *Dispatches from the Front*, p. 165.

[20] Responding to Michel Villey, Alasdair MacIntyre, and others, Brian Tierney points to the pre-fourteenth-century origins of modern rights theories. He writes: "The doctrine of individual rights was not a late medieval aberration from an earlier tradition of objective right or of natural moral law. Still less was it a seventeenth-century invention of Grotius or Hobbes or Locke. Rather, . . . it was a characteristic product of the great age of creative jurisprudence that, in the twelfth and thirteenth centuries, established the foundations of the Western legal tradition." See Tierney, *The Idea of Natural Rights* (Atlanta: Scholars, 1997), p. 42.

[21] See Ramsey, *Speak Up for Just War or Pacifism* (University Park: Penn State University Press, 1987), pp. 73–75.

[22] Ronald Sider, *Christ and Violence* (Scottdale, Pa.: Herald, 1979), p. 45. See also Ronald Sider and Richard Taylor, *Nuclear Holocaust and Christian Hope* (New York: Paulist, 1982), pp. 111–13; and John Howard Yoder, *The Politics of Jesus* (Grand Rapids: Eerdmans, 1972).

of autonomy, the debatable assumption here is that it is impossible to distinguish between justifying violent resistance to evil and justifying hatred or aggression toward one's enemies. Love never hates or objectifies human beings, seeking always the good of others,[23] but this leaves open the issue of whether lethal force might not sometimes be loving. It is quite compatible with the Golden Rule, for instance, to say, "Were I an aggressor, I would want someone to stop me with force if necessary."

Hauerwas's defense of pacifism is often deft, particularly when it seeks to unmask various forms of political idolatry. A dynamic church is frequently necessary to form those virtues that can stand against abuses of state power. Hauerwas himself reminds us, however, that the church is not God's kingdom and remains forever dependent upon the Holy Spirit.[24] I would only emphasize that the church (like any finite community) can itself become an oppressive, idolatrous, even demonic body that prophetic individuals must challenge in the name of a transcendent faith. God speaks to individuals as well as groups, and Christians must keep in mind all three love commands in formulating a sound ecclesiology as well as a sound personal ethics. A Kierkegaardian "absolute relation to the Absolute," relativizing *all* temporal associations, is the sine qua non for Christlike love.[25] The basic issue remains: Does the logic of such love, communicated by the Spirit, dictate refusal of all resort to violence? We may begin to answer this question by turning to the work of Reinhold Niebuhr.

REINHOLD NIEBUHR AND PROPHETIC CHRISTIANITY

On Reinhold Niebuhr's view, "prophetic Christianity" is distinctive for maintaining a tension between immanence and transcendence, between a concern for history and the natural order and a recognition that full redemption of that order comes from God and only at the end of history. If we lose sight of the fact that God is Creator of the world, we tend to deny the meaningfulness and (original) goodness of temporal reality; if we forget that God is also the world's Judge and Redeemer, we tend to a

[23] Romans 12:9 reads: "Let love be genuine; hate what is evil, hold fast to what is good." Here I take the word "hate" to mean "vigorously reject or avoid," rather than "will calamity for," and it is noteworthy that Paul does not say "hate *who* is evil." Jesus' suggestion that a disciple ought to "hate father and mother" (Luke 14:26) should also be seen as "vivid hyperbole," as the NRSV makes clear; see *The New Oxford Annotated Bible*, NT note p. 105. On the irreconcilability of love of God and hatred of neighbors, see 1 John 4:20.

[24] Hauerwas, *Christian Existence Today*, pp. 59–62. See also p. 196, where Hauerwas perceives that even "communities of virtue risk becoming ends in themselves."

[25] See my analysis of *Fear and Trembling* in *Love Disconsoled*, chap. 6; and compare also Hauerwas, *Christian Existence Today*, pp. 159–60.

pantheistic complacency. Truly prophetic faith, in contrast, recognizes that ultimate meaning can be exclusively identified with neither temporality nor eternity. The kingdom is "both here and not yet."

This attempt to live between the extremes of naturalism and otherworldliness defines Niebuhr's genius, but it forces him to say some quite paradoxical things, especially about Jesus Christ:

> [Jesus'] Kingdom of God is always a possibility in history, because its heights of pure love are organically related to the experience of love in all human life, but it is also an impossibility in history and always beyond every historical achievement. Men living in nature and in the body will never be capable of the sublimation of egoism and the attainment of the sacrificial passion, the complete disinterestedness which the ethic of Jesus demands. The social justice which Amos demanded represented a possible ideal for society.[26]

Interpretation of these words is subject to the very same problems and temptations faced by prophetic religion itself; we want to eliminate the paradox by ignoring one or the other pole of opposition. Thus some commentators accent the impossibility of Christian love, at least on the group level, and construe Niebuhr as saying that we must simply leave *agape* behind as a political ideal, favoring justice instead.[27] Yet this misses his exquisite, sometimes tortured ambivalence. Also simplistic is any move which so accents the "possibility" of Christian love that politics is believed compatible with nonviolence and pacifism. The second reading is not very tempting as Niebuhr-exegesis, but the first is not altogether implausible. Niebuhr himself is not always consistent here. He too lapses occasionally into a philosophical contrast of the horns of the dilemma (suggesting an either/or), when faith demands accepting the "contradiction" as such (affirming both/and). In *Moral Man and Immoral Society*, for example, he writes:

> A rational ethic aims at justice, and a religious ethic makes love the ideal. A rational ethic seeks to bring the needs of others into equal consideration

---

[26] Niebuhr, *An Interpretation of Christian Ethics* (New York: Seabury, 1979), p. 19.

[27] See Hauerwas, *Resident Aliens*, p. 76. Even as careful a critic as Barbara Hilkert Andolsen writes:

> Because of Niebuhr's acute awareness of human selfishness, especially corporate selfishness, where economics and government are concerned, he reduced *agape* to a remote star. Christians can use *agape* as a reference point to get their moral bearings, but in the public world the total actualization of love will never be reached. Thus according to Niebuhr sacrificial love is the operating norm for personal life; justice, the standard for social life.

See Andolsen, "*Agape* in Feminist Ethics," p. 148.

with those of the self. The religious ethic . . . insists that the needs of the neighbor shall be met, without a careful computation of relative needs.[28]

Given his frequent claims that *agape* is nonresisting while politics is built on the balance of power, it is tempting indeed to ascribe to Niebuhr a sharp (almost cynical) discontinuity between love and justice, Christianity and politics; but this too easily resolves the central paradox of prophetic morality. In spite of himself, Niebuhr forgets at times that Christian ethics must combine both horizontal and vertical referents, as when he asserts that "neither natural impulses nor social consequences are taken into consideration" by Jesus and that we are to love all our neighbors "not because they are equally divine, but because God loves them equally."[29] This is contrary to his own best insights concerning God as both Creator and Redeemer. To contend that moral universalism is based *solely* on our reflection of or obligation to "the loving will of God,"[30] rather than also on the needs and potentials of our fellow creatures, is to do violence to the biblical doctrine of creation in which a loving Deity makes human beings in God's own Image, and calls them "good."

Reminiscent of Kierkegaard's pseudonyms, Niebuhr's characteristic trope is to resist all reductive gambits and to depict Christianity paradoxically. The law of love, for example, is both a cogent norm and an impractical ideal; it is neither simply possible nor simply impossible, but rather an "impossible possibility."[31] A philosophical turn of mind will immediately pounce on this as contradictory, and so it is on one level. Niebuhr's point, however, is that prophetic religion avails itself of myths and mysteries that transcend philosophical reason. Any rationalistic attempt to dismiss the love command as impractical and therefore irrelevant, and any romantic attempt to preach it as fully realizable and therefore straightforwardly binding, evacuates Christian piety of its distinctive tension. Faith believes in a higher unity, a transcendent Personality, that despite current appearances will ultimately reconcile the contradictions of our moral lives. Because complete reconciliation takes place only at the end of time, all political utopias are relativized; but because the stage is decisively set within time, political engagement is ethically essential. "Prophetic Christianity . . . demands the impossible," and yet "the prophetic tradition in Christianity must insist on the relevance of the ideal of love to the moral experience of mankind *of every conceivable level.*"[32] Any-

---

[28] Niebuhr, *Moral Man and Immoral Society* (New York: Scribner's, 1960), p. 57.
[29] Niebuhr, *An Interpretation of Christian Ethics*, pp. 28, 30; and cf. p. 131.
[30] Ibid., p. 69.
[31] Ibid., p. 37.
[32] Ibid., pp. 62, 63; emphasis added.

thing else encourages a less than mature faith and is founded on a less than adequate anthropology.

Niebuhr's depiction of prophetic religion is deeply informed by his Augustinian-Kierkegaardian conception of human nature. The various forms of theological liberalism, naturalism, and idealism all fail to understand "that though man always stands under infinite possibilities and is potentially related to the whole of existence, he is, nevertheless, and will remain, a creature of finiteness."[33] Man himself is a paradox, a tense unity of opposites that might be called "an impersonal personality." Men and women are compounded of body and soul so as to be free but determined by physical and biological circumstances, invariably sinful but capable of a degree of self-transcendence and reformation. Both horns of the dilemma of selfhood must be grasped simultaneously, thus a qualitatively similar dynamic appears on the individual as on the collective level. Earthly moral perfection is out of reach, but because fallen humanity is still made in the Image of God rigorous moral responsibility is unavoidable. No creature is now capable of the righteousness of Christ, but anticipation of adoption as Son or Daughter compels upon every individual the *Imitatio Christi*, the absolute rule of *agape*.

What may be said by way of criticism of Niebuhr's position? In a phrase, I think that he is less sensitive than he ought to be to the fact that he seeks to eff the ineffable. (S.K. was more self-conscious about the limits of his "irrationalism"; Christianity appeared absurd to his pseudonyms, but not to the believer himself.) One must distinguish, for example, between an ideal itself being contradictory or counterproductive and our pursuit of it being flawed, even inevitably flawed. If, although our moral efforts are halting, the ideal itself is theoretically and practically appropriate, then it still makes sense to *try* to realize that ideal. If, on the other hand, it is unintelligible or destructive even to strive for the ideal, then in what sense is it still a valid measure of success or failure? Niebuhr's use of the language of paradox fails to distinguish between these two scenarios adequately. He does speak in places of the eschatological overcoming of the oppositions of human existence; but he does not discriminate rigorously enough between an apparent or temporary contradiction and a real and enduring one, thus inviting the charge of irrationalism or various reductionist readings designed to avoid this charge. Niebuhr's own retreats from the prophetic, mentioned earlier, are due to the failure to make clear that ultimately faith does not oppose, but rather completes, reason, and love does not contradict, but rather sustains and fulfills, justice.

Is it possible to formulate Niebuhr's insights into Christian ethics so as to avoid the problems just described? I believe so, and the cue may be

---

[33] Ibid., p. 72.

taken from Niebuhr himself. At his most lucid, Niebuhr acknowledges that love and justice, Christianity and politics, are not in their natures opposed. In these contexts he supplements (or replaces) the language of "paradox" with that of "approximation." "A religion which holds love to be the final law of life stultifies itself if it does not support equal justice as a political and economic approximation of the ideal of love."[34] The key word in this sentence is "final." Love and justice may *seem within history* to be contradictory, due to human ignorance; they may temporarily *be* so, due to human sin; but if they are forever and irremediably at odds, even *beyond history* and *independently of sin*, then a stark dualism prevails in which it is absurd to affirm both love and justice and in which eternity breaks covenant with time. Such Manichaeanism cannot be Niebuhr's considered opinion any more than it could be Augustine's.

Just as faith may appear *contra rationem* while actually being *supra rationem*, so love may appear *contra justitiam* while actually being *supra justitiam*. The essential distinction is between a truth that cannot be fully rationalized (and thus calls for myths) and a garden variety absurdity that is against reason (and thus necessarily false). Niebuhr never backs away from the claim:

> Love is both the fulfillment and the negation of all achievements of justice in history. . . . the achievements of justice in history may rise in indeterminate degrees to find their fulfillment in a more perfect love and brotherhood; but each new level of fulfillment also contains elements which stand in contradiction of perfect love.[35]

But the hard edge of this paradox is softened when we note that the qualifying phrase "in history" is repeated twice. If these phrases do not mitigate the contradiction of love's being both fulfillment and negation, justice's being both approximation and contradiction, then Niebuhr is simply a misologist. I urge the more charitable reading.

Niebuhr is neither misologist nor relativist. Such charges fail to grasp that, for him, Christian belief is finally beyond paradox, even as Christian ethics is beyond tragedy.[36] On the latter score, although he claims to reject "absolute standards," Niebuhr does not merely leave love behind

---

[34] Ibid., p. 80.

[35] Niebuhr, *The Nature and Destiny of Man*, vol. II (New York: Scribner's, 1964), p. 246.

[36] See Niebuhr's *Beyond Tragedy* (New York: Scribner's, 1938), esp. the preface and chap. 1. In vol. I of *The Nature and Destiny of Man*, he writes: "Though the religious faith through which God is apprehended cannot be in contradiction to reason in the sense that the ultimate principle of meaning cannot be in contradiction to the subordinate principle of meaning which is found in rational coherence yet, on the other hand the religious faith cannot be simply subordinated to reason or made to stand under its judgment" (New York: Scribner's, 1964), p. 165.

for the sake of political expediency. Indeed, love itself tends to become an absolute, however much it may elude discursive articulation:

> For the Christian the love commandment must be made relevant to the relativities of the social struggle, even to hazardous and dubious relativities.[37]
>
> [Man's] freedom consists in a capacity for self-transcendence in infinite regression. There is therefore no limit in reason for either his creativity or his sin. There is no possibility of giving a rational definition of a just relation between man and man or nation and nation short of a complete love in which each life affirms the interests of the other. . . . *Love is the only final structure of freedom.*[38]

The problem here is not with irrationalism or nihilism but with a potentially too easy consequentialism in which love, claiming to transcend justice, actually falls below it in embracing too violent means to political ends. Enter Paul Ramsey.

Paul Ramsey and Love Transforming Justice

Paul Ramsey is the worthy inheritor of Reinhold Niebuhr's prophetic legacy, as well as a faithful steward working interest on the principal. Ramsey's signal contribution is to retrieve Augustine's view of charity and in its light to elaborate the love/justice relation so as to avoid both Niebuhr's hard paradoxes and his tendency to soft consequentialism. At the heart of Ramsey's view of Christian politics is a principled love that seeks innovatively to restrain evil.

> Sometimes love does what justice requires and assumes its rules as norms, sometimes love does more than justice requires but never less, and sometimes love acts in a quite different way from what justice alone can enable us to discern to be right. When one's own interests alone are at stake, the Christian governs himself by love and resists not one who is evil. When his neighbor's need and the just order of society are at stake, the Christian still governs himself by love and suffers no injustice to be done nor the order necessary to earthly life to be injured.[39]

An adequate account of love avoids contradictions, for these may contribute to an unduly pessimistic view of human nature and thus to an

---

[37] Niebuhr, *An Interpretation of Christian Ethics*, p. 121.

[38] Niebuhr, "Christian Faith and Natural Law," in *Love and Justice: Selections from the Shorter Writings of Reinhold Niebuhr*, ed. by D. B. Robertson (Glouchester: Peter Smith, 1976), p. 50; emphasis added. See also Niebuhr, *The Nature and Destiny of Man*, vol. I, pp. 285, 295–96. For more on Niebuhr on love and justice, see Gene Outka, *Agape: An Ethical Analysis*, chap. 3.

[39] Ramsey, *War and the Christian Conscience*, p. 178.

impoverished view of moral responsibility. Love is not left behind on the political plane in favor of natural justice, nor does it stand in an irrational tension with it. Love may sometimes assert its autonomy and transcend (but not violate) natural categories of merit, but it characteristically informs and transforms (modern) justice by simultaneously altering its motive and placing limits on its means. With respect to motive, we are to will the good for all creatures for whom Christ died—friend and foe, guilty and innocent—thus vengeance and the unchecked will to power are ruled out. The desire to protect the innocent from unjust attack *is* a part of love's inspiration, however; thus, especially on the corporate level, impassivity and nonresistance are also ruled out. With respect to means, because effectively willing the good for the innocent neighbor may sometimes require the use of violent force, just wars are a possibility, according to Ramsey. But because unbridled lethal means would themselves contradict the end of love, poisoning wells and obliteration bombing (all forms of direct attack on the innocent) are *not* a possibility. This last insight accounts for the centrality and inviolability of the principle of discrimination (noncombatant immunity) in Ramsey's account of *jus in bello*, and it represents a corrective to Niebuhr's occasional readiness to embrace a too purely utilitarian approach to political means.[40]

Behind Ramsey's axiology lies his eschatology. Just as the belief that temporal life is not the greatest good leads some Christians to in-principle pacifism (out of a denial of self), so this same belief leads Ramsey to the just use of force to restrain evil (out of love of neighbor). Although it is hard to settle this dispute on purely theological grounds, Ramsey has a powerful case. On the face of it, it is logically odd to derive an in-principle prohibition of killing from a denial of the absolute value of living. To admit that some things are in themselves more important than temporal existence suggests that both living and dying (one's own and others')

---

[40] Ibid., pp. 190–91, 269–70. In "Perpetual Peace," Immanuel Kant writes:

A war of extermination, in which the destruction of both parties and of all justice can result, would permit perpetual peace only in the vast burial ground of the human race. Therefore, such a war and the use of all means leading to it must be absolutely forbidden. . . . these infernal arts [assassination, poisoning, breach of capitulation, and incitement to treason], vile in themselves, when once used would not long be confined to the sphere of war.

Kant here does for proportionality what Paul Ramsey does for discrimination. Ramsey shows how violating discrimination is self-defeating: it is incompatible with the law of love and its work of protecting the innocent. Kant shows how violating proportionality is self-defeating: it leads to the "undoing of the very spirit of peace," to preserve which is one of the main moral reasons for going to war. See "Perpetual Peace," trans. by Lewis White Beck, appearing in *The Enlightenment: A Comprehensive Anthology*, ed. by Peter Gay (New York: Simon and Schuster, 1973), pp. 789 and 788–89.

may be subordinated to a greater good. Short of doing something evil in itself (*malum in se*), even killing may be a proportionate means precisely because death is not the worst calamity. Taking the life of an aggressor to defend the innocent may serve both parties, or at least be compatible with willing the good for both. Although a "hard saying," it may sometimes be better/more just to be killed than be permitted to become a successful murderer, better/more just forcefully to restrain evil than to allow the political triumph of the murderous. As Thomas Aquinas saw, an external action and its consequences can add to the malice of an interior action/intention,[41] so it may be to an aggressor's moral benefit to nip his offenses in the bud.

Ramsey focuses, understandably, on the neighbor to be defended, and there is no question but that defense of the innocent will be the primary motive for the just warrior. Nevertheless, the strong agapist will also insist on asking what love for the aggressor requires, or at least permits. Even the victimizer remains a neighbor, a creature of God, and although there will seldom if ever be philial relations on the modern battlefield, there can still be regard for the other's basic humanity. You will not have a warm fuzzy feeling for the party trying to kill you and/or others, but you can remain open to several concrete practices designed to limit war's ferocity: refusing to use weapons (e.g., mustard gases) that horribly maim or disfigure, declining to attribute personal guilt to a draftee ignorantly prosecuting an unjust war, allowing trapped or retreating forces to surrender, offering benevolent quarantine to those who do surrender, and so on.[42] In even risking some of his or her own troops ("friendlies") in order to ensure discriminate and proportionate tactics, the "just" warrior may actually be inspired by something like Christian charity and its call to costly service (even to enemies).[43]

Yet there are inescapable limits here. Because I can and should forgive an aggressor, Augustinians suggest, I may be called not to defend *myself* by taking another's life; but I cannot forgive *for others* who may come under his unjust attack.[44] The same love that would forgive all injustice

---

[41] Aquinas, *Summa Theologiae*, I-II, Q. 20, arts. 4 and 5; I thank Jean Porter for this reference.

[42] Late in the Gulf War, NATO forces under U.S. command utterly wiped out a retreating Iraqi tank column from the air. This carnage seems cruel, a violation of *jus in bello* or at least of the spirit of charity that would repeatedly offer surrender to a bested adversary. All direct attacks on noncombatants are violations of discrimination, but the fire bombing of Dresden toward the end of World War II also comes to mind as especially brutal, revenge without even the semblance of strategic "necessity." I thank Todd Whitmore for reminding me of the Gulf War incident.

[43] Cf. Michael Walzer's revision of the traditional principle of double effect, in *Just and Unjust Wars* (New York: Basic, 1977), pp. 155–59.

[44] Augustine considered lethal self-defense morally wrong for Christians because it entails preferring one's own life to that of another for whom Christ died. Only the public defense

may also forcefully check the hand of the aggressor. Aware of the evils of paternalism, and with fear and trembling, I quote *The City of God*:

> Just as it is not an act of kindness to help a man, when the effect of the help is to make him lose a greater good, so it is not a blameless act to spare a man, when by doing so you let him fall into a greater sin. Hence the duty of anyone who would be blameless includes not only doing no harm to anyone but also restraining a man from sin or punishing his sin, so that either the man who is chastised may be corrected by his experience, or others may be deterred by his example.[45]

Like Augustine, Ramsey teaches us to avoid the assumption that all war is unmitigated moral failure, at most a prudent second-best engaged in because we are incapable of doing what love demands on the political level. The belief that all war results either because we try and fail to avoid it or because we fail even to try, is inadequate. All war is evil in the sense of being destructive and in itself undesirable, but not all war (much less all politics) is wicked or to be avoided. Reinhold Niebuhr's comments on love and justice can contribute to misunderstanding here. To the extent that he *seems* on occasion to say that on the group level we must leave behind the ideal of selfless love (*agape*) and settle for justice (*suum cuique*), he invites a romantic response. "Let us not compromise with the world but cling to what we know is right, no matter how difficult or costly" is the call of some Christian pacifists. If, as evident in Ramsey, love and justice are not finally in opposition, however—conceding that love itself may demand different things in different circumstances—then any necessary link between Christian virtue and political nonviolence is far less plausible. In fact, the issue then becomes whether, by failing to protect innocents from unjust attack, pacifism represents not admirable perfectionism but dereliction of duty.

Ramsey sought to distance the phrase "love monism" as a characteriza-

---

of innocent others could be free of inordinate self-assertion, on his view. See Augustine, *On Free Choice of the Will* [395], trans. by Anna S. Benjamin and L. H. Hackstaff (Indianapolis: Bobbs-Merrill, 1964), bk. 1, chap. V, pp. 10–13. My own opinion, elaborated further in chap. 4, is that self-defense against unjust attack may *sometimes* be ruled out by charity, including forgiveness, but that it may occasionally be permissible. I too may be a relevantly innocent party and thus come under the protection, even the violent protection, of a proper self-love. This is especially true if, as is often the case, the aggressor threatens both myself and the wider community with grievous harm. If I do not defend myself in this case, I may be abandoning the common good as well as God's will for my life. For helpful criticism on these points, I am indebted to Darrell Cole, "Legitimate Christian Violence and Charitable Self-Defense" (unpublished paper).

[45] Augustine, *The City of God*, bk. XIX, chap. 16, p. 876. Cf. Reinhold Niebuhr's observation in *The Nature and Destiny of Man*, vol. II, p. 88: "as soon as the life and interest of others than the agent are involved in an action or policy, the sacrifice of those interests ceases to be 'self-sacrifice.' It may actually become an unjust betrayal of their interests."

tion of his position,[46] but whatever the terminology, he improves on Niebuhr by avoiding the latter's occasional drift into dualism. Ramsey's insistence on "love-informed justice" and on justifying actions "in terms of countervailing requirements of *agape*" locates the standard Niebuhrian tensions between self/others and conscience/power within love itself.[47] *Love does not choose between justice and mercy, for these two goods are internally related to agape.* Although substantive tensions may remain, this means we should not flinch from calling Ramsey's corpus a defense of the "loving war tradition." (Just war is an "alien work," but still a work, of love.) It also suggests, ironically, that he shares to a degree Joseph Fletcher's conviction that justice is "love distributed." It may be that on the interpersonal level a loving distribution is often all one way, thus talk of justice tends not to arise; but this is still a limiting case of justice, at least not an injustice. On Ramsey's view, the in-principle pacifist is not holding out for the moral ideal (much less for supererogation) and merely disagreeing with the just war theorist over what is feasible in a fallen world; rather, he or she is disagreeing on the ideal itself.

We are no doubt imperfect and incapable of acting always in love. But to say with Niebuhr that "the world is only partially amenable to the strategy of the cross," is not to say (rightly) that we are only partially capable of realizing love's strategy, but rather to say (relevantly) that love's strategy is not always noncoercive. *It is not that in the political sphere we leave love behind, but rather that here love leaves (or may leave) nonviolence behind.* For a proponent of *bellum justum*, the question is not whether love sometimes permits violent restraint of evil (it does), but whether it ever categorically demands it. In the latter case, in-principle pacifism must seem less than fully responsible; but to the extent that mercy is an ineliminable aspect of love, it is hard to defend an *imperative* to violence as an outgrowth of Christian charity (even in direst situations). It is better, I think, to see just war as permissible for Christians, rather than as obligatory.

A further clarification of the responsiblity of and to love may be had by reviewing the work of Juan Segundo.

JUAN SEGUNDO AND LIBERATED ETHICS

Juan Segundo's thoughts on "Christian love" and "political violence" may first be approached via the adjectives rather than the nouns in those two phrases. What Segundo thinks about love and violence is more deeply

---

[46] Ramsey, "A Letter to James Gustafson," *Journal of Religious Ethics* 13, no. 1 (spring 1985): 74–75.

[47] Ramsey, *The Just War* (New York: Scribner's, 1968), pp. 247 and 460.

and self-consciously conditioned by his account of Christianity, politics, and their interrelation than is the case with the other theologians I have discussed, with the possible exception of Niebuhr. This is not an unforeseen implication of his work but part of its basic intent. Segundo's conception of and commitment to human liberation, especially as these are worked out in *The Liberation of Theology*, prevent him from giving a priori accounts of love and violence which might then "prove" that they exclude one another on purely logical grounds. On his view, there is no ahistorical essence of love that might entail nonviolence, just as there is no ahistorical essence of violence that might entail nonlove. In any concrete context, the theological meaning of love and violence will depend on our understanding of a host of contingent facts, including the nature of the church, the state, the economy, and theology itself.

Let me begin, therefore, by briefly describing Segundo's views on theology and liberation. My chief concern is to ask whether his work represents an advance over—a liberation of—that of Hauerwas, Niebuhr, or Ramsey. My answer will be that, for the most part, the later Segundo (i.e., of *The Liberation of Theology*) falls short of the insights of these other authors as well as those of his former self (i.e., of *A Theology for Artisans of a New Humanity*).

Early in *The Liberation of Theology*, Segundo advances a recurrent thesis: "We must realize that there is no such thing as an autonomous, impartial, academic theology floating free above the realm of human options and biases."[48] This means that any belief system that claims universal validity or unmediated access to atemporal reality is false and an obstacle to solving real problems; it encourages an empty, and inherently conservative, spirituality. Human life is characterized by such complexity and ambiguity that choices must be made without benefit of neutral perspectives or absolute rules. Not even Holy Scripture can escape being conditioned by time and place.

> The Bible is not the discourse of a universal God to a universal man. Partiality is justified because we must find, and designate as the word of God, that *part* of divine revelation which *today*, in the light of our concrete historical situation, is most useful for the liberation to which God summons us.[49]

Because our social situation is constantly changing and facing us with new challenges, our theology (exegesis, sacraments, ecclesiology, etc.) must also change and adapt, or else die. To the extent that classical theology pictures an immutable and impassive God and fixed and incorrigible dogmas, it denies the need for openness to history and thus frustrates the

---

[48] Segundo, *The Liberation of Theology*, trans. by John Drury (Maryknoll: Orbis, 1982), p. 13.

[49] Ibid., p. 33.

liberation of actual human beings. It contributes often to an otherworldliness leading to political quietism and moral insensitivity. But, the later
Segundo contends, "There is no doubt that the picture of God in the
Bible is a very different one, presenting us with a passionate God who
suffers along with his people."[50] In this age in which "politics is the fundamental human dimension," theology is deeply implicated in every critical social choice, either for good or for ill. If it would be liberating,
Christian theology must come to grips with the social sciences (especially
sociology and economics) and realize that to preach an apolitical love is a
"distortion" of the gospel message itself. Partially correcting the Medellín
documents of the Latin American bishops, Segundo suggests that political commitment to the oppressed and appropriation of the gospel message go hand in hand, each supporting the other, although the hearing of
the gospel usually comes first temporally.[51]

As we have seen, Paul Ramsey places primary emphasis on the nature
of Christian love, allowing it to define political ends (justice) and limit
political means (discrimination and proportionality). Some forms of liberation theology (e.g., Hugo Assmann's) simply reverse this ordering, making political praxis prior to and interpretive of the content of faith, but
the later Segundo rejects such a move. He says explicitly that "no one
can enter into the revolutionary process without forming some idea for
himself of the goal of the process and the proper means to be used to
achieve it."[52] For Segundo, priority cannot be given to political commitment; but it is also clear that no single religious creed can be the immutable touchstone of all action. Creed and commitment are related dialec-
tically, such that political ends (liberation) and means (revolution and
violence) do *help* to define and limit the nature of love. Ramsey believes
that love rules out some things categorically as *malum in se* (e.g., coun-
terpopulation warfare), but in *The Liberation of Theology* Segundo commits himself to no such absolutes. Variables of time and place, theology
and history, may prompt us to alter even our most fundamental beliefs
and entrenched patterns of behavior.

The later Segundo's analysis of the relation between faith and ideologies brings many of the above themes to a head. He clearly wishes to
distinguish the two notions. Faith "claims to possess an *objectively* absolute value," while ideologies have no such "*pretensions*"; faith embodies
the "permanent and unique" content of divine revelation, while ideologies represent "changing" reflections on particular means and ends and

---

[50] Ibid., p. 46.
[51] Ibid., pp. 71, 84–85.
[52] Ibid., pp. 101–2.

are "bound up with different historical circumstances."[53] Yet in the end this looks to be a distinction without a difference. No concrete content can be given to Christian faith, not even *agape*. "If someone were to ask me what I have derived from my faith-inspired encounter as a clear-cut, absolute truth that can validly give orientation to my concrete life, then my honest response should be: nothing."[54]

Segundo (unlike Hauerwas) sees some forms of political violence as compatible with biblical faith and the example of Christ. He (like Ramsey) construes Jesus' admonitions to "resist not evil," "turn the other cheek," and forswear the sword as tactical rather than in-principle, as historically conditioned expressions rather than the essence of love. While Ramsey thinks that some moral deeds and rules *are* essential to love, however, the later Segundo's contextualism leaves any enduring content to love extremely hard to specify. The difference between Ramsey's view and Segundo's occasionally resembles that between rule- and act-agapism,[55] but it actually goes deeper. At times, *agape* itself seems for the later Segundo not to be permanently valid. He endorses the opinion that "the only perduring rule is that one should try to display the most effective and wide-ranging love possible in a given situation," but he also allows that "the concrete kind of love proclaimed by Jesus constitutes an *ideology*."[56] This is the source of my primary criticism.

Especially in his later work, Segundo is so concerned not to give comfort to the forces of theological or political reaction that love and covenant fidelity become devoid of content. Violence is not ruled out by Christian faith, but we are hard-pressed to know when, where, how, or why it might be ruled in. No action or instrument is evil in itself, thus, "We cannot decide whether love or egotism is at work by examining the means employed."[57] But are there no limits, then, to what might be done in the name of God? May we lie, steal, torture, or murder even for temporal goals? These questions are especially urgent in light of the incipi-

[53] Ibid., pp. 106–7, 116. In his earlier work, "ideology" is a much more pejorative term. In fact, "the alienating sin of the world is 'ideology,'" Segundo writes in *Evolution and Guilt*, thus making the notion very close to the antonym of "liberation." See *A Theology for Artisans of a New Humanity*, vol. 5, p. 52.

[54] Segundo, *The Liberation of Theology*, p. 108.

[55] For a discussion of this distinction, see Ramsey, *Deeds and Rules in Christian Ethics* (New York: Scribner's, 1967), esp. pp. 104–22.

[56] Segundo, *The Liberation of Theology*, p. 155; see also p. 116.

[57] Ibid., p. 164. Segundo goes so far as to claim "that *violence is an intrinsic dimension of any and all concrete love* in history" (ibid., p. 161). For a criticism of this as "badly exaggerated," see Gene Outka, "Discontinuity in the Ethics of Jacques Ellul," in *Jacques Ellul: Interpretive Essays*, ed. by Clifford G. Christians and Jay M. Van Hook (Urbana: University of Illinois, 1981), pp. 219–20.

ently totalitarian claim noted above that "politics is the fundamental human dimension" and the related notion that "the only truth is liberation itself."[58] One does not have to be an advocate of the status quo or of otherworldliness to want more detailed criteria for moral judgment, criteria that are consistent and informed (however fallibly) by Scripture, reason, and tradition. The observation that God sides with the oppressed, although important, is not a sufficient basis for discriminating ethically between complex political means and ends. It suffers from the same moral ambiguity as the Marxist claim that history favors the proletariat; unqualified, it may give license to the oppressed to become oppressors.[59] One may adopt what the early Segundo calls "an evolutionary outlook"[60] and acknowledge the provisional character of all ideology, but to contend that no belief can apprehend a permanent truth is to assume either the unattainability of truth per se or the perpetual flux of all reality, including God. Both are substantive ideas and require argument; neither follows from human finitude or fallibility alone.

The later Segundo's emphasis on the importance and open-endedness of human choice flirts with an extreme form of moral voluntarism. With respect to the parable of the Good Samaritan, he writes:

> Jesus does not end up his parable saying that every human being *is* our neighbor. His point is that we can make any given human being our neighbor if we take advantage of the countless opportunities offered us in life. That is a very different point.[61]

But one must not confuse loving someone in a particular way because they are your *near* neighbor with their *becoming* your neighbor *simpliciter* only because you *choose* to love them. Segundo's exegesis of the Good Samaritan blurs the fact that I may recognize other human beings as creatures of God, all of *equal value*, and yet not take this as demanding for them *identical treatment*.[62] His discussion of "deutero-learning" (learning how to learn) is a welcome contribution to pedagogy; but in the absence of substantive things *to* learn, its final significance is ambiguous at best.

If, in effect, we must view the whole of faith as one more radically contingent ideology, then theology's liberation is virtually indistinguishable from its demise. *The Liberation of Theology* laudably deflates dogma-

---

[58] Segundo, *The Liberation of Theology*, p. 118.

[59] The early Segundo himself warns against the mere reversal of tyranny. See *Evolution and Guilt*, p. 69.

[60] Ibid., pp. 47, 59, and passim.

[61] Segundo, *The Liberation of Theology*, p. 159.

[62] For more on this general distinction, see Outka, *Agape: An Ethical Analysis*, pp. 19–20, 90–91.

tism and sectarianism, which is surely its main point; but to the extent that it embraces in the process an extreme consequentialism-cum-contextualism—the end justifies the means, and there are few if any permanently valid ends—it threatens to undermine both love and justice. Segundo is aware of the dangers associated with many of his remarks. But this does not alter the fact that even on a generous reading his position offers minimal support for the principles and institutions necessary for the survival of morality and politics themselves. It is hard not to conclude that in *The Liberation of Theology* Segundo purchases political relevance at too high a price, fostering not liberation but a relativism in which love and justice may be left behind.[63] He is more clearly committed to the ineliminable centrality of love in his earlier work, *A Theology for Artisans of a New Humanity.*

> Christ used two different formulas to describe the road which leads to salvation. When he was referring in general to God's judgment on humanity, the thing required of man was simply real love. When he referred to the function of the Church and spoke about it to the apostles, he tied in salvation with faith and the sacraments. . . . Christ was talking about the same thing in both texts: real love.[64]

"*Efficacious* love is the only demand imposed by Jesus for all time," Segundo writes in a subsequent volume of *A Theology for Artisans;* and although he repeatedly emphasizes there the evolutionary character of Christian morality, he also insists that the most adequate reading of the gospel is one in which both in-principle pacifism and a purely contentless or utilitarian love are overcome in favor of a "complex" view of how and why love may sometimes employ violent tactics.[65] Segundo nowhere provides the sort of helpful details that Ramsey does (e.g., on discrimination and proportionality), but the early Segundo's position is decidedly more nuanced than *The Liberation of Theology.*

What the later Segundo says about minorities and the Christian church is very difficult indeed to defend. A vanguard must "relieve the masses of

---

[63] An extended discussion of the relation between means/ends and faith/relativism appears in *The Liberation of Theology*, pp. 170–81. There are sections here in which both contextualism and consequentialism are considerably muted, and any defense of Segundo must rely on these and related passages as normative. The difficulty is in making him consistent, however. On p. 215, for example, he condemns the "inhuman means" employed by the church to convert people, "mass means that are intrinsically opposed to liberation." Such language directly contradicts his earlier claim that "We cannot tell whether love or egotism is at work by examining the means employed" (p. 164). Apparently, certain sorts of violence and coercion may be "categorically" ruled out after all.

[64] Segundo, *The Community Called Church*, p. 52; see also p. 66.

[65] Segundo, *Evolution and Guilt*, pp. 120–21.

the burden of relative options," he maintains;[66] and although the former
are not to constitute an abusive "elite," for practical reasons they must
liberate the many in ways beyond their capacity to effect or appreciate.
What are we to make of this? Christianity's aiming at the masses only
seems *im*practical when its goal is considered to be most basically political, which is dubious. But even more troubling is the analogy Segundo
suggests between members of the religious vanguard and medical doc-
tors.[67] With this, Christianity becomes a complex intellectual skill beyond
the reach of most. A physician serves others by restoring health, not by
imparting medical knowledge itself, thus a basic inequality perdures between doctor and patient. Christian faith, in contrast, serves others via
self-communication. Grace leaves both speaker and hearer, agent and patient, in possession of the same end (Jesus Christ). If Segundo wishes to
avoid elitism, different images are called for.[68]

Separatism, Apology, and Political Idolatry

In his 1795 essay "Perpetual Peace," Immanuel Kant contends:

> The state of peace among men living side by side is not the natural state
> (*status naturalis*); the natural state is one of war. . . . A state of peace, there-
> fore, must be *established*, for in order to be secured against hostility it is not
> sufficient that hostilities simply not be committed; and unless this security is
> pledged to each by his neighbor (*a thing that can occur only in a civil state*),
> each may treat his neighbor, from whom he demands this security, as an
> enemy.[69]

Social peace must be established politically, according to Kant, and surely
he is at least *partially* correct that this requires a civil state. Although it is
often also the agent of injustice, the modern state is currently a necessary
(although obviously not a sufficient) condition to *build* a tolerable peace
on earth. After the Fall, even Christians may grant that war is a common
(if not "natural") condition (cf. Matt. 24:6). Just as rendering unto self
(self-love) is best secured by loving God and neighbors in the *Imitatio
Christi*, however, so "rendering unto Caesar" (political prudence) is best
accomplished by Christians by loving God and neighbors in the *Pax
Christi*. This is the enduring truth behind Hauerwas's remarks on the

[66] Segundo, *The Liberation of Theology*, p. 209; and compare *Evolution and Guilt*, pp. 68–69.

[67] Segundo, *The Liberation of Theology*, pp. 210–11.

[68] See Segundo, *Evolution and Guilt*, p. 68, and *The Community Called Church*, p. 90. Christians are "the minority" but must steer between "mass mechanisms on the one hand or elitism on the other" (*Evolution*, p. 131).

[69] Kant, "Perpetual Peace," pp. 789–90; second emphasis added.

church as "polis" and "counter-story."[70] The state and its institutions are not the only relevant agencies, nor by any means the most important; for Christians, the community of the faithful is the primary vehicle of grace and thus the most salient social body. But these realities do not settle the normative question about violence, unless one thinks that all unjust force is limited to, if not caused by, the nation-state as such.

A subscriber to just war theory believes that various forms of state coercion, including ones that employ violence—armies, national guards, police forces, prisons, and the like—are, when suitably controlled, permissible (if not required) elements in the political building of peace. These are not the only elements, however, and Christian just war thinking becomes objectionable accommodationism when it forgets this. A Christian pacifist rejects violent state coercion as incompatible with the example of Jesus, but the history of the church itself makes clear that aggression is not limited to the nation-state or to "worldly" politics, and that the political building of peace is required in some form in any case. It may be, as Hauerwas claims, that in a world without foundations, "all we have is the church,"[71] in the sense that Jesus Christ as handed down in and through ecclesial tradition is the governing norm of all Christian behavior. But it is not the case that all we *are* or *are called to serve* (*and to be served by*) is the church; we are embedded in the wider world.

Christians as both individuals and groups, as both members of the church and citizens of the state, are *simul justus et peccator*, in Luther's phrase. The priority of love forbids any absolute distinction between "the church" and "the world" such that charity rules in one but not the other, even as it rules out any simple conflation, such that Christian identity is conformed to secular culture. If just war becomes mere apology for being "effective" by any means necessary, it is obviously irreligious. Yet if pacifism means political separatism from the civil state, this may itself breach the peace because absenting oneself from that social nexus inspires fear in others not similarly at liberty. As Augustine notes, "so long as the two cities [of God and earth] are intermingled, we [Christians] also make use of the peace of Babylon."[72]

These facts seem to place the burden of proof on pacifists like Hauerwas. Hauerwas is not Rousseau, of course, identifying peace with the state of nature, any more than Ramsey is Hobbes or Kant, embracing a similarly misleading equation for war. Both Christian theologians recognize that neither the longing for peace nor the avoidance of war may be

---

[70] Hauerwas, *In Good Commpany: The Church as Polis* (Notre Dame: University of Notre Dame Press, 1995).

[71] Ibid., chap. 2.

[72] Augustine, *The City of God*, bk. XIX, chap. 26, p. 892.

our prime moral focus; fidelity to God is means and end. Both theologians eschew Enlightenment contract theory in favor of an evangelical
vision of the church's place in the larger human community; indeed,
both share an eschatological faith that unites them against both secular
ethical theory and their own Methodist Bishops' pastoral letter on nuclear war. Hauerwas observes: "It is Ramsey's and my common conviction that—contrary to the Bishops' claim [in "In Defense of Creation"]—the nuclear crisis has not posed questions of faith that point
beyond just war or pacifism." He adds: "I (and Ramsey . . .) urged the
Bishops to avoid . . . 'survivalist' rhetoric, noting that what we must fear
as Christians is not our deaths at the hands of an unjust aggressor but
how as Christians we might serve the neighbor without resorting to unjust means."[73]

Two complementary vices are possible here: (1) an inadequate appreciation of the rights and responsibilities of civil governments such that
nearly all political activity is seen as profane and legitimate means and
ends of state are ruled out, and (2) an inadequate circumscription of
these same rights and responsibilities such that nearly all political activity
is baptized and illegitimate means and ends are ruled in. Seldom is either
error found in pure form, but (1) is sometimes approximated by Hauerwas, in spite of himself. In seeking to avoid secular chauvinism, he may
discourage good and faithful people from entering politics, thus abandoning it to the barbarians. Although well-aware of the dangers of idolatry and what he earlier called "the Christendom mentality,"[74] the later
Juan Segundo is haunted by a Marxist version of error (2). By not limiting violent resistance, his comments may encourage unscrupulous people
to stay in politics, thus securing it for the barbarians.

With respect to *jus in bello*, Hauerwas and arguably the later Segundo
(certainly Michael Walzer)[75] provide a graphic illustration of how right
Ramsey is to insist on the ordered pair of discrimination (noncombatant
immunity) and proportionality (a positive cost-benefit analysis). These
men miss the Ramseyan mean, which, in emphasizing the governance of
love, is Niebuhr's prophetic faith rendered consistent and free of moral
dilemmas.[76] Hauerwas expands discrimination so as to undo the combat-

---

[73] See his epilogue to Ramsey's *Speak Up for Just War or Pacifism*, pp. 149–50.

[74] Segundo, *The Community Called Church*, p. 49. Although the early Segundo sees the
church and the world as "two distinct aspects of an indivisible unity," he still contends that
the church "would appear to be faithful to her rationale and mission if she evinced a clear
commitment to collaborate in the work of authentic human development, without getting
mixed up in the political government of the state; or even if she reacted strongly against
political regimes that violate man" (ibid., p. 97).

[75] See Walzer, *Just and Unjust Wars*, pp. 251–68.

[76] Gene Outka has maintained that, in fact, Niebuhr's remarks on *jus in bello* are rather

ant/noncombatant distinction and thereby radically contracts the proportionate activity of the state; and Walzer allows *jus ad bellum* considerations to override discrimination and thereby permits murder in the name of national interest. Ramsey, in contrast, insists that discrimination and proportionality form both an ordered *pair* and an *ordered* pair in the economy of *agape*; neither one alone is sufficient and, although both are necessary, one does not even consider proportionality if discrimination cannot be met.[77] One may not directly take innocent life even to ensure national survival, but one may restrain political aggression in a just cause. In short, *agape* is politically active but self-limiting.

Absence of violence is always an end, but proximately it is to be insisted upon only so long as nothing of superior moral import (e.g., justice) is sacrificed. We must distinguish between a prideful or nationalistic self-assertion and love's defense of innocent others from unjust attack. It may be that most wars do not accomplish the latter, but this is a factual question and thus cannot provide support for a categorical pacifism. Without a perfectly general principle, grounded in love, to settle disputes concerning whether and when to employ force, in-principle pacifism is by definition ruled out. Nonviolence can only be a rule of thumb for *agape*, what Ramsey calls a "summary rule" and others call a "prima facie duty."

This accent on context would not mean that *all* political judgments are relative or that there are no ethical absolutes, however. The principle of discrimination could still be viewed as absolute because in violating it one would be attacking that very value (love's defense of innocent life) seen to validate the use of the sword in the first place. Just as it can never be correct to affirm a theoretical paradox, so it can never be correct to perform a practical perversity. Attempting to believe in a contradiction undermines all thought, just as attempting to act on a contradiction undermines all praxis. Segundo's work is troubling at times precisely because of its failure to appreciate the centrality of principles of justice—too much is put up for grabs at once.

I have argued that the difference between just war theory and pacifism is not adequately captured with reference to distinctions such as "hate versus love" or "compromise versus fidelity." The same can also be said about "apology versus separatism." Particularly in liberal democratic contexts, we do better to ask how to resolve (or at least understand) the tension, internal to love itself, between judgment and mercy. Consider,

---

thin, probably even incompatible with viewing noncombatant immunity as exceptionless. If so, this is a palpable difference from Ramsey. See Outka, "The Protestant Tradition and Exceptionless Moral Norms," in *Moral Theology Today: Certitudes and Doubts* (St. Louis: The Pope John Center, 1984), pp. 150–54.

[77] Ramsey, *The Just War*, p. 431.

for example, the relation between killing a would-be murderer and allow-ing him or her to kill. The consequence in both cases is the same (a physical death), but the other moral factors (deontological and theologi-cal) are reckoned differently by the two traditions. Just war theory sees the murder of the innocent as an evil more to be prevented than the killing of a murderer (either subjectively or objectively "guilty") is an action to be avoided. Pacifism takes the opposite line, proposing that love tolerates a murder more readily than it kills anyone at all. Both agree that one may not murder to prevent deaths, even to prevent more murders, but this does not settle the basic dispute.

Are *Agape* and Violence Always Antithetical?

Is there, in fact, anything about *agape* that rules out violence a priori, as a matter of consistency? This will depend in part upon how the term is translated, but the fact that *agape* is directed toward and received from both God and our neighbors makes uniform translation difficult. Be-tween human beings, phrases such as "personal respect" and "equal re-gard" are plausible paraphrases.[78] Concerning God, these are less appro-priate—terms such as "self-surrender" and "fidelity" being more so. In neither case, however, is it clear that all forms of violence are self-defeat-ing or incompatible with love's ends.

The three reasons commonly set forth for believing that agapic love rules out all violence are:

(1) Violence thrives on hatred and brutalizes both agent and patient by fos-tering animosity and vindictive motivation (an aretological argument).

(2) Violence fails to show proper respect for the other, inasmuch as it short-circuits appeal to the other's conscience and, especially when lethal, cuts off the possiblity of free repentance and reform (a deontological argument).

(3) Violence does not deter evil but contributes to an endless cycle of ven-geance and retaliation that makes matters worse, especially in the long run (a consequentialist argument).[79]

---

[78] Outka, *Agape: An Ethical Analysis*, passim. One should not take "equal regard" to imply lack of passion, however; see Vacek, *Love, Human and Divine*, pp. 160–62.

[79] Martin Luther King, Jr., touches on all three reasons:

[Violence] is impractical because it is a descending spiral ending in destruction for all. The old law of an eye for an eye leaves everybody blind. It is immoral because it seeks to humiliate the opponent rather than win his understanding; it seeks to annihilate rather than to convert. Violence is immoral because it thrives on hatred rather than love. It destroys community and makes brotherhood impossible.

See *The Words of Martin Luther King, Jr.*, ed. by Coretta Scott King (New York: New-market, 1983), p. 73.

A fourth reason is distinctly relevant to Christians:

(4) Violence is incompatible with the life and lessons of Jesus Christ as related in Scripture (an exegetical/hermeneutical argument).

Let me briefly consider (1)–(4) in turn.

(1) *Reply to the Aretological Argument*: When I teach "The Morality of Peace and War," I show the episode from the PBS "World At War" series entitled "Genocide." It details the planning and execution of the Nazi "Final Solution" concerning the Jews in Europe, before and during World War II. In addition to documentary footage of the rise of Himmler and the SS, the employment of mobile firing squads then gas chambers for mass extermination, the deception of the *Judenrat* and the resistance of the Warsaw ghetto, and so on, the video also shows interviews with the survivors of the Holocaust. The film is the best argument I know of for pacifism, but also the best for just war. The horrors of aggression and hatred are sickeningly manifest on the bodies of all, victims and victimizers, and the issue of how to respond is urgent.

On the one hand, one cannot but wonder what a broad commitment to nonviolence and noncooperation with evil would have meant for the Nazi leadership's ability to carry out its genocidal intentions. What if every city in France, Poland, Holland, even Austria had acted like the Huguenot town of Le Chambon, which peacefully yet resolutely shielded thousands of Jews from Vichy, as well as from the Nazis?[80] Nonviolent opposition was no doubt more difficult within Germany itself, but Peter Schneider has recently argued that, even there, "the supposed choice between unquestioning obedience and death-defying resistance is much too crude: you could resist without automatically risking your life."[81] The scores of German civilians who did hide and save Jews illustrate that personal courage might have preserved life much more often than it did. Finally, what if the governments of France, Britain, the United States, even Russia had brought real political and economic assistance to Germany in the 1920s or put real political and economic pressure on Germany in the 1930s? Enlightened politics just might have prevented world war.

On the other hand, there is no denying the radicality of the Nazi evil and the basic nobility of many who chose to resist it with violence. At one point in "Genocide," a Hungarian Jew named Dov Paisikowic recalls wondering while in Auschwitz: "Where is the whole world? Where is the

---

[80] See Philip Hallie, *Lest Innocent Blood Be Shed* (New York: Harper and Row, 1979).

[81] Schneider, "Saving Konrad Latte," *New York Times Magazine*, February 13, 2000, p. 53. See also Daniel Goldhagen, *Hilter's Willing Executioners: Ordinary Germans and the Holocaust* (New York: Knopf, 1996), which argues that even German police and military personnel were often given the chance to opt out of genocidal killing—a chance which few took advantage of.

United States? Where is Russia? Do they know what is happening here in the extermination camps at all?" Those words must sting just warrior and pacifist alike. Many did know. And by the summer of 1942, if not well before, it may have been impossible to stop Hitler's killing machine without the use of the sword. In any case, the claim that everyone willing to take up arms against Nazism was moved by vindictiveness or idolatry is simply not credible when one reads letters, views films, or listens to interviews of the time.[82]

If nonviolence is the vocation of some Christians, there may also be a place for violent resistance lest one be brutalized by apathy or lack of compassion. Nonviolence does not dictate indifference or inaction, of course; on the contrary, it normally rules these out as immoral. But, similarly, justified war does not necessarily require hatred or vengeance; it would preclude these at its core by insisting on proper authority, just cause, right intention, proportionality, and so on.[83] Given what goes on in military training—pressures to objectify the "enemy" and to follow orders without question—being a Christian soldier is manifestly a perilous occupation, and many souls may not be able to resist the temptation either to hate or to surrender conscience to a temporal authority. I am grateful, however, to those who are willing to risk life and limb and to face the trials and ambiguities of combat in order to protect the innocent. If governed by love of God and neighbors, *all* neighbors, this is service open to self-sacrifice in a highly admirable sense.

The events associated with 1940–45 suggest that it is not always possible to achieve justice, or perhaps even to be fully loving, without the use of some violence. To make true peace we may sometimes have to unmake unjust war by main force, even while refusing to hate those who are our enemies and for whom Christ died. Put most pointedly, Christian violence may, *in extremis*, be the content of political love. (Just war may be an "alien work" of those "resident aliens" who call themselves Christians.) The key point, however, is that *the governing factor is love, not political violence per se—neither withdrawal from it nor participation in it.* If I cannot as a matter of fact employ violence, even in a just cause, without hating my neighbor (who although unjust continues to be God's creature), then pacifism is the only faithful alternative.

(2) *Reply to the Deontological Argument*: Appealing to the conscience

---

[82] Hauerwas asks at one point, "What is war but the desire to be rid of God, to claim for ourselves the power to determine our meaning and destiny?" (*Against the Nations*, p. 196). In answer, he contends, without qualification, that war is "but the manifestation of our hatred of God" (ibid.). As Hauerwas knows in cooler moments, this is not an adequate account of the motives of many of those who fought against Hitler—Dietrich Bonhoeffer, for instance.

[83] See, for example, Aquinas, *Summa Theologiae*, II-II, Q. 40, art. 1.

of an aggressor is clearly part of any moral response to evil. Jesus himself repeatedly refuses to write sinners off as beyond hope, aiming instead to wound their hearts and thereby call them back to faith and love. Because killing another prevents her or his temporal reform, a very good case can be made that capital punishment of disarmed criminals (including first-degree murderers) is un-Christian. Who has the righteousness to visit such an ultimate penalty on someone who, being incarcerated, is in theory no longer a lethal threat to society? (Life sentence without parole may be required here.) In the context of war, however, the aggressor represents an *ongoing* menace to the life and health of others. If the aggressor cannot be restrained nonviolently, one may have to choose between violent defense of the innocent and the toleration of a "peace" in which a malevolent conscience prevails. I see no deontological argument that *requires* one to prefer such "peace" over justice.

A defense of the just war tradition will usually appeal to a preference for justice over "peace" in the narrow sense. But this leaves open whether the tradition ought morally to exclude pacifism ("categorical just war") or ought to take its place alongside pacifism as morally permissible ("elective just war"). I side with those who see just war as a responsible Christian option but not an absolute requirement of faith. As the U.S. Catholic Bishops put it, "The Christian has no choice but to defend peace, properly understood, against aggression. This is an inalienable obligation. It is the *how* of defending peace which offers moral options."[84] Neither just war nor nonviolent resistance is deontologically *malum in se*, and one or the other must be embraced when the common good is put in peril.

(3) *Reply to the Consequentialist Argument*: The tendency for violent means to get out of hand is about as well documented as any sociological datum, so the argument that war contributes to a cycle of futility is powerful indeed. Yet this is precisely why traditional just war criteria have insisted on employing violence only as a last resort, with a clear declaration of causes and aims, and with attention to proportionality and discrimination. One of the central inspirations behind just war theory, as Paul Ramsey emphasized, is to limit the use of force to avoid the spiral of retaliation so common in human history. It is an empirical question, in any given case, whether and how this can be done. So I need not tarry longer on this objection than to say that consequences matter, as do motives and acts, but that on balance D-Day, for example, brought good consequences.

(4) *Reply to the Exegetical/Hermeneutical Argument*: Richard Hays has

---

[84] See National Conference of Catholic Bishops, "The Challenge of Peace: God's Promise and Our Response" (Washington, D.C.: United States Catholic Conference, 1983), p. 23.

recently argued that "the point [of the Book of Matthew] is that the community of Jesus' disciples is summoned to the task of showing forth the character of God in the world. That character is nowhere more decisively manifest than in the practice of loving enemies (5:44–45), a practice incompatible with killing them."[85] For all his insight, Hays seems too quick here. Loving enemies is surely incompatible with hating them, with willing evil for them, but it has seemed plausible to the majority of Christian theologians (e.g., Augustine and Niebuhr, as Hays notes) that killing an enemy may be consistent with loving that enemy himself or herself. Perhaps only Eva Braun had erotic feelings for Hitler. But is it not likely that assassinating Hitler would have been a more agapic act toward Hitler himself, as well as toward his potential victims, than letting him become a successful mass murderer? Is it not possible, for instance, that Dietrich Bonhoeffer was loving "*der Führer*" as a neighbor even in plotting to kill him?

Hays goes on to maintain that "the church's embodiment of nonviolence is—according to the Sermon on the Mount—its indispensable witness to the gospel."[86] But if we take the Sermon on the Mount literally and categorically, Jesus himself must be indicted for inconsistency on two counts. Matthew 5:39 reads: "But I say to you, Do not resist an evildoer. But if anyone strikes you on the right cheek, turn the other also."[87] On its face, as Ramsey points out, the Sermon calls for *nonresistance*, not merely nonviolence, and it requires a specific expression of that nonresistance: cheek-turning. Jesus, for his part, resisted evildoers, sometimes quite vehemently (as when, in John 2:13–16, he drove the money changers out of the temple); moreover, as Augustine notes,[88] Jesus did not always turn the other cheek (as when, in John 18:23, he responded to being struck with the challenge, "Why do you strike me?"). Some see the injunction to turn the other cheek as relevant only to a personal insult given via a slap with the back of the right hand, while Augustine maintained that "what is here required is not a bodily action, but an inward disposition."[89] On either of these readings, violent resistance to a public evil, aimed at oneself and others, may be compatible with the

---

[85] Hays, *The Moral Vision of the New Testament*, p. 329.

[86] Ibid.

[87] The KJV translates Matt. 5:39 with "resist not evil," while the NRSV has "do not resist an evil*doer*." The Greek word *poneros* permits either reading, and a just warrior might maintain that the point in both cases is not to despise the one who does evil as a person but rather forcefully to resist the latter's evil intention or action—a case of loving the sinner but "hating" the sin.

[88] Augustine, "Letters," CXXXVIII, p. 177.

[89] Augustine, *Contra Faustum* [402], XXII, 74–79, in *The Political Writings of St. Augustine*, p. 166.

injunction, given the proper motive. Augustine may risk a too exclusive accent on aretology, holding that "the real evils in war" are "love of violence, revengeful cruelty, fierce and implacable enmity, wild resistance, and the lust for power, and such like."[90] But he has a point in refusing to find a perfectly general rule of action in Matthew 5:39.

Hays too declines to read the Matthew passage as propounding literal and categorical rules. "Instead, as a 'focal instance' of discipleship, [the directive to 'turn the other cheek'] functions metonymically, illuminating the life of a covenant community that is called to live in radical faithfulness to the vision of the kingdom of God disclosed in Jesus' teaching and example."[91] Yet once the metonymic function of this and similar directives is granted, the interpretation of what faithfulness requires in concrete circumstances is much more open-ended than a blanket rejection of violence can allow. There are other exegetical and hermeneutical alternatives. Why not see Matthew 5:39 as a vivid prohibition on being conformed to evil, akin to Paul's injunction, "Do not be overcome by evil, but overcome evil with good" (Rom. 12:21)? Dietrich Bonhoeffer's decision to participate in the plot to kill Hitler is a poignant case of a devout Christian seeing resort to violence as a necessary act of atonement for the German church's apostasy under Nazism.[92]

Again, goodness rules some things out and others in. Love never hates and always forgives, for instance; to deny this would indeed be to be overcome by evil. The means one employs in confronting an enemy must be chosen carefully, moreover, lest one erode the very evangelical values one would defend. The age-old irony of much "just war" is that it "destroys the village in order to save it." No doubt, first of all and most of the time, a faithful love will choose nonviolence as the surest means of both preserving one's own soul and affirming an aggressor's conscience and sanctity before God. But even for the strong agapist, "violent love" is not always a contradiction in terms. The shape of God's own justice and mercy, revealed in Scripture and history, indicates that evil may sometimes be restrained by coercive force. "God retains the evil will of the devil within limits by violence," as Elizabeth Anscombe has pointed out.[93] Human beings do not possess the righteousness of God, to be sure, and this will limit what they may do to check or punish an aggressor. (As noted, capital punishment of disarmed murderers may be too akin to a

[90] Ibid., p. 164.

[91] Hays, *The Moral Vision of the New Testament*, p. 329.

[92] See L. Gregory Jones, *Embodying Forgiveness* (Grand Rapids: Eerdmans, 1995), pp. 24–28.

[93] Anscombe, "War and Murder," in *War and Morality*, ed. by Richard Wasserstrom (Belmont, Calif.: Wadsworth, 1970), p. 43.

direct assault on the innocent to be tolerated by a charity aware of its finitude.) But the avoidance of hubris is the point, not of violence per se.

In the *Old Testament*, *shalom* encompasses all those things that comprise right relation with God, our neighbors, and ourselves—including justice.[94] Most broadly, it implies full spiritual and bodily well-being in company with others and as such is, for Christianity, both a Christological and an eschatological concept. Complete human wholeness, in which body and soul, desire and conscience, judgment and mercy, are at one, is both realized in Christ and generally awaits the end of history (cf. the images in Isa. 2:1–4; 11:1–9). For those within time, there will be approximations and trade-offs; the lion does not yet eat straw like the ox. Not all of the components of *shalom* can be achieved simultaneously, although all are relevant. Duties to God may be in tension with commitments to others, and commitments to others may be at odds with duties to oneself. Genuine goods may sometimes come into conflict. One must sometimes sacrifice physical safety for moral integrity, for example, and ethical ambiguity, as well as weakness of will, is inseparable from much of historical existence.

As many have pointed out, the either/or represented by *shalom* and its opposite is not peace/war but faith/sin. "Shalomism" (faithful action serving God and others) may often ally itself with nonviolence, but for their part the *Old Testament* prophets certainly did not understand war as categorically contrary to the will of God. Today the phrase "holy war" suggests a no holds barred fanaticism, a form of unbridled bellicism. But this is largely alien to the biblical concept.[95] In fact, the prophetic understanding of holy war as a battle ordained, directed, *and limited* by God stands in marked contrast to many of the supposedly "just" wars waged by nation-states for political ends. God's own covenant fidelity (*ḥésed*) sets the standard, and again such fidelity is a tandem of judgment and mercy that is both active and self-limiting—both dynamic and kenotic. The internal complexity of God's steadfast love, at least as we view it, makes a single, more specific criterion for the resolution of moral conflict impossible. Scripture allows that conflict situations (together with their attendant opportunities) will be with us "until justice and peace embrace" (cf. Psalm 95).

---

[94] On these topics, see E. M. Good, "Peace in the OT," in *The Interpreter's Dictionary of the Bible*, ed. by G. A. Buttrick, vol. 3, pp. 705–6; C. L. Mitton, "Peace in the NT," in *ibid.*, p. 706; E. R. Achtemeier, "Righteousness in the OT"; P. J. Achtemeier, "Righteousness in the NT"; and Donahue, "Biblical Perspectives on Justice."

[95] See James Turner Johnson's critique of Roland Bainton's account of holy war in *Just War Tradition and the Restraint of War* (Princeton: Princeton University Press, 1981), pp. 230–35.

CONCLUSION

We are at last in a position to answer summarily the question: What must Christian love be like to hold together, in a unity, such opposing principles as violent defense of the innocent (just war) and nonviolent embodiment of forgiveness (pacifism)? For strong agapists, love is a hypergood, as described earlier. Such a value "trumps" all others in that it can never be correct to surrender it in favor of some other good; but, more to the point, it is not even *possible* fully to realize another good if charity is absent. Love always takes priority because it is the very core of the divine Personality in which human nature is realized rather than sacrificed. The priority of *agape* to political philosophy, for instance, means that no calculation of social utility (e.g., preservation of the nation) can outweigh the obligation to love neighbors, including aggressive strangers.

Agape is, and knows itself to be, of such surpassing worth that love itself is its primary object. Love wants to generate more love. This is not to say that the agapist is chiefly concerned with his or her own subjective feelings or dispositions. The experience of love is attended by intrinsically valuable internal states, but Christian love's central aim is obedience to God in promoting the well-being of others. The point is that *love serves others most profoundly by making them loving in their turn. Agape*'s "bestowal" of value—its treating human beings as if fully lovable—contributes to their actually becoming so. Again, a loving will is not the only good, as Jesus' reaction to the poor and afflicted suggests, but, as participation in the life of God, it is fundamental. In the Gospels, Jesus shows deep concern for others' physical and psychological wholeness: he cares about the everyday interests of incarnate human beings. But he respects wants and meets needs so as to bring people out of immediate absorption in them. He touches individuals not merely to calm their private fears or to heal their personal infirmities—as important as these deliverances are—but to make them publicly charitable like himself. The graciousness of Jesus' actions astonishes others into a similar altruism because they are able (if momentarily) to forget themselves and attend to the world and its suffering.

Love's emphasis on self-communication helps to explain why judgment and mercy are irreducible components of *agape*. Both tend to multiply charity. On the one hand, *agape* may forcefully defend the innocent not simply to sustain their bodily life but to preserve and enhance their potential for just community. Such a defense clarifies for the innocent their worth, and it may impress upon their attackers the fact that those under threat are due respect. On the other hand, *agape* may embody nonviolence because this attitude can also, in turn, prick the consciences of the unjust, as well as summon potential victims to heroism. In a culture like our own that increasingly glorifies belligerence, traditionally by men and now also by women, nonviolence has its corrective place. Forgiveness is always a call of love (chapter 4), moreover, but what form this takes will depend on context. Individuals and situations differ sufficiently that both just war and pacifism can be faithful responses to aggressive strife, as well as potent means to avoid further strife.

POSTSCRIPT: SILENCE, SPEECH, AND SEPTEMBER 11

The terrorist attacks of September 11, 2001, make scholarly reflections on Christian love and political violence seem, simultaneously, irrelevant and indispensable. The murder and destruction were so cold-blooded and horrific that words are beggared as moral reactions, yet the meaning of the lives lost and the suffering and solidarity of those left behind must be honored. Words are ethicists' essential means to condemn the injustice done, to affirm the justice to be done in response, and to express the grief that not even justice can fully allay. (Donations of blood, time, money, and/or emotional support are central means for us all.) If one believes, as I do, that ultimately it is the love of God about which we must try to speak, then the task is doubly difficult: both to name a profound evil and to counter this name with the Name that is above every name. (And what to say when the evil is itself done in the name of God?!) The most immediate danger is that, in trying to make sense of things, we will indulge in false consolations (or false alarms) that further harm people. But meaningful silence is something that one can only work up to, with patience and after lament.

Unhelpful Languages

I begin by describing four ways in which it is *not* helpful to talk about Tuesday, September 11, and its aftermath. First, some of the headlines appearing on Wednesday, September 12—like "Doomsday Comes to America" or "America Shaken to Its Foundations"—were alarmist. It is important not to give the terrorists more "credit" than they are due. They effectively murdered many people and destroyed much property— as I note, the enormity of the crime can stun one into muteness—but they have not "shaken our country to its foundations." The foundations of this democracy are as stable or unstable as they were on Monday, September 10, because the true foundations are moral, not material or even personal. We must grieve our fallen fellow citizens, as well as the many from other nations who were killed; and we must punish the malefactors. But, with God's help, the republic goes on in its finite, fallen way. It is our collective response that may undermine us, inwardly, not any external assault. We already go wrong if we think of apocalypse as something that can be forced on us by other human beings.

Second, I don't think we should use the language of "divine judgment" in this connection. To do so is to suggest that God wills the murder of innocent people as an expression of divine justice. That I find incredible. I see nothing "divine" in the terrorism. Directly killing innocent persons is wrong no matter who does it, the United States (as in the bombing of Dresden and Hiroshima during World War II or in the Mi Lai Massacre in Vietnam) or Muslim extremists (as in the attack on the World Trade Center, the Pentagon, and Flight 93). To think that God would use the direct slaying of innocents as an expression of the holy will seems worse than absurd. The United States has much to answer for in the world, and many have understandable reason to despise us, but the events of September 11 were human evil, not divine judgment. God may have permitted them in permitting human free will, but nobody should claim to be the hammer of God while they wipe out civilians, including women and children. (The Pentagon is, one might claim, another matter, but a plane full of innocents was destroyed in that action too.) To suggest otherwise is to wound still further those who are struggling to find the heart to live after the slaughter of their loved ones. Whether it is to "blame the victims," it is surely to blaspheme God.

The problem with the language of "divine judgment" is that if one group is seen as God's instrument in murdering the members of another group, then the second group can plausibly claim to be God's instrument in murdering in retaliation. And then we are off to the races with holy wars on all sides. To be sure, the United States has blood on its hands, and had its policy decisions of the past fifty-five years been wiser, the current situation might have been avoided. (Actions, both private and public, do take on a certain momentum.) We must confess and rectify our sins, but this does not entail condoning or valorizing the unjust actions of wicked men. Forgiving our enemies itself presupposes naming their (and our) sin for what it is.

Third, it is unwise to call the suicide hijackers "cowardly." If, as Aristotle argued, courage is a mean between the extremes of cowardice and rashness, then the hijackers were as far away from cowardice as you can get (as Jeffrey Stout has noted in correspondence). We badly misunderstand our adversaries if we do not see that they are neither courageous nor cowardly; they are moved by an obscene rashness that stems from perceived injustice coupled with perverted doctrine. We must not underestimate their willingness both to kill and to die, even as we should not underestimate our own capacity for excessive violence. Genuine fortitude and solidarity are the remedies here, lest we become victims of the age-old irony of war (in this case, an unconventional war): that in seeking to defend cherished values (and persons) we undermine those very values (and persons). We are aware intellectually and reminded repeatedly that, in seeking to protect democratic freedom and tolerance, we must not vilify or attack Muslims as such. But do we have the courage to deal humanely with those "indefinitely detained"? We are aware intellectually and reminded repeatedly that, in seeking to know and do God's will, we must not conflate that will with mere national interest. But do we have the humility to accept that God remains America's transcendent Judge and Redeemer, even as God is Lord over all nations, ideologies, and peoples?

Fourth, I wish that the conflict before us could be characterized as purely or even mainly "political," as though the sole or chief motive of the terrorists were to protest decisions of the U.S. government or to consolidate their own power in Afghanistan, Iraq, and elsewhere. But matters are not that simple. The symbolism of September 11, if I may call it that, proves otherwise. Both the Pentagon (an arm of government) and the World Trade Center (a hub of commerce) were attacked, and the weapons used were ordinary people on airliners (private citizens using private transportation). Some speculate that Flight 93, the plane downed in Pennsylvania, was headed for the White House or Congress, but in our secular setting these are emblems of American civil religion. The only major sites more palpably beyond the narrowly "political" would be the Statue of Liberty and the National Cathedral. Do we presume that these are immune or exempt?

Admittedly, there is no stark boundary between politics and culture; they interpenetrate. Yet it must be said that the terrorists do indeed hate much of Western, especially American, culture. The murders of September 11 were evidently retaliation for distinct actions taken by the American government: our backing of the corrupt regime in Saudi Arabia, our disastrous bombing of the Sudan and Afghanistan by the Clinton administration, our stationing of troops on Saudi soil, and, perhaps above all, our ongoing support of Israel. But the murders were also motivated by a hatred of fundamental aspects of Western faith, morals, and mores. The members of al-Qaeda detest a range of Western values, sacred and profane, going all the way back to the Crusades and the Enlightenment and coming all the way forward to Hollywood, McDonald's, and women's liberation. I see no point in denying that Christianity, democracy, capitalism, and feminism all have real enemies; only a simpleminded cultural relativism tempts us to deny this.

Do I endorse, then, Samuel Huntington's language of a "clash of civilizations"? No, because that diction also tends to blind us to important truths. History, language, tradition, and religion both shape and express who we are, but civilizations/cultures are not singular, monolithic, unchanging things with wills of their own. Huntington emphasizes that "the lines between [civilizations] are seldom sharp" and that "the composition and boundaries of civilizations change,"[96] but his nuance is hard to sustain when the "clash" catchphrase is thrown around. Huntington himself speaks of "cultural fault lines,"[97] thus (in spite of stated intentions) encouraging the impression that civilizational contrasts are like immutable natural phenomena. One ought not to deny the reality of systems and structures that outstrip any given individual's knowledge and will. Collectives remain the products of those who people them, however, and people can be self-critical and other-regarding. Moreover, even traditional societies are highly complex and variegated. There is not just one form of Islam, as Huntington notes, any more than there is one form of Judaism or Christianity.

We must not lose sight of the fact that the terrorists remain a very small minority within the diverse Muslim world, but, at the same time, we must never forget that large segments of any alienated or threatened population can be radicalized. It is important to realize that parts of the Qur'an (and Islamic Sharia generally) call for forgiveness and the curbing of anger, with some passages seeming to forbid the kind of aggressive and indiscriminate assault that we saw on September 11 (see Qur'an 3:134; 2:190; 17:33).[98] (Think as well of the poems on divine and human love by the great Sufi mystic, Rumi, who was born in the war-torn thirteenth century in what is now Afghanistan.) Yet it is also important to acknowledge that other parts of the Qur'an call for denial of friendship to, a "curse" on, "ruthless" treatment of, even the beheading of, "unbelievers" (3:118; 2:88–89; 2:161–162; 48:29; 47:4).[99] Surah 3:141 maintains that God acts in history to "test the faithful and annihilate the infidels," and 9:123 says straightforwardly (?), "Believers, make war on the infidels who dwell around you." A charitable reading of "unbelievers"/ "infidels" does not include pious Jews and Christians, since these share with Muslims a common revelation from God: Torah and gospel (2:62;

---

[96] Huntington, "The Clash of Civilizations," *Foreign Affairs* 72, no. 3 (summer 1993), taken from http://www.alamut.com/subj/economics/misc/clash.html, p. 3.

[97] Ibid.

[98] The sayings (*hadith*) of the Prophet Muhammad more or less explicitly prohibit the direct slaying of women and children, even in (holy) war, although it is doubtful that this amounts to a full doctrine of noncombatant immunity as understood in modern Western just war theory. See John Kelsay, *Islam and War: A Study in Comparative Ethics* (Louisville: Westminster/John Knox, 1993), pp. 59–67.

[99] All quotations from the Qur'an are from *The Koran*, trans. by N. J. Dawood (London and New York: Penguin, 1999).

2:136; 4:162–163; 5:46–47; etc.). But what of Hindus, Buddhists, pagans, atheists, et al.? Surah 3:19 proclaims, moreover, that "the only true faith in God's sight is Islam," while 3:20 goes on to suggest that Jews and Christians should "become Muslims."[100]

Thus does a divine vision of unity easily slip into a demand for religio-political hegemony; even God's prophets can be made the invidious tools of one-upmanship. Osama bin Laden and his associates can quote Scripture to their purposes, but they would deny any charitable reading and rancorously set Muslims against all non-Muslims. This Manichaeanism of "us against them" is the main thing that makes them so dangerous[101]—that coupled with the prospect of their acquiring weapons of mass destruction.

That said, the Christian Bible also offers a mixed picture of God's will in relation to violence and nonbelievers. We too have shadow texts and practices, as is evident from medieval pogroms, the religious wars of the sixteenth and seventeenth centuries, and contemporary strife in Northern Ireland; we too can claim license and precedent for a vengeful God and unbridled war, if we choose to. (Notoriously, 1 Sam. 15:3 has the Lord say to Saul: "Now go and attack Amalek, and utterly destroy all that they have; do not spare them, but kill both man and woman, child and infant, ox and sheep, camel and donkey." See also Deut. 20:16–18, and cf. Surah 17:16.) Neither the West nor the Middle East can retreat behind ancient texts or past histories, however, as though these alone settle or unsettle the morality of the present. Respect for the sanctity of life and tolerance for religious differences have to be affirmed anew in each generation and by every faith. Rather than a "clash of civilizations," therefore, we should recognize in this moment a "*test* of the *civilized*."

Testing Questions

Will Jews, Christians, Hindus, Buddhists, pagans, atheists, et al. insist that the ongoing U.S. response to terrorist attacks be just, that is, discriminate and proportionate? And will Islamic imams and mullas condemn and curtail, in no uncertain terms, the terrorist minority claiming to act in the name of Allah and His Prophet?

Will the defenders of Western democracy be consistent and apply democratic principles in all relevant cases around the world, including with

[100] The Qur'an's attitude toward Jews and Christians is ambivalent, but the following is representative: "Had the People of the Book accepted the Faith, it would surely have been better for them. Some are true believers, but most of them are evil-doers" (3:110).

[101] A similar "circling of the wagons" can be seen in the reaction of the early Christian church against the Jewish synagogues that rejected them; cf. the Gospel of John's references to "the Jews."

reference to a Palestinian state? And will the defenders of Middle Eastern orthodoxy find ways to live up to the best teachings of their holy books?

Will we Americans recognize and address the immorality that does exist in our society—racism, sexism, the glorification of hedonism and violence, the economic exploitation of the Third Word, and so on? And will the world community continue to hold the Taliban and their allies accountable for the political tyranny they put into place (especially concerning the treatment of women), as well as for the cultural envy and animosity they helped to unleash (even unto mass murder)?

Testosterone, Taliban, terrorists civilized by testiness, technology, the *New Testament*? Best to keep more concrete questions before us, and not to let imprecise or prevaricating language cloud either the questions or our answers. Behind all the testing questions is the issue of whether there is enough agreement on basics—God, man, woman, sex, marriage, family, liberty, equality, hierarchy, food, money, territory, war, peace, prosperity, and so on—to sustain civil conversation. The issue is as old as Amos and the Hebrew Bible, Thucydides and "The Melian Dialogue," and Plato and *The Republic*. Contemporary philosophical idioms often make us skeptical, but lived experience suggests that suffering and injustice are universally intelligible human phenomena, as are compassion and fairness. Human differences are real and important, and one hardly need say that just peace does not come easily to disparate nations or ethnic groups. Nevertheless, it is neither parochial nor imperialistic to talk sincerely of "human rights." I myself have remarked on the limits of "rights" and "claims," the need to ground such a vocabulary in "love of God and neighbor." Even so, commitment to human rights, although controversial, is one of the best hopes we have for *checking* Western imperialism, as well as non-Western tribalism.

What, Then, Is to Be Said and Done?

I don't have a lot to say about military tactics, but I can offer two autobiographical observations by way of moral summary. First, as I make clear in the preceding chapter, I am not a pacifist, although I respect many who are committed to pacifism. I hold that the use of force, even lethal force, is sometimes justified in defense of innocent life and a just peace. To the extent that governmental authorities have been able to identify them, those responsible for the atrocities of September 11 should be brought to justice or, as President Bush has said, justice should be brought to them. "Justice" is the operative word here, however. Disproportionate or indiscriminate retaliation can only be immoral, as well as counterproductive. To keep America accountable, there is no substitute for coalition-building within the United Nations, together with reliance on international police organizations and the World Court. Inaction, of the wrong sort, would invite additional attacks, at home and abroad. But the continued military action—I write this in late October 2001—must not be seen as sufficient or self-justifying.

Second, I subscribe to Christian just war teachings. To the extent that we cannot identify those responsible or we cannot act with real justice in relation to them and others, then diplomacy, police prevention, and non-violent resistance are our only recourses. If, for instance, we cannot keep our bombing in Afghanistan from killing a lot of civilians—and apparently quite a few have been killed already—or if we cannot assist in the creation of a decent social order after the fact, then we must be content with what H. Richard Niebuhr once called "the grace of doing nothing." Inaction, of the right sort—to state the obvious, no use of nuclear or biochemical weapons—may sometimes be the best we can do. Use of lethal force is not the only form of action, but, in addition to being morally wrong, an indiscriminate or disproportionate military response will only radicalize Arab moderates. If terrorism is an international problem, international law must play a key role in the solution.

Above all, Christians must be of good courage and sustain (and be sustained by) that peculiar combination of action and inaction, speech and silence: prayer. In praying, we are not so much speaking to God as letting God speak to us over the din of our pain and fear. Without prayer, the virtues of faith, hope, and love are not possible; and without these, we become what the terrorists would make us: brutal and brutalizing, like themselves. But did not the terrorists themselves "pray," intensely? Yes, but only so to speak. We imagine that this was mostly a human monologue, an attempt to shout down God with the fervor of conviction. Without that "holy stillness" (Kierkegaard) that opens the heart to God's will, all of us turn prayer into self-assertion. Terrorism raises this idolatry into an infernal (and deadly) art that Allah Himself has condemned.

The West has real enemies, to repeat, but Christians would love their enemies. Whatever democrats, capitalists, and feminists may recommend—and I leave to another context whether and how a Christian can be a member of these groups—Christians struggle, with God's help, to forgive those who do evil against them. Forgiveness does not rule out restraining and punishing the guilty (see chapter 4), but it does eschew hatred and accept some risk and sacrifice for the sake of others. (Today, accepting risk may mean something as simple as getting on an airplane or as complex as refusing to torture a prisoner.) But did not the suicidal terrorists themselves embrace "self-sacrifice," in the extreme? Yes, but only so to speak. Virtuous sacrifice absorbs the suffering of others and turns it into eternal life, while terrorism projects suffering onto others and turns it into untimely death. A Messiah retranslates "fault lines" to direct violence away from the guilty and the innocent alike, whereas a terrorist would find security, or at least release, in stammering violence against the innocent above all.

Even zealots may have been wronged, of course. Just as the fact that you are paranoid does not mean that no one is out to get you, so the fact that you are a terrorist does not mean that your every claim is unjust. For pious Christians *and Muslims*, nonetheless, doing evil that good might come confounds the difference between revelation and blasphemy. To doubt this is to mistake inarticulateness for sagacity, to romanticize mayhem into martyrdom. This is an especially tragic development if it leads individuals, admittedly sinful, to default on their obligation to defend the common good by moral means.

Because an ugly and immoral violence is all too common in human relations, we owe it to our near neighbors to promote "homeland security." The Lord knows that creatures have need of this. There are many homelands and some without a homeland (e.g., the Palestinians), however, and the means to the relative end of safety matter. We do well to recall that security is always partial in time, and that a Christian's true home is in eternity. Whatever or wherever heaven may be, absolute invulnerability on earth only comes six feet under it. In the end, remaining faithful to Christlike ideals, refusing to hate or to return evil for evil, is the surest way to deny terrorists "victory." As participation in God's own holiness, such charity approaches a beauty deeper than speech. It is the substance of real victory, a gift of grace that does not depend on any one book, creed, or country. (Neither the Bible nor the Qur'an, neither Christianity nor Islam, neither America nor Palestine is going to save the world, but God.) The incarnate Word, beyond all mortal words and military triumphs, is marked finally by guns, grief, bombs, and bombast falling meaningfully . . . silent.

FOUR

Forgiveness as an Eternal Work of Love

*God in Christ has forgiven you. Therefore be imitators of God,
as beloved children, and live in love, as Christ loved us and
gave himself up for us, a fragrant offering and sacrifice to God.*
—Ephesians 5:1–2

If you want to see the brave, look at those who can forgive.
—*Bhagavad Gita*

The prophet Isaiah gives us some of the most memorable images of peace and peacemaking in the Bible: "they shall beat their swords into plowshares, and their spears into pruning hooks; nation shall not lift up sword against nation, neither shall they learn war any more" (Isa. 2:4). Yet this same Isaiah also speaks a harsh word of condemnation against the house of Jacob and counsels *against* forgiveness for idolaters and other sinners: "do not forgive them!" (2:9). In a remarkable 1997 piece entitled "A Prayer for the Days of Awe,"[1] our own prophet, Elie Wiesel, also movingly addresses both us and God. He does not accept any theological "answers" to: "Where were you, God of kindness, in Auschwitz?" He insists rather that "Auschwitz must and will forever remain a question mark only: it can be conceived neither with God nor without God." But because "it is unbearable to be divorced from you so long," Wiesel reconciles with God, realizing in fact that he never really lost his faith.[2]

Reconciliation with God does not mean forgiveness for the Nazis, however. Wiesel speaks for, and as one of, the survivors of the camps in declaring that "they do not forgive the killers and their accomplices, nor should they." And he speaks directly for himself in adding, "Nor should you, Master of the Universe." In his 1985 address to President Reagan before the latter's visit to the cemetery at Bitburg, Wiesel declared, "I too wish to attain true reconciliation with the German people,"[3] but this apparently did not mean forgiveness for the Nazi killers any more than

---

[1] Wiesel, "A Prayer for the Days of Awe," *New York Times*, October 2, 1997, p. A15.

[2] See also Wiesel, *All Rivers Run to the Sea* (New York: Schocken, 1995), p. 84, where similar points are made.

[3] From the transcript of his remarks in the *New York Times*, April 20, 1985, quoted by Donald W. Shriver, Jr., *An Ethic for Enemies: Forgiveness in Politics* (Oxford: Oxford University Press, 1995), p. 97.

making up with God now does. Note that, while Wiesel eloquently speaks out against the persecutors of his people, Isaiah is concerned over Judah's own prosperity and recommends not forgiving members of the house of Jacob itself.

A DUBIOUS DICHOTOMY

For Christians, the possibility of forgiveness is at the very heart of the gospel.[4] From Jesus' claiming authority to forgive sins (Matt. 9:6) to his instructions to his disciples to repeat the Lord's Prayer (Matt. 6:12), forgiveness is inseparable from the good news of the kingdom. Debates about the exact *nature* of forgiveness—as well as when it is or is not appropriate—often revolve around an apparent either/or, however. Either forgiveness is unconditional, an act of pure grace without strings, or else it entails critical judgment of a range of requirements to be met if forgiveness is to be properly forthcoming. The exponents of pure grace speak of God's "everlasting love" for Israel (Jer. 31:3) or of Jesus' direction to forgive "seventy-seven times" (Matt. 18:22), while the advocates of critical judgment insist on the sacramental necessity of contrition, confession, satisfaction, and the like, reminding us of Jesus' words: "If another disciple sins, you must rebuke the offender, and *if* there is repentance, you must forgive" (Luke 17:3; emphasis added).

There are valid concerns on both sides of this debate, and it would be a fundamental mistake simply to contrast the *Old* and *New Testaments* here, identifying the *Old* with condemnation and the *New* with forgiveness. Yahweh, the God of both *Testaments*, is both righteous and merciful—Psalm 7:11 affirms that "God is a righteous judge, and a God who has indignation every day," yet Nehemiah addresses God in the second person with "you are a God ready to forgive, gracious and merciful" (9:17)—and Jews and Christians are called on in their Scriptures to embody both justice and love. (What else would we expect when Jesus, Paul, and most of the early disciples were Jews?) But how is this balancing to be done without compromising either virtue?

Pure gracers fear that, in our litigious society, forgiveness is being politicized. When a narrow justice-as-giving-each-his-or-her-due is considered the chief (if not the only) social virtue, then forgiveness ceases to be a work of love and becomes a political bargaining chip, they believe. Forgiveness loses its character as a spontaneous self-giving, aimed at healing, and becomes at best a modus vivendi, at worst itself an instrument of

---

[4] See my "The Gospels and Christian Ethics," in *The Cambridge Companion to Christian Ethics*.

vengeance. We dangle forgiveness before our enemies in order to manipulate them into cooperating with us or in order to punish them for not doing so. We may owe forgiveness to others so long as they antecedently comply with certain public criteria; but, no compliance, no forgiveness. This calculating attitude enmeshes forgiveness in economies of exchange, according to pure gracers. Forgiveness is corrupted, they maintain, when we fail to see its utter gratuitousness, its astonishing hopefulness. For them, mercy overcomes the past and looks to a restored future without conditions.

Critical judgers, on the other hand, worry that unconditional forgiveness sacrifices justice on the altar of a bogus charity. A purely unmerited forgiveness abandons standards for responsible action in favor of a "cheap grace" (Bonhoeffer) that gives free rein to villainy.[5] A forgiveness that does not require repentance and atonement simply fails to confront evil, the argument goes, in both others and oneself. Indeed, to forego punishment of the wicked or to accept injury from the wanton is to affront both justice and truth; it encourages sadism and self-assertion on the part of victimizers and masochism and self-deception on the part of victims. An infinitely patient forbearance represents a loss of nerve before the agonistic realities of the world, a failure of self-respect, and is a sure sign of religious and moral decadence. Christian mercy is all too often dishonest, critical judgers suspect: resentment masquerading as virtue.

Despite genuine cogency on both of these sides, I want, Anglican that I am, to propose a middle way. The terms of the familiar dispute about forgiveness represent a dubious dichotomy.[6] Forgiveness is neither a passive remission of punishment premised on a blind verdict of acquittal nor a contractual agreement cannily designed to make us more peaceful or cooperative. That is too limited a set of alternatives. The dynamics of forgiveness, at least when biblically understood, suggest that forgiveness is a *means* to truthful moral judgment and the resistance of evil, rather than to their avoidance, and that compassionate forbearance *empowers*

---

[5] For a discussion of Bonhoeffer on this point, see Jones, *Embodying Forgiveness*, pp. 13–18.

[6] The debate over forgiveness is paralleled by similarly protracted and dubious discord over self-love. Either self-love is a prideful temptation, a virtual oxymoron, to be supplanted by self-sacrificial service to others, or else it is the one thing needful, the indispensable starting point, in our appreciation of other people and of life in general. In religious contexts, the detractors of self-love associate it with the original sin and construe it as the opposite of love of neighbor and obedience to God, while the champions of self-love equate it with the wellspring of virtually all interpersonal affections (*agape*, *eros*, and *philia*) and refer to Matthew 22's "as thyself" for partial corroboration. Strong *agape* seeks to overcome this opposition, but the ambivalence of the Christian tradition is writ large in the works of Augustine and thus hard to eradicate. See Oliver O'Donovan, *The Problem of Self-Love in St. Augustine* (New Haven and London: Yale University Press, 1980), passim.

repentance and atonement, rather than requiring them as detached pre-conditions. Forgiveness may even endorse punishment—with her usual insight, Simone Weil calls punishment "a *need* of the soul"[7]—as an expression of love's taking justice seriously.

We tend to accept a stark contrast between grace and judgment only because we tend to confuse the means and ends of charity and of virtue generally. The ultimate end of charity, its very substance, is joyful participation in the life of God and God's creatures; the expression of such virtue includes actions and attitudes as seemingly antithetical as forgiveness and punishment, mercy and judgment, self-sacrifice and self-realization, and other-regard and prudence. The call to forgiveness is fundamental, however, precisely because Yahweh is characterized by *ḥésed* (steadfast love). In spite of Matthew 6:14–15, Luke 6:37, and related passages, we do not forgive others in order subsequently to be forgiven, but rather because we have *already been* forgiven, most basically by God. More on this later.

Once we comprehend forgiveness as Eternity's work of love, as a good gift given first from above, we can see how the usual contrast between mercy (frequently allied with love of neighbor) and justice (frequently allied with self-love) is overdrawn. Mercy and justice characteristically involve different means, and there can be short-run tension between them, but for Christians the basic end is the same: the joyful imitation of God, conformity to God's holy will. As I have emphasized, love sometimes rises above the narrow computations of justice, but it never dips below justice to give less than is due. More to the point, mercy makes justice possible by extending the gratuitous care (including forgiveness) to the needy that enables them to grow into responsible persons who can deserve both praise and blame. Or so I will argue in this chapter.

The position I defend has notable affinities with an emphasis on "pure grace," but it also attempts to respond to the legitimate concerns of critical judgment.

THREE THESES ABOUT FORGIVENESS

I begin this section with two relatively uncontroversial theses: *(1) Forgiveness presupposes freedom.* When we forgive another, it is normally for something that she has done by choice. She may not have anticipated all of the consequences of her action, and there need not be active malice; but the forgiven thought, word, or deed must have been an option within

---

[7] Weil, "Draft for a Statement of Human Obligations," in *Selected Essays, 1934–1943*, trans. by R. Rees (Oxford: Oxford University Press, 1962).

her power to exercise or not to exercise at some point. At the limit, the choice may have been unconscious, but it must nevertheless have stemmed from a will not necessitated by anything external. Responsible decision must have been possible at some point or else we have an amoral fatalism in which praise/blame, and thus forgiveness, are out of place.

(2) Forgiveness presupposes guilt. Even if not all candidates for forgiveness flow from positive malice, there must be some kind of turpitude for forgiveness to be well-founded. We are contrite, or ought to be, because we have somehow trespassed. Yet just how much intentionality is required is hard to say. Usually, one must know or be able to know that what one is doing is morally dubious, but we do sometimes blame/forgive people for sheer thoughtlessness or ineptitude. Again at the limit, the vice in question may have been so deeply entrenched that the individual could not really have done otherwise *at the moment*, yet in this case we are faulting/forgiving the antecedent habituation that left the person in bondage. That habituation must originally have been both free and culpable, or else nonmoral categories like "fate" or "biology" override.

What of original sin? Don't the Fall and the subsequent structures of evil imply that human freedom is now an illusion, that sin is inevitable? Moreover, don't traditional doctrines of providence assert that grace is irresistible for the elect and that damnation is unavoidable for the reprobate? Theologians from Augustine to Calvin to Kathy Tanner have seemed to some to evacuate fallen creatures of moral responsibility—Augustine holding, for example, that we are currently unable not to sin—but at a Methodist School of Theology like Candler perhaps I will be forgiven for assuming a more libertarian doctrine. To say that all have sinned and fallen short of the glory of God is not to say that this was somehow necessitated. We know of no one who has not sinned, as Barth observes, and personal and institutional injustice is virtually inescapable by individuals and groups. But if living together in time and the flesh means sinfulness as such, then creation is not in fact good. To put less fine a point on it, if hard double predestination is the case, ethical ideals are illusions and forgiveness makes no sense.

Alternatively, I continue with a very controversial third thesis: *(3) The offer of forgiveness presupposes nothing more than freedom and guilt.* In particular, there are no other preconditions (such as contrition, confession, or satisfaction) for when willingness to forgive is appropriate. Forgiveness is a gift, literally a giving-in-advance and without qualification, a bestowal of worth that covers a multitude of sins. It may be called supererogatory, but it is not merely optional for Christians. Forgiveness is above and beyond the usual call of duty, that is, but it is nonetheless an indispensable calling. You can't owe forgiveness as an agent or earn it as a recipient, in the standard senses of "owe" and "earn." Even as charity is the wellspring of rights and duties but is not itself a right or a duty in the modern sense, so forgiveness is beyond all appraisive questions of merit or desert or contract. When we are forgiven by God or other people, this is an unforced flower of grace. To be sure, Scripture "commands" love of neighbor (Matt. 22:36–40), and related prescriptions cover forgiveness as well (Matt. 18:21–22). But such injunctions stem from the overflowing goodness of God rather than the calculation of human worthiness. The insistence on forgiveness in particular is too monumental to entail either duties for agents or rights for patients, in the modern sense.[8] Modern duties normally correlate with rights, and both notions imply claims and counterclaims, but it would be more than odd to speak of a "right" to be forgiven that corresponds to another's "duty" to forgive. Rights and duties have their place, especially in adversarial political contexts, but the biblical calls to love and mercy make rights and duties possible by addressing human needs and potentials that are prior to (or at least independent of) any contingent achievement or personal obligation. Most basically, forgiveness issues first from grace-filled gratitude for and subsequent imitation of God's steadfast love for creatures, and, then, from appreciation of the human need and potential for mercy.

THE PURPOSE OF FORGIVENESS

The purpose of forgiveness is commonly said to be reestablishment of right relation between two alienated persons, but this cannot be the exclusive objective. Emory University dedicated the 2000–2001 school-year to Reconciliation, and few commitments could be more worthwhile. But if reconciliation is defined as repairing or restoring an ongoing relation to another human being, then it is not synonymous with forgiveness. Reconciliation is surely not a *precondition* for the offer of forgiveness, and it may be no objective at all. For we can forgive people we know we will never see again in this life, such as the dead, or who we plausibly anticipate will forever despise and ill-use us. Forgiveness may be a necessary condition for reconciliation, Wiesel notwithstanding, but it is not sufficient.

Think of a wife who is abused by an alcoholic husband or a friend who is repeatedly betrayed by a dishonest comrade. The wife may forgive her husband in the sense that she may refuse to hate him, and the friend may willingly let go of feelings of resentment. But this does not mean that

---

[8] One may talk of "religious duties" or "the demands of holiness," but these phrases are at home in theological or ecclesial settings that consciously prescind from reciprocal justice between contentious human beings.

either one need stay in the relation in question. Patience is long-suffering, and one may credibly argue, on biblical and sacramental grounds, that even a battered spouse ought not to divorce the guilty party. Nonetheless, there may be overwhelming reasons permanently to part company, to absent oneself and give the relation over to God. One may owe this to oneself and to others (for example, children) who would also be at grave risk.

Partially to uncouple forgiveness from restored relation in this way is not to belittle reconciliation—far from it. We all pine for the Spirit that will say a healing word to unite the races, the sexes, all nationalities, and all creeds. I said in a previous chapter that sometimes the best way to realize a goal is not to value it too highly or to aim at it too directly. Jesus endorses a similar principle in instructing the disciples not to let the left hand know what the right hand is doing (Matt. 6:3). In the present context, this means affirming the priority of forgiveness as participation in God's own holiness, no strings attached, then letting earthly estrangements take care of themselves.

The least one might say is that reconciliation with, and obedience to, God must precede and ground reconciliation with, and service to, humanity. Martin Luther King, Jr., used to insist that he was committed to "the ministry of Jesus Christ" first, and on that basis to specific social agendas, such as civil rights and peace protest.[9] His social activism flowed directly from loyalty to the Heavenly Father—"I just want to do God's will"[10]—and he refused to separate fidelity to God from concern for the poor and oppressed. But he did not simply equate any political cause with Christian faithfulness. As he put it, "I must be true to my conviction that I share with all men the calling to be a son of the living God. Beyond the calling of race or nation or creed is this vocation of sonship and brotherhood."[11] Being a son of God requires eschewing aggression and forgiving other human beings, but the Creator/creature distinction remains. The two love commandments are intimately linked, in other words, but the *first* has priority.

FORGIVENESS AND SACRIFICE

I indicated above that, even having forgiven someone, one might still withdraw oneself and others from grave risk. Now a critic will say, "But does not agapic love run risks and embrace sacrifices? Aren't Christians enjoined to find their lives by losing them, to follow Jesus even unto

---

[9] King, "A Time to Break Silence," in *I Have a Dream*, p. 139.

[10] King, "I See the Promised Land," in ibid., p. 203.

[11] King, "A Time to Break Silence," in ibid., p. 140.

death if necessary?" Yes, to be sure: there is no gaining the crown without accepting the cross. We all live by the kindness of strangers who, like the Good Samaritan, put themselves out—think, most importantly, of the suffering presence of God in Christ—but we must never forget that Christian charity is not mere imprudence. Jesus himself flees danger when his hour has not yet come, Jesus himself withdraws from the multitude for the quiet of solitude, and Jesus himself freely (however dreadfully) consents to his Passion rather than having it compelled upon him by force. Forgiveness is a *form* of self-sacrifice; in letting go of the *lex talionis* one is, indeed, foregoing various justified retaliations, various wounded self-understandings. Any proper conception of forgiveness must reflect three things, however: (1) openness to sacrifice is not the whole of charity— one must also speak of unconditional willing of the good and of equal regard; (2) even though forgiveness sacrifices some of the claims of justice, it may nonetheless resist injustice and even withdraw from relation to the unjust; and (3) sacrifice is itself premised on its being both constructive and consensual.

So here's the point: motives, acts, and effects all matter. Overcoming in a marriage, a congregation, or a nation, may mean getting back to "we." But if I stay in a troubled relation because I think I am a piece of garbage and deserve nothing better than abuse, that is masochism; if I stay in a troubled relation because I think I have no other choice, that is cowardice; if I stay in a troubled relation because I want to earn my way into heaven, that is bribery; if I stay in a troubled relation even though it harms all involved, that is profligacy. In contrast, if I freely remain in such a relation because I feel called by God to be a vehicle of grace, that is fidelity; if I freely remain in such a relation because I passionately believe that, in spite of the pain, my sacrifice will be redemptive for others, that is charity; if I freely remain in such a relation because I trust that I will grow from the experience, that is hope; if I freely remain in such a relation simply because God has commanded it, that is obedience. But, lastly, if I freely *withdraw* from such a relation because anything more than forgiveness would be to pander to evil, that is wisdom.

Need I say, the besetting temptation for *most* of us in this autonomous age, particularly us males, is not inordinate loyalty or undue perseverance. Overzealous self-surrender is not *usually* the problem; just the opposite. The key, of course, is to make an idol of neither self-sacrifice nor self-realization. There is nothing wrong with proper self-love, but it is typically the bloom of charity, not its root or inspiration. We do indeed find our lives by losing them in God. Even the second great love commandment, which presumes love of self as a norm (Matt. 22:39), is arguably superseded by Jesus' final commandment: "that you love one another *as I have loved you*" (John 15:12; emphasis added; see also John 13:34).

Because we do not naturally know how to love (or forgive) ourselves, faith, hope, and love must look first to God's guidance and power, and second to the neighbor's needs and our shared potentials, rather than to our own antecedent preferences. As Jesus himself says to God, before the Passion, "not my will but yours be done" (Luke 22:42).

FORGIVENESS "DEFINED"

How, more concretely, might we understand forgiveness? I'm partial to the phrase "cessation of againstness," the resolve to continue to will the good for others rather than to despise them, in spite of any hostility and transgression. As such, forgiveness *may* make another feel accepted and acceptable, and thereby bolster his or her self-esteem; forgiveness *may* help induce repentance and thus contribute to another's moral reform; forgiveness *may* even make enemies into friends. But it need not do any of these. I might *hope* that forgiveness is appropriated by a guilty party as a means to "at-one-ment"; harmony-as-restored-relation is *often* an ideal fruition of mercy. But, again, forgiveness is not offered with reconciliation as either a precondition or a necessary effect. Or it *shouldn't* be, if it is to be spontaneous, Christlike virtue.

My offer of forgiveness wills the good of the other by making his tawdry past no longer exist for me, save in a special (almost impersonal) form of memory. Such a redemption of time requires the inbreaking of eternity, saying to the offender, "It is with me as if you had never transgressed, even as God has forgiven my sin." This "cessation of againstness" is a teleological suspension of the ethics of merit, an altruism that rises above justice (narrowly defined as *suum cuique*) without offending against it. "Mercy triumphs over judgment" (James 2:13), but it does not humiliate it. To respond to an infidelity with permanent hostility might be reciprocally fair, for example, but it is not loving. Love would ideally empower another to be self-giving, and thus forgiving, in her turn; but, again, repentance and reform follow, if they follow, only at a distance. Love is not first a technique; it is a presence that serves and suffers. It is a steadfast refusal of ill-will characteristic of a sacred heart— but who is capable of this without special grace? Although love does not forget temporal offenses, it recalls them from the point of view of eternity (i.e., in light of God's mercy *and* judgment). Not to re-member sin at all is to dis-member time, but to re-member eternally is to re-deem time by seeing all sin (past, present, and future) as already vanquished by Almighty God.

Forgiveness is an "eternal" work of love in two senses, then: it is Eternity's work *on* time (on us), and it is our perpetual task *within* time (within us). In this life, we can never simply have done with mercy, once and for all, since we will forever be called on to forgive, at least ourselves.

GIVING AND RECEIVING: A CLARIFYING DISTINCTION

At this point, I want to introduce a clarifying distinction: between the *offer* or *extension* of forgiveness, on the one hand, and its *acceptance* or *appropriation*, on the other. Contrition, confession, and reparation may well be essential to the *appropriation* of forgiveness by the sinner, but they cannot be the preconditions of the *offer* of forgiveness by the one sinned against, or else the latter has ceased to be an imitator of God's kenotic love. The unconditional offer of forgiveness is itself the best hope of sparking moral reformation in others, but it does not wait on that reformation. Jesus asks his Father to forgive the Romans even as they crucify him, and Scripture reminds us over and over again that God, although wrathful at times with Israel, will not remove the covenant of peace (Isa. 54:8–10), that God recognizes and condemns wickedness yet is full of mercy and offers pardon (Isa. 55:7)—more broadly, that God loves humanity first (1 John 4:10) and while we are still sinners (Rom. 5:8).

Armed with the distinction between giving and receiving forgiveness, we can now see the possible point of some difficult passages in the Bible. Matthew 6:14–15 reads: "if you forgive others their trespasses, your heavenly Father will also forgive you; but if you do not forgive others, neither will your Father forgive your trespasses." Does this not make divine forgiveness conditional, after all? Aren't we being invited to trade our earthly forgiveness for heavenly reward? Perhaps still more daunting to unconditionalists, like myself, is Matthew 12:31. There Jesus states that "blasphemy against the Spirit will not be forgiven." Is not this assertion of an unforgivable sin out of character for the Christ, even a little petulant?[12] It does indeed seem at odds with the exhortation to forgive "seventy-seven times" (i.e., without limit) found in Matthew 18:22. What are we to make of this? The key to harmonizing these verses is to see that realized forgiveness has two sides or moments: the offering and the accepting. The example of Christ points unmistakably, I believe, to an unflagging willingness to extend forgiveness to everyone who sins against us (see Luke 11:4). But the offer of forgiveness alone does not ensure a cessation of againstness on the other side; in addition to the generous giving, without precondition, there must be an active receiving, without prevarication. For forgiveness fully to "take," so to speak, both parties

---

[12] See Mitchell, *The Gospel According to Jesus*, pp. 193–94.

must acknowledge the wrongdoing, then refuse hatred and let go of the past—if not reestablish relations. Without confession, contrition, and restitution on the part of the sinner, however, this process cannot be completed.

When Jesus maintains that blasphemy against the Spirit is unforgivable, he is gesturing, I believe, toward this truth. To mock the Paraclete is to deny that God is just and that one is in need of divine forgiveness; it is to refuse, in turn, all mercy that might placate that justice and communicate that forgiveness. Blasphemy makes it impossible, not for God to *extend* forgiveness, but for us sinners to *grasp* it. Something similar may be said about Matthew 6:14–15: if we do not forgive, God will not forgive us, not because God will cease to make overtures but rather because we will be too bitter to hear them. God's *ḥésed* is steadfast, but we may become willfully inured to it. To the extent that each of us freely turns away from God, the neighbor, and ourselves, the Bible suggests that every man is his own Adam and every woman her own Eve. Similarly, to the degree that each allows past sin to rule and thus says no to forgiveness, whether for others or for oneself, every person is Christ's Pilate—crucifying the Lord and his gospel anew.

And how might Pilate forgive himself, both giving and receiving mercy simultaneously? If the offer to forgive *others* is unqualified, a notable asymmetry may seem to emerge when the focus becomes *self*-referential. First-person forgiveness is parasitic on repentance, one might argue; when I forgive myself, I appear to have to assume regret in advance. This appearance is misleading, however. The reflexive offer of, or desire for, forgiveness does not so much *require* contrition as itself *constitute* contrition. (It is also very near to entailing both confession and atonement.) I cannot want to forgive myself without being sorry for what I have done. I can double-mindedly refuse my own offer, but this is simply to say that I can, as always, play Herod and decline grace.

Six Possible Reasons for Unconditional Forgiveness

So far I have baldly asserted three main propositions. Adequately defending these theses would require explaining forgiveness from the roots up and in much more detail: why, how, when, and so on. But a problem immediately presents itself. Giving reasons for forgiving may seem a self-contradiction. If forgiveness is to be unconditional, must it not be unmotivated; and if forgiveness is to be spontaneous, must it not be without technique? Asking why we ought to forgive is like asking why be moral, even as asking how to forgive is as odd as asking how to breathe. These misgivings are understandable, but they should not stymie us. One can in fact distinguish between *consequences of* forgiving and *motives for* forgiving, as well as between *motives for* forgiving and *preconditions on* forgiving. One might be moved by thankfulness to God, for instance, to give to others without demanding reciprocity. Like a student of yoga learning to inhale and exhale more naturally, one can learn to forgive precisely by ceasing self-consciously to calculate.

We must always be wary of instrumentalizing forgiveness, making it a means to an extrinsic end. Nevertheless, I want briefly to describe six possible reasons for forgiving. It is not the case that all six reasons need always come into play in every case of forgiveness. What, on some occasions, is sought with conscious deliberation (e.g., to influence the consciences of others) may be, on other occasions, either missing from the moral equation altogether or an unreflective by-product of action, a "mere" consequence that is not part of one's original intentions.

The first possible reason for forgiving is self-referential: *humility based on consistency.* All have sinned and fallen short of the glory of God, and all have need of and/or ask for forgiveness. One should not deny to others what one requires for oneself (cf. again Matt. 6:14–15). Acknowledgment of the ubiquity of moral guilt, and thus of the universal need for forgiveness, is the initial step toward mercy: "Let anyone among you who is without sin be the first to throw a stone" (John 8:7). This is but a practical application of the positive Golden Rule of Matthew 7:12: "In everything do to others as you would have them do to you." This self-referential reason to refuse to retaliate in kind, in spite of costs, is not unique to Christianity. While Platonists speak of "not returning injustice,"[13] however, Christians talk of "becoming children of God."

A second possible reason is again self-referential: *liberation from personal torment.* Although forgiveness wills the good *for* the wrongdoer, forgiveness can also be the final declaration of independence *from* the wrongdoer. It refuses to be conformed to and thus controlled by his or her sin, and this refusal is liberation from hatred, resentment, anxiety, and other crippling emotions that lead to despair and vendetta. This is the great mystery: in losing ourselves and loving God with our whole hearts, we find ourselves; similarly, in pardoning another and imitating God's

---

[13] Plato's *Crito*, 49B8–C10, reads: Socrates: "Hence we must never commit injustice." —Crito: "No." —Socrates: "Nor return injustice when we have suffered it ourselves, as the many believe, since we must *never* commit injustice." —Crito: "Evidently not." —Socrates: "What then? May we harm [anyone], Crito, or not?" —Crito: "Surely not, Socrates." —Socrates: "And should we return harm, when we have suffered it ourselves? Would this be just or unjust?" —Crito: "We should never return it." —Socrates: "For to harm human beings is no different than committing injustice against them." —Crito: "What you say is true." —Socrates: "Therefore, we must never return wrong or do evil to a single man, no matter what he may have done to us." (Gregory Vlastos translation, distributed in a 1979 lecture at Yale)

grace, we are sparing ourselves torment. This suggests one way to understand the old saw, "forgive and forget": to fore-give is not to wipe away all memory of sin—that would be irresponsible—but it is to fore-get, to get one's life back in advance of anything another might do or not do.

The third possible reason to forgive is other-regarding: *to touch the consciences of others.* Forgiving can be a sign to another of God's redeeming presence. By turning the other cheek and refusing to retaliate, one who forgives may prick the conscience of the wrongdoer. In this case, forgiveness has more than epistemological significance, however; it both testifies to and substantively communicates God's love. The claim that love ought to move me to forgive another is straightforward and plausible, but in a typical deepening of a traditional theme, Jesus also makes the obverse point that forgiving another elicits love in her. The causality works in both directions:

> "A certain creditor had two debtors; one owed five hundred denarii, and the other fifty. When they could not pay, he canceled the debts for both of them [RSV: forgave them both]. Now which of them will love him more?" Simon answered, "I suppose the one for whom he canceled the greater debt [RSV: forgave more]." And Jesus said to him, "You have judged rightly." (Luke 7:41–43)

Jesus implies that loving others is both a mark and a fruit of having been forgiven oneself. "Therefore I tell you, her sins, which were many, have been forgiven, hence she has shown great love. But the one to whom little is forgiven, loves little" (Luke 7:47). One does not forgive others on the condition that they perform in some specified way, to repeat, but rather because one has been forgiven oneself. That said, forgiving is a work of love that often both wants and tends to elicit love. If charity aims to make others loving in their turn, the greatest gift, then forgiving unconditionally can be a potent means to this end.

The fourth possible reason is again other-regarding: *solidarity aimed at furthering the kingdom.* Persons who are slanderous, treacherous, murderous, and the like have declared their hatred for the community to which they belong. If the Christian doctrine of creation is correct, however, all belong first and foremost to the community of God's children. Race, gender, nationality, and religious affiliation are secondary, since all human beings are made in the divine Image. To forgive is to honor this commonality by refusing to hate in return. Even if one dare not invite another back into one's physical company, one might still hope that he or she enjoy the society of God. This does not mean that swindlers keep their jobs, abusive spouses are allowed back in the home, rapists are turned loose in the streets, and serial killers get public housing. It means, rather, that an indelible humanity is recognized. What God has joined together—Creator and finite creatures—cannot be put altogether asunder, even by sin. The sanctity of human life need not be earned, nor can it be surrendered. Convicted felons may well be sent to prison and unjust aggressors may even, in the extremity of war, be killed, for they have no right to threaten the innocent. They remain persons summoned to Christ's kingdom, however, regardless of their posture. There is no necessary contradiction between some forms of retributive punishment and heartfelt forgiveness, I believe, but the latter requires basic consideration for all come what may: for example, no torture, no death penalty once disarmed, no direct assault of noncombatants, benevolent quarantine for captive soldiers, and so on.

Again, forgiveness cannot be merited, either negatively by undergoing the lash and ceasing to threaten or positively by showing repentance and making amends. It is a gift. Forgiveness may sometimes decline overtly to punish, depending on circumstances, but what is forever incompatible with forgiving is hating the other, willing evil for him or her. This is what it means to call forgiving "an eternal work of love." Love always offers forgiveness, meaning it steadfastly wills the good for the other, and it frequently invites fellowship with the other. Yet the tactics of forgiveness are variable. Forgiveness does not pander to evil by ignoring or tempting it; forgiveness may employ confrontation and reprimand as means of encouraging contrition and satisfaction. But "cessation of againstness" is not contingent on these things. One does not repent in order to be forgiven, although being forgiven may help one to repent.

The fifth and sixth reasons for forgiveness are theocentric and, therefore, the most fundamental. I have held them until last in my list to highlight the fact that they obtain even if other reasons fail. These are the most distinctive Christian reasons to forgive, and the example of Christ suggests that one or the other ought always to be part of one's motivation and not a mere afterthought or double effect.

The fifth reason is *gratitude moved by grace to Imitation*. One forgives others out of appreciation for the forgiveness God has gratuitously shown oneself. Moreover, forgiveness is eucharistic; to show mercy unconditionally is to participate in the holiness of God. One is merciful in order to love as God loves, as Roberta Bondi puts it.[14] One is to "love your enemies and pray for those who persecute you, so that you may be children of your Father in heaven" (Matt. 5:44–45). Real enemies and persecutors are attended to, not God alone, but creatures are to forgive in order to model God's sublime self-expenditure, God's sending rain "on the righteous and the unrighteous" (ibid.). Persons made in God's Image

[14] See Roberta Bondi, *To Love as God Loves* (Philadelphia: Fortress, 1987), esp. chap. 3 on "Humility."

are to imitate "his indiscriminate bestowal of light" (in Simone Weil's phrase).[15] That indiscriminateness is writ largest on the cross. As Saint Paul observes, "God proves his love for us in that while we still were sinners Christ died for us" (Rom. 5:8). A pious thankfulness is arguably the sentiment most characteristic of Christian charity, at least when considered vertically in relation to God. It is not fear of physical death but gratefulness for ransomed life that makes one a religious soul. Even when we despair of being consistent or becoming perfect, even when we despair of converting others or building the kingdom, God can still open our musty selves to the Son's light, with grace.

The sixth reason is closely related to the fifth: *the direct commandment of Christ*. Jesus says in Luke 6:32–36:

> "If you love those who love you, what credit is that to you? For even sinners love those who love them. If you do good to those who do good to you, what credit is that to you? For even sinners do the same. If you lend to those from whom you hope to receive, what credit is that to you? Even sinners lend to sinners, to receive as much again. But love your enemies, do good, and lend, expecting nothing in return. Your reward will be great, and you will be children of the Most High; for he is kind to the ungrateful and the wicked. Be merciful, just as your Father is merciful."

Matthew 18:21–22 reads:

> Then Peter came up and said to him, "Lord, how often shall my brother sin against me, and I forgive him? As many as seven times?" Jesus said to him, "I do not say to you seven times, but seventy times seven." (RSV)

I am told that there is a clever novel entitled *491*. The significance of the name, I gather, is that one may forgive seventy times seven, but on the 491st offense: Pow! The critical nerve must then kick in, literally with a vengeance. This novel notwithstanding, clearly Jesus intends to say that forgiveness does not keep tabs: it is uncalculating and endless. This is not to say that the forgiveness of any one of us is actually inexhaustible; although these vary, we all have our practical limits. But the mercy of God is infinite: for God and with God, "all things are possible" (Mark 10:27; and see also Luke 18:27), and we are commanded (and empowered) to follow the divine perfection as best we can.

Jesus explicitly equates being "perfect" with universal love (Matt. 5:46–48). The paradox, however, is that in mandating mercy and unconditional love Jesus himself appeals to the idea of "reward." In the quoted passage from Luke 6, Jesus seems to reintroduce *self*-interest and concern

---

[15] Weil, *Waiting for God*, p. 97.

for *heavenly* reward even as he enjoins other-regard and eschewal of earthly gain. So we are presented yet again with the issue of the relation of self-love, love of neighbor, and obedience to God. The first point to make here is that sometimes Jesus' references to "reward" from God or "treasure in heaven" make a point about the *consequences* of certain actions or attitudes, not directly about what one's intentional *motives* ought to be (see, e.g., Matt. 6:18). But the second point is that this is not uniformly the case. At times, Jesus does indeed tell his listeners to do something specifically *in order to* accrue eternal profit or avoid eternal loss (see, e.g., Matt. 6:1). What are we to make of this?

I draw two lessons. The first is that self-perfection has a proper, if limited, place in the scheme of moral motivation. As with self-love generally, concern for spiritual profit and loss is legitimate for individuals and groups. One does well to acknowledge that one is a sinner and to ask for mercy from God, for instance (Luke 18:13–14). The second lesson, however, is that heavenly reward (and punishment) is not like the earthly kind and thus displays a different dynamic. "Treasures in heaven" are not limited resources and not subject to corruption (Matthew 19–20), so they need not be anxiously grasped. God knows when one fasts "in secret" and can be counted on to "reward" one out of the sight of other human beings (Matt. 6:17–18), and perhaps out of one's own sight. "When you give alms, do not let your left hand know what your right hand is doing," Jesus instructs his disciples (Matt. 6:3), and one might apply this same principle to assisting *oneself*. The self should be like one's left hand; fidelity to God and neighbor need not entail an anxious and self-absorbed existence. Even one's own soul is not, first of all, something to be seized or served but something to be forgotten—forgotten by you so that it might remember, and be remembered by, God. "All who exalt themselves will be humbled, but all who humble themselves will be exalted" (Luke 18:14).

Ultimately, as Luke implies, self-surrender and self-possession are one in Christ. But first of all and most of the time forgiveness is more akin to self-emptying (a divine *kenosis*) than self-cultivation (a human design). To be willing to forgive is inevitably to suffer, moreover. Eternity enters time by way of the cross, and the Crucified One says "Father, forgive them" even as he dies (Luke 23:34). As the *Bhagavad Gita* observes, "If you want to see the brave, look at those who can forgive." Suffering is not sought for its own sake, which would be perverse, but here is no relentless pursuit of happiness, no modern "eudaimania." Forgiveness can be an eternal work of self-love, an act of self-realization, precisely because it stems from a truthful understanding of who one is (a sinner), who has saved one (God), and who else is or might yet be saved (the neighbor).

FORGIVENESS AND PUNISHMENT

But how can I both punish someone and claim to forgive him or her, especially if forgiveness makes the past offense no longer exist for me? Let me begin by considering two less than fully satisfying explanations. First, one might maintain that forgiveness is entirely an attitude of the heart, a matter of what motivates action, rather than any form of external action or inaction. Saint Augustine maintained, for instance, that the injunction to "resist not evil" and to "turn the other [cheek]" (see Matt. 5:39, KJV) is a call to "an inward disposition" of patience and benevolence toward aggressors but not a strict rule of nonresisting outer behavior.[16] On this view, one must give up subjective hostility and resentment toward wrong-doers, and one must always avoid "recompensing evil for evil";[17] but one might still forcefully check and discipline them for their own good, as well as for the sake of public order. Second, one might argue that forgiveness is a first-person-singular affair, what I do in my own case, while punishment looks to the general welfare and the protection of third parties. Here too Augustine provides a model that might be applied to forgiveness. He held that a Christian ought not to defend himself or herself against violent assault, since this would betray "lust" for things that can be lost against one's will, but that one may take up the sword to defend one's neighbors, since this can be done in other-regarding charity.[18] Analogously, one might argue that both forgiving and refusing to punish others are always called for when the offense is against oneself, but that one might carry out retribution against those who are harming or have harmed others. One must still refuse to hate in the latter case, since willing the good is the essential core of all forgiveness, but one might employ punishment as a *tactic* when this is aimed at sustaining the social fabric beyond one's individual claims or interests.

The "Augustinian" model is highly suggestive, but it can be overdone. If forgiveness is interpreted *purely* inwardly, it opens the door to a crude situationalism. I cannot plausibly be said to have surrendered hostility to others if I viciously beat them or perpetually berate and ostracize them, no matter how much I may claim to have "forgiven" them in my heart. Because I am not a disembodied soul timelessly contemplating myself but rather a psychosomatic creature in historical relation with others, my concrete actions and effects matter, as Augustine well knew. My moral stature is partially defined by how I behave and what I achieve, as well as

---

[16] Augustine, "*Contra Faustum*," XXII, and "Letters," CXXXVIII, both in *The Political Writings of St. Augustine*, pp. 166 and 177.

[17] Ibid., p. 178.

[18] Augustine, *On Free Choice of the Will*, bk. 1, chap. V, pp. 10–13.

by who I wish to be. One may look *primarily* to motives for the ethical tenor of an act or outcome—Augustine is arguably right that far—but it would be folly to think that good intentions alone are enough for virtue. Forgiveness is a process that has internal roots but also external expressions, so the question is not whether punishment is somehow "outer" while forgiveness is "inner," but rather whether punishment is itself sometimes a manifestation of (or at least compatible with) a forgiveness that refuses to hate.

The difficulty with seeing forgiveness as *requiring* that one forego retributive justice (including punishment) in first-person-singular cases but not in others is that it may deny individual worth. If I can check and discipline evildoers for the sake of neighbors, out of love, why can't I do the same for my own sake, since I too am beloved of God in whose Image I am made? I have emphasized that self-forgetfulness is a hallmark of Christlike love, but it does not seem plausible to assert that inordinate self-love or "libido" will *always* be involved in a vindication of one's own just claims. I may willingly rise above justice and give up my life without resistance, perhaps to touch the conscience of an attacker. But I may also be motivated by a sense of God's will for my life and what will most profoundly check evil in a particular context to stay the hand of my assailant. (Jesus himself shows a prudent concern to save himself from assaults that are premature and unproductive [e.g., Matt. 12:14–15; John 7:1–9], even as he opens himself to radical sacrifice when the time is right.) Both the rising above justice and the appealing to justice must refuse hatred, to repeat, but a proper love that aims at constructively willing the good may ground both tactics. Or, if vice *is* always operative in resisting those who trespass against me, it will almost as easily be operative in resisting those who sin against my friends or my tribe or my country. It is one thing to say that, as an individual, I cannot forgive in the name of others (see below), but it is quite another to say that I must not punish in my own name or that I may punish in another's name. Once again we are left with the question of whether punishment is ever an expression of forgiveness, or at least not essentially at odds with it.

My next major thesis is: *(4) Punishment is often love's taking justice seriously.* If I have been the victim of a crime, I may both forgive the criminal and want him to be put in jail to protect myself and others from future harm. If love ever embraces such punishment, however, it is not as an alternative to offering forgiveness. In addition to aiming at public safety, punishment may even be a method of empowering the offender to *receive* forgiveness. The issue for the agapist is not "*Should* I forgive this person for wronging me?" but rather "*Can* I forgive him or her?" My *offer* of forgiveness as "cessation of againstness" need not be conditional to recognize that the *appropriation* of that forgiveness depends on the other party. Here, to repeat, is where contrition, confession, and satisfaction have their proper place: as means of *accepting* forgiveness. The forgiver, like the forgiven, must be free; again, forgiveness is not a strict duty of justice that others can demand as a dignity right, although it is always noble. Even when forgiveness embraces the tactic of limited and constructive punishment, a "just" possibility is foregone, since one might have chosen a perpetual hostility never open to reconciliation.

The relation between punishment and forgiveness is admirably described by Augustine in *The Enchiridion*:

> The man who pardons the sinner . . . gives alms; and the man who corrects with blows, or restrains by any kind of discipline one over whom he has power, and who at the same time forgives from the heart the sin by which he was injured, or prays that it may be forgiven, is also a giver of alms, not only in that he forgives, or prays for forgiveness for the sin, but also in that he rebukes and corrects the sinner: for in this, too, he shows mercy. Now much good is bestowed upon unwilling recipients, when their advantage and not their pleasure is consulted.[19]

An obvious danger in these sentiments is that others' legitimate choices will be overridden by an overweening paternalism. Concern over a "killing compassion"[20] led me to argue in chapter 3 that only the restraint of serious injustice can warrant the use of violence, and I would make a similar point about punishment. Love only resorts to punishment when there has been a proven offense and when the retributive steps will likely benefit all concerned; punishment is not a proper means of indoctrination or conversion or crowd control.

That said, the truly pressing question for my purposes here is not "How do I check paternalism?" but rather "Do I have the moral resources to forgive with a pure intention, utterly gratuitously? Do I have confidence that lack of resentment is virtue's optimal way with vice?" If I cannot forgive without violating self-respect, then it is better not to try; and if I cannot resist or punish another without lapsing into hatred, then again it is better not to attempt it. But both of these incapacities betray my own limits, not those of love. Love is supremely confident yet without enmity, even if we never fully realize this ideal. Jesus himself challenged and resisted evildoers (e.g., the cleansing of the temple), even as he asked his Father from the cross to forgive his executioners. God used the substitutionary punishment of the Son as an instrument of forgiveness, rather than as its denial (cf. Isa. 53:5).

This strong endorsement of unconditional forgiveness is not a prescrip-

---

[19] Augustine, *The Enchiridion on Faith, Hope, and Love* [421], trans. by J. F. Shaw (Washington, D.C.: Regnery, 1961), LXXII, p. 85.
[20] See Hauerwas, *Dispatches from the Front*, pp. 164–76.

tion for in-principle pacifism, in my estimation, since I may take up the sword to defend innocent others or myself from direct attack without abandoning love (chapter 3). Armed resistance to social injustice is in some circumstances permissible, if not obligatory, and, to reiterate, refusing to hate or to launch a vendetta is not the same thing as declining to stay or even to strike a wrongdoer's hand. The one thing needful is the courage to do good to those who spitefully use us, to refuse to return evil for evil. Forgiving others is always incarnating Goodness and the best one can hope for in doing well by them. It may ultimately redound to my benefit, both physically and spiritually, but it will certainly cost. As Kierkegaard notes, "true self-denial . . . always involves suffering for the good that one does"; indeed, "suffering is the mark of the God-relationship."[21]

IS FORGIVENESS IRRESPONSIBLE?

Someone may still object that the type of forgiveness I have described is irresponsible. Does it not amount to a condoning of sin? As Miroslav Volf observes, "The powerful emotional pull of revenge is not the only reason we resist forgiving. . . . Our cool sense of justice sends the same message: the perpetrator *deserves* unforgiveness; it would be unjust to forgive."[22] Might not forgiveness disastrously pander to evil by encouraging even more wrongdoing than is otherwise necessary? No, for two reasons.

First, there is a distinction between denying that an action is culpable (condonation) and refusing to hold a grudge or to become vindictive in the face of a recognized wrong (forgiveness). The saint more clearly discerns and more emphatically resists injustice than the rest of us, but she absorbs its ill effects by expending herself rather than by lashing out in hatred. She relies on the charisma of goodness in interpersonal relations; she *is* that charisma incarnate in the flesh. Second, although love is not paralyzed by the limitless demands of social utility, neither is love blind to the consequences of its actions. It hopes for the best, but its best hope is to be itself: forgiving come what may. Forgiveness is compatible with schooling others retributively to see their folly, but this consummation is neither a necessary condition nor a universally governing motive. Forgiving is always marked by sacrifice of a right—cancellation of a debt—if only the right to claim self-righteousness or to despair over another's soul. But confrontation, resistance, even wrath may accompany forgive-

[21] The first quotation is from Kierkegaard, *Judge For Yourself!* trans. and ed. by Howard V. and Edna H. Hong (Princeton: Princeton University Press, 1990), p. 207; the second is from Kierkegaard, *Journals and Papers*, vol. 4, ed. and trans. by the Hongs, assisted by Gregor Malantschuk (Bloomington: Indiana University Press, 1975), #4682, p. 408.
[22] Volf, *Exclusion and Embrace* (Nashville: Abingdon, 1996), p. 120.

ness. One can, and often should, be indignant at another's sin or one's own; yet love always wills the good and refuses to hate. Indifference is also unforgiving because it writes others off the rolls of fellow humanity.

We must keep clear two distinctions, then: hatred versus anger and vengeance versus retribution. Hatred entails directly willing evil for another, wishing ultimately that he or she no longer exist; this is ruled out by charity, which always wills the good. Anger, on the other hand, may be a righteous indignation that confronts the wrongdoer as such; this is quite compatible with loving the other and hoping for his reform. Vengeance I take to be synonymous with unbridled vendetta against another, even unto the utter destruction of all he holds dear: "You raped my sister, so I'll wipe out your whole damn family!" Retribution, in contrast, is a measured attempt to right the scales of justice, even to benefit the transgressor. No serious moral wrong will ever be entirely expunged or compensated for by strict retributive justice,[23] but retribution aims to "make the punishment fit the crime." Vengeance, for its part, is limitless and without constructive purpose, thus incompatible with other-regarding love.

Again, love transcends and transforms justice, but it never embodies injustice. Love may help us see that what we think is justice is actually self-defensiveness and self-deception. We would rather indict the foible of another, the "mote" in our neighbor's eye, than acknowledge our own massive sin, the "plank" in our own. Indeed, we may be so touchy and quick to accuse because, on an unconscious level, we are aware of our guilt and wish to cover it up. We may even take a social convention expedient for an elite group, like slavery or patriarchy or child-sacrifice, to be a command of God. But it is nonetheless possible to forgive out of love and still exercise a corrective hand that stops short of hatred and vengeance. The sine qua non is that any retribution and distribution be impartial and other-regarding, for then I have surrendered ill-will and may reestablish the necessary conditions for harmony. As Volf puts it:

> Forgiveness is not a substitute for justice. Forgiveness is no mere discharge of a victim's angry resentment and no mere assuaging of a perpetrator's remorseful anguish, one that demands no change of the perpetrator and no righting of wrongs. On the contrary: every act of forgiveness enthrones justice; it draws attention to its violation precisely by offering to forego its claims. . . . Moreover, forgiveness provides a framework in which the quest for properly understood justice can be fruitfully pursued.[24]

[23] Ibid., p. 122.
[24] Ibid., p. 123.

Love sometimes stoops to embrace justice, as a concession to or corrective of human weakness and sin. I might bind myself in promise to visit a sick colleague who asks this of me, for instance, even though I intended to visit him out of friendship all along (cf. chapter 2). In this way I become duty-bound; an erstwhile kindness becomes an obligation of justice. But when love transcends strict justice, as in foregoing reparations, the charisma of goodness can be still more catching. Mercy is Immanuel, incarnating love in and through us.

CAN FORGIVENESS BE CORPORATE OR VICARIOUS?

It will be protested that mercy cannot be exercised politically, that it is not a corporate virtue. As admirable as forgiveness might be between individuals, no one can or should forgive in the name of others who have been wronged, the argument will run. Take President Reagan's visit to the German military cemetery at Bitburg, as well as to the former concentration camp at Bergen-Belsen, in May 1985. The trip caused considerable controversy in the United States and Europe for several reasons. First, the cemetery contained the graves of forty-nine members of the Waffen SS, the SS being among the most atrocious criminals of the Second World War. Second, prior to arriving, Reagan said that young German draftees who died in World War II "were victims [of the Nazis] just as surely as the victims in the concentration camps," thus seeming to equate the deaths of Hitler's legions with the deaths of the Jewish victims of the Holocaust. Third, and perhaps most important, Reagan appeared to some to be forgiving the Nazis for their crimes. Although Reagan had already accepted Chancellor Helmut Kohl's invitation, Elie Wiesel made an impassioned plea for the president not to go to Bitburg, maintaining that "That place, Mr. President, is not your place. Your place is with the victims of the SS."[25] What does this affair tell us about guilt, innocence, and mercy?

The Bitburg/Bergen-Belsen visit could have been one of Ronald Reagan's finest hours, had he and his advisors been more sensitive. To be sure, nobody can forgive in the stead of someone else, short of an explicit proxy. (A priest, for example, might be seen as having a presumed proxy from God.) To repeat, free choice is internal to both forgiveness and the need to be forgiven; mercy cannot be compelled or usurped. Still, a head of state or a head of government can acknowledge, as few others can, the

---

[25] "Nazi Victim Confronts Reagan: Holocaust Survivor's Dramatic Appeal Rejected," *Chicago Tribune*, April 20, 1985, p. C1.

fallibility and vulnerability of us all. He or she can note that we live as nations and as private citizens by a grace that precedes and overarches us. We are potentially free yet perpetually dependent and liable to sin and hurt others. We all *need* forgiveness and are *capable* of giving it; this is the point Reagan tried to make, however awkwardly. His speech, although obviously written by someone else, captured some of the pathos of war and the longing for peace: the fact that all parties to a protracted conflict are losers, even if all are not equally culpable. The reaction to Reagan's visit and his call for "a spirit of reconciliation" that breaks past cycles of destruction was rather different inside Germany. Evidently, it had a heal-ing effect for many there, although it also elicited anti-Semitic comments from some and seemed to "rehabilitate" the SS in the eyes of others.[26]

I do not for a minute suggest a moral equivalence between Nazis and their victims, or that the Jewish survivors of the Holocaust or the presi-dent of the United States, Israel, or anywhere else should forgive in the name of the Six Million dead. No one but God can command another to forgive, and the enormity of the Nazi evil may make it effectively unpar-donable for many. The Holocaust was not merely mass murder but the product of an outlaw civilization that would base itself on race slavery and genocide,[27] the denial of the very idea of God's sovereignty and holi-ness and humanity's dignity and sanctity. If anything is, Nazism is that blasphemy against the Spirit which Jesus says "will not be forgiven" (Matt. 12:31). It is important, however, to see in what sense the sin is "un-forgivable." It is unforgivable not because offering forgiveness would be wrong, but because the evil itself perpetually refuses divine grace and human community. The Nazi mind will not receive pardon even if of-fered, just as it refuses the chastisement of punishment, because it will not acknowledge the call to love and be loved. Its quest for total domi-nation of others means total dissolution of itself, a setting of itself beyond contrition on the one hand and mercy on the other. Blasphemy against the Holy Spirit is the one unforgivable sin because, as noted, in cursing God's saving presence in the heart, it intentionally denies that humans are fallible and in need of grace. It mocks God's goodness itself and so de facto cannot be redeemed, rather like the "abomination that desolates" mentioned in Daniel 9:27; 12:11.

Thus one wonders if Isaiah and Elie Wiesel, for all their moral author-ity, go too far in protesting *against* forgiveness. No Christian, believing like myself that "salvation is from the Jews" (John 4:22), may fail to take

---

[26] See Shriver, *An Ethic for Enemies*, pp. 97–102.

[27] See William Styron, "Hell Reconsidered," in *This Quiet Dust* (New York: Random House, 1982). Styron is elaborating themes from Richard Rubenstein's *The Cunning of History*.

Wiesel's heartfelt words with utmost seriousness. As a Gentile born post-Shoah, I am aware of the limits of my credentials to speak on these matters, but Judaism itself leaves me with misgivings here. This century, and those that follow, must not fail to be haunted by the words of Simha Rottem, thinking to himself among the ruins of the Warsaw ghetto: "I'm the last Jew. I'll wait for morning, and for the Germans."[28] But faithfully remembering the Holocaust and wisely refusing all theodicies in the face of it does not dictate that one *reject as wrong* forgiveness by God, or by another, of the abominable criminals. It requires that one not forget the radicality of their evil and not take for granted the miracle that would be its forgiveness by the victims. It requires, in addition, that one begin by acknowledging one's own complicity in this or related evils and asking for pardon.[29] But then forgiveness may come.

The second volume of Wiesel's recent autobiography suggests two possible motives for his refusal of forgiveness: (1) shock and dismay over "the passivity of the doomed" during the Nazi Holocaust, and (2) the fact that "memory is everything" and that "to forget is to abandon."[30] Wiesel will not be resigned and nonresisting before evil, and, above all, he is "afraid of forgetting"[31] the victims of injustice. But why should these admirable resolves require a refusal to offer forgiveness to the victimizers? Wiesel is one of the most eloquent champions of moral memory in our time, and he and his literary characters are well aware that God is a God of justice and of charity.[32] He is correct, moreover, that if forgiving means forgetting, in the usual sense, it is better *not* to forgive. Yet Hebrew Scripture itself teaches that it may be possible both to resist

---

[28] Simha Rottem (known as "Kajik"), in *Shoah: An Oral History of the Holocaust*, by Claude Lanzmann (New York: Pantheon, 1985), p. 200.

[29] On Sunday, March 12, 2000, the "Day of Pardon," Pope John Paul II offered the following "Confession of Sins Against the People of Israel":

> God of our fathers,
> you chose Abraham and his descendants
> to bring your Name to the Nations:
> we are deeply saddened by the behaviour of those
> who in the course of history
> have caused these children of yours to suffer,
> and asking your forgiveness we wish to commit ourselves
> to genuine brotherhood
> with the people of the Covenant.
> We ask this through Christ our Lord.

(Taken from the Vatican Web site.) Although he did not mention the Holocaust by name, the pontiff clearly had this great atrocity in mind, among others.

[30] Wiesel, *And the Sea Is Never Full* (New York: Knopf, 1999), pp. 356, 357, and 363.

[31] Ibid., p. 410.

[32] Ibid., p. 364.

and to be merciful, both to remember and to forgive—with God's assistance.[33]

The prophet Jeremiah is a striking example of the tension between collective justice and mercy playing itself out in an individual conscience, with mercy finally getting the upper hand. Jeremiah is concerned with the interrelation of his God, his people, and himself. He suggests repeatedly that the "abominations" of Judah and Israel, including giving children as burnt offerings to Baal (Jer. 7:30–31; 19:4–5), have destined the people for severe divine punishment. Indeed, Jeremiah quotes: "I have taken away my peace from this people, says the LORD, my steadfast love and mercy. Both great and small shall die in this land; they shall not be buried, and no one shall lament for them" (16:5–6). More characteristic, however, is the conditional formulation:

> If you truly amend your ways and your doings, if you truly act justly one with another, if you do not oppress the alien, the orphan, and the widow, or shed innocent blood in this place, and if you do not go after other gods to your own hurt, then I will dwell with you in this place, in the land that I gave of old to your ancestors forever and ever. (7:5–7)

As insistent as Jeremiah is on a horrible retribution from God (e.g., 5:9; 19:7–9; 20:11–12), there is still some hope for reconciliation if the prophetic warning is heeded. As candidly as he questions God's way with the world, especially his enemies, Jeremiah is still confident that God is "in the right" (12:1).

Jerusalem was eventually burned in 587 B.C.E. by King Nebuchadrezzar. During the siege, Jeremiah was arrested for his dire forecasts, but he continued to demand from prison that his fellow countrymen surrender to the Babylonians. The Babylonian king was a "servant" of Yahweh and an instrument of God's judgment, according to Jeremiah, therefore sure to win (21:3–10; 27:6–8). This claim did not contradict the prophet's affirmation that "Truly in the LORD our God is the salvation of Israel" (3:23) and that "the days are surely coming, says the LORD, when I will restore the fortunes of my people, Israel and Judah" (30:3; see also 50:19). But the destruction of the Temple and the consequent exile of many of the people did dictate a new phase of Israelite religion—new forms of trial and comfort, sin and pardon (30:3ff.). Jeremiah even speaks of "a new covenant with the house of Israel and the house of Judah" written "on their hearts" (31:31–33), but this is a function of God's "everlasting love" and "continued . . . faithfulness" (31:3). In spite of the fact that the prophetic warnings are not heeded, that the prophet

---

[33] For a defense of the possibility of social/political forms of forgiveness, coupled with an insistence that forgiving is not forgetting, see Shriver, *An Ethic for Enemies*, esp. chap. 4, where Reagan's visit to Bitburg cemetery is analyzed sensitively and at length.

himself is incarcerated, and that holy Jerusalem is razed, God remains loving toward the Chosen People, in Jeremiah's definitive estimation. God's "new" and enduring covenant with Israel, that is, is a miracle of corporate forgiveness and healing.

Can Jeremiah still represent us, without gerrymandering? This would be astonishing. Even the Babylonian conquerers were not the systematic enslavers and murderers that the Nazis were, and I have little doubt that had I lost a family member in the Holocaust, I would find it virtually impossible to offer forgiveness to the perpetrators. On the other hand, perhaps the final, horrific triumph of Nazism would be if Jews and Christians ceased to believe in God's patience and mercy.[34] The Nazis wanted to appropriate and expunge all memory of the Jewish people, but perhaps the final, glorious victory of Judaism would be if Jews and Christians remembered how God forgives and calls us all to a similar holiness. Yahweh's own way with the world suggests that the Nazis are "unforgivable" only in the sense that, as supreme blasphemers, they are unable to receive forgiveness, not because we or God cannot or should not offer it.

THE QUESTION OF IMMORTALITY, AGAIN

The question of immortality plays a complex role in Christian attitudes toward forgiveness. Some contend that faith in immortality is necessary to forgive unconditionally, since the willingness to "bear all things" (1 Cor. 13:7) requires that we anticipate compensation for the just and torment for the unjust in heaven. We can refuse vendetta in time only because we are confident that God will punish malefactors in eternity.[35] If we eschew malice and self-assertion in this life in favor of mercy and self-giving, yet are not resurrected after death, then we are to be pitied, simply wretched, the argument goes (cf. 1 Cor. 15:17–19, 29–30). For we will have bet on a loser and lost our chance for worldly happiness, or at least catharsis.

This "Pauline" line is time-honored, but I want nevertheless to argue that it is problematic. If forgiveness is conformity to God's will, then it is its own reward, the experience of eternity in time. Forgiveness cannot fundamentally depend on externals, therefore, whether these are negotiated with the Deity as rewards/punishments or extorted from human beings as prerequisites. A Final Judgment of my temporal life, on which

---

[34] As Wiesel writes: "I was determined to remain a Jew even in the accursed kingdom. My doubts and my revolt gripped me only later. . . . I had seen too much suffering to break with the past and reject the heritage of those who had suffered." See Wiesel, *All Rivers Run to the Sea*, pp. 82–83.

[35] Cf. Volf, *Exclusion and Embrace*, p. 302: "The certainty of God's just judgment at the end of history is the presupposition for the renunciation of violence in the middle of it."

my eternal destiny depends, may encourage me to self-examination. Yet by the same token, being convinced of an endlessly extended existence may discourage me from attending to myself and others here and now. Immortality makes mercy seem far less urgent.

Nothing said here (or in chapter 2) rejects everlasting life as a blessed hope. The strong agapist is not among those who "say there is no resurrection of the dead" (1 Cor. 15:12); she simply denies that postmortem resurrection should be a forced belief for Christians. The ambiguous and even contradictory *New Testament* pictures of resurrection (both Jesus' and believers')[36] suggest the wisdom of leaving the prospect of an afterlife a mystery rather than a dogma.[37] Christian hope is not primarily inspired by uncertain evidence of immortality, but rather by an unconditional commitment to embody God's goodness. The strong agapist may well affirm Tennyson's "hope to see my Pilot face to face / When I have crost the bar."[38] But she will also allow that, if we would love our finite lives and consequently forgive our flawed selves and fractious neighbors, this ought to be done without strings. Inwardly there should be penance for sin, voluntary submission to God, but postmortem duration is best seen as an outward trapping rather than a conscious motivation for forgiveness and other acts of charity.

This is what it means to overcome the world: no longer to fear that death can rob charity of its meaningfulness, come what may. No doubt, the early Christian community proclaimed that God had raised Christ

---

[36] As J.D.G. Dunn observes: "What Luke affirms (Jesus' resurrection body was flesh and bones), Paul denies (the resurrection body is *not* composed of flesh and blood)!" See Dunn, *The Evidence for Jesus* (London: SCM, 1985), p. 74, quoted by Wedderburn, *Beyond Resurrection*, p. 66.

[37] The Nicene Creed ends with "We look for the resurrection of the dead, and the life of the world to come. Amen." The phrase "look for" seems a happily undogmatic expression of hope, and an Anglican (like myself) gladly employs it in the rite of the Holy Eucharist. See *The Book of Common Prayer* (New York: Seabury, 1977), p. 327. The Apostles' Creed, on the other hand, concludes with "I believe in . . . the resurrection of the body, and the life everlasting. Amen." This wording is more difficult to square with the epistemic humility counseled by Scripture, especially since the old Roman formulation requires "assent to the doctrine of *resurrectio carnis* [resurrection of the flesh] not *mortuorum* or *corporum* [of the dead or of the body]." (See Bynum, *The Resurrection of the Body*, p. 26.) Insofar as the Apostles' Creed implies a need for the resurrected body's material, fleshy continuity, it insists on more than the Gospels and Saint Paul (and Origen and Aquinas, for that matter) warrant. (See ibid., p. 10.) The Apostles' Creed has a significant place in the historical affirmations of the church, thus the strong agapist suggests that bodily resurrection "should not be" a forced Christian belief, not that it "has not been." Moreover, this suggestion is not motivated by a Docetic or Gnostic conviction that resurrection must be purely spiritual/psychic; again, the agapist would avoid all dogmatic formulations of what and even whether postmortem resurrection must be.

[38] Lord Tennyson, "Crossing the Bar," in *Selected Poems and Idylls of the King*, ed. by Myra Reynolds (Chicago and New York: Scott, Foresman, 1913), p. 356.

from the dead, in part to express its conviction that God had vindicated the life and teaching of the man Jesus and to announce its loyalty to and imitation of Jesus as Yahweh's Messiah. To the extent, however, that the Resurrection was meant to remove the sting of Jesus' unexpected and "shameful" death, it tempts us today to ignore or belittle the cross. If the cross cannot be accepted on its own terms, as a sign of love's willing yet costly sacrifice, then we still need to forgive ourselves and others for being fallible and dependent and/or to forgive God for creating a world in which people are what they are.

As noted, Jesus permits and even recommends seeking "reward" from God and storing up "treasure in heaven," but we must not forget that the Lord does not give the way the world does. "Peace I leave with you; my peace I give to you. I do not give to you as the world gives. Do not let your hearts be troubled, and do not let them be afraid" (John 14:27). To be delivered from fear and to experience the forgiveness of sins (both as forgiver and forgiven) is already to know eternity. Whether and how "this perishable body must put on imperishability, and this mortal body must put on immortality" (1 Cor. 15:53), the logic of a truly fearless and forgiving *agape* does not definitively establish. Like the early church, we are still trying to determine a suitable ending to Mark, the oldest Gospel. Do we end with Mark 16:8 and the mysteriously empty tomb, with the resurrection appearances of Jesus a mere promise, or do we include the highly didactic and likely redactional 16:9–20? I would only observe that a dogmatic insistence on immortality as the necessary consequence of or rationale for forgiveness quickly dilutes *agape* by entangling it in economies of exchange.

May We/Must We Forgive God?

Now we come to one of the most difficult questions of all: May we/must we forgive God? Even if free human beings perpetrate sins and must be held accountable for them, how could God *permit* the magnitude of moral evils we see throughout history? And what of diseases and natural disasters not attributable to human agency: earthquakes, floods, famines, and the like? Echoing God's question to Jonah, do we do well to be angry with God over such things?

Consider this true story from the *San Jose Mercury News.* A nine-year-old girl comes home to find her two younger brothers playing in the backyard with their father's shotgun. Surprised to find it out of its case, she fears that the gun might be loaded, so she rushes to take it from them. While she is carrying it back to the house, the family dog jumps up on her and knocks her down; as she falls, the shotgun slips from her hands, hits the ground, discharges, and blows her younger brother's head off. What makes this actual event so horrible is not just the grisly death but the fact that it should have resulted (however partially and indirectly) from good intentions so grossly and contingently miscarried. Can't we imagine that this girl may never be able to forgive herself? Don't we fear that she may never be able to accept herself (or others) because of her "dirty hands"? Needn't she forgive her father for carelessly leaving a dangerous weapon accessible to children? Might it be necessary for her even *to forgive God* for creating a world in which such a tragedy can occur?

Or consider Sophie in the novel *Sophie's Choice*, forced by a Nazi officer to choose which of her children will be saved and which will be gassed. Must Sophie forgive God for creating the world a veil of tears where people can be undone in this way? Even if one judges, commonsensically, that the Holocaust was perpetrated by free human beings rather than directly by God, is it right nevertheless to be angry with God for permitting such evil (cf. Jonah 4:9)? I side with those who hold it better to live in a world where freedom and guilt (hence forgiveness) are possible, than in one where they are not. I accept as an article of faith, that is, that the finite freedom on which forgiveness trades has a point. Yet the complaint of Ivan Karamazov over the suffering of one innocent child rings in one's ears. Is freedom worth it? The free will defense, the appeal to human responsibility, only goes so far in "accounting for" evil. Calamity is the result of both human malevolence and natural accident, and theodicies or anthropodicies that would explain away affliction are false consolations.[39]

With what, then, are we left? Even though God, the Holy One of Israel, is not culpable, as such, it is appropriate to hold God to the divine promises of love and justice. And this means learning how to lament.[40] Many of us have largely forgotten how to rend our garments and have a knock-down argument with God over the ills of the world, including our own. Perhaps we have never really learned how to sit on the mourning bench as or with Job, feeling or sharing pain without denying it. It is ultimately more faithful to beseech (and assist) God to make the divine justice and mercy manifest than to claim that the Deity is somehow beyond human accosting or that the world is fine as it is.[41] God's essential depths remain a mystery, beyond sensual desire and rational discernment, but partial revelations are possible. If we consciously deny our alienation

---

[39] See *Love Disconsoled*, pp. 169–74.

[40] See Nicholas Wolterstorff, *Lament for a Son* (Grand Rapids: Eerdmans, 1987).

[41] See chap. 2, "Is God Just?" and compare David R. Blumenthal, *Facing the Abusing God: A Theology of Protest* (Louisville: Westminster/John Knox, 1993).

from God, we will likely either unconsciously blame God for what is genuinely our fault, and thus not admit our need for mercy, or unconsciously blame others for what is really no one's fault, and thus not admit their innocence (cf. the parable of the vineyard).

Both Job and the author of Lamentations knew that anger is something that has to be worked through, however fitfully, in cries before God that eventually become dialogues with God:

> The LORD has become like an enemy; he has destroyed Israel; He has destroyed all its palaces, laid in ruins its strongholds, and multiplied in daughter Judah mourning and lamentation. (Lam. 2:5)

> The thought of my affliction and my homelessness is wormwood and gall! My soul continually thinks of it and is bowed down within me. But this I call to mind, and therefore I have hope: The steadfast love of the LORD never ceases, his mercies never come to an end; they are new every morning; great is your faithfulness. "The LORD is my portion," says my soul, therefore I will hope in him. (3:19–24)

> Let us test and examine our ways, and return to the LORD. Let us lift up our hearts as well as our hands to God in heaven. We have transgressed and rebelled, and you have not forgiven. (3:40–42)

> The crown has fallen from our head; woe to us, for we have sinned! Because of this our hearts are sick, because of these things our eyes have grown dim: because of Mount Zion, which lies desolate; jackals prowl over it. But you, O LORD, reign forever; your throne endures to all generations. Why have you forgotten us completely? Why have you forsaken us these many days? Restore us to yourself, O LORD, that we may be restored; renew our days as of old—unless you have utterly rejected us, and are angry with us beyond measure. (5:16–22)

Note in these representative passages the oscillation between accusing God and confessing human sin, between mourning and hoping, between referring to God in the third person and addressing God in the second person ("great is *your* faithfulness"), between speaking intimately in the first-person singular and declaring corporately in the first-person plural, between resigning to heartsickness and guilt and pleading in agitation for divine remembrance and renewal. All these pairs go hand in hand in learning how to forgive; they are part of the worship of a faithful God by finite people.

Isaiah, Elie Wiesel, and many of the Christian saints also know that forgiveness is a process and may take some time. The ancient progression from despair over God to hope in God does not come quickly or easily, and it is crucial to avoid false consolations that explain away suffering and sin. May we, in the end, forgive God? Yes, we might conclude paradoxically, and God will forgive us even this.

CONCLUSION: THE AESTHETICS OF FORGIVENESS

My concluding thesis on forgiving is: *(5) Forgiveness is a seeing with our third eye, "beyond the frontier of guilt and shame,"* [42] *as well as a being seen by God*. Anger in the aggrieved is often justified, even as expiation from the aggrieving is often constructive, but there is never an obligation *not* to forgive. Rather than an external turning of the other cheek, forgiveness is a denial of cheek altogether. A forgiving love is stronger than any principle of retaliation in kind, more generous than any rational justice. Even if temporarily indignant, it is, with the aid of providence, never hateful. Becoming self-consciously hateful would be an unforgivable sin: the refusal both to give and to receive forgiveness itself. Such a refusal denies the witness of the third eye, that inner ability to stand apart from our thoughts and deeds, as well as those of our enemies, and to see the universal need for redemption. Since all are in need of mercy, to eschew forgiveness is to reject a necessary condition for one's own well-being. To despise oneself in this way is blindness, not merely a dimming of one's own moral vision but a denial of God's oversight of the world. In turning the heart from hate and leaving vengeance to the Lord, one is, in a sense, turning a "blind eye" to wrong. But this is not the blindness of ignorance or indifference; it is a seeing with the spiritual eye of forgiveness even when it "overlooks" faults.

I know of no better pictorial representation of forgiving mildness and its relation to moral vision than Hieronymus Bosch's "Christ before Pilate" (1513–1515).[43] In that work (figure 1), Jesus is surrounded by nine beastial tormentors, and his eyes are cast downward, almost closed. Patience before affliction has made him resigned but not resentful, even as detachment from mercy has caused those around him to degenerate into brutality. The only persons looking directly at Jesus are Pilate (lower right), who is about to wash his hands, and a crude figure evidently about to take a bite out of the back of the Savior's head (upper left). All the rest are either dour or blasé and quite inhuman looking; some with multiple nose- or earrings; many with bizarre paramilitary garb; and all with piti-

---

[42] Michael Ignatieff, *The Needs of Strangers* (New York: Penguin, 1984), p. 71.

[43] Though "Christ before Pilate" is usually attributed to Bosch, both the date and the painter of this oil and tempera work are disputed. In what follows, I write as an ethicist making phenomenological observations rather than as an art historian making empirical claims, thus this dispute is largely irrelevant for my purposes.

Bosch's *Christ before Pilate, 1513–1515*. Princeton University, McCormick Art Museum.

less, distorted features. It is as though to fail to see or be seen by the long-suffering Christ reduces individuals to animality or mechanism. Such is the power of love's gaze, the opposite of the evil eye.

It is tempting to equate "Christ before Pilate" with "Christian Charity before Social Justice," but the "justice" portrayed would be perverse, an image of judgment without wisdom or compassion. Pilate looks with a jaundiced appraisive eye on Christ's innocence (cf. Luke 23:14), and he attempts to assuage his conscience by denying responsibility for Christ's impending death (cf. Matt. 27:24). Pilate sees the holy victim, but he is evasive. The would-be cannibal is also not merely oblivious: he responds to Christ's visible presence with a basic, if rough, form of communion. "If . . . you bite and devour one another," Paul warns the church at Galatia, "take care that you are not consumed by one another" (Galatians 5:15). Jesus himself invites the world to "eat my flesh and drink my blood" (John 6:54) and thus to undo the disastrous eating in the Garden that leads to death. Indeed, although Bosch is pre-Trent, his Christ holds the thumb and index finger of his right hand pinched together, as the priest does after the consecration in the Tridentine mass.[44] Thus Christ celebrates the sacrament of others' salvation, offering without recrimination his body as bread. Pilate washes his hands without eating, while the cannibal would eat cruelly, but Jesus' forgiving mildness still touches these two souls, however briefly and incompletely. Their actions lead the spectator to suspect that, on some level, they both see that not internalizing Christ's innocence leads to consuming oneself and others with guilt. This distinguishes them from those in the painting almost entirely animal because morally unseeing and unseen.

Christ's suffering is real and profound, but it seems remarkably free of bitterness; his face is characterized by a tolerant, if somber, forbearance. Bosch's Jesus is saddened by the self-destructive sinfulness of others rather than moved to hatred or vengefulness by his own pain. Rather than resentment, in short, Bosch depicts the eternal beauty of Christ's forgiveness.

Some remarks by Nietzsche, the master psychologist of *ressentiment*, are germane here. In *The Gay Science*, Nietzsche writes:

> I do not want to wage war against what is ugly. I do not want to accuse; I do not want even to accuse those who accuse. *Looking away* shall be my only negation. And all in all and on the whole: some day I wish to be only a Yes-sayer. Let us stop thinking so much about punishing, reproaching, and improving others! . . . Let us rather raise ourselves that much higher. Let us color our own example ever more brilliantly. Let our brilliance make them look dark. No, let us not become darker ourselves on their account, like all those who punish others and feel dissatisfied. Let us sooner step aside. Let us look away.[45]

Nietzsche associates his "Yes-saying" refusal to reproach with love of fate (*amor fati*), while Jesus' forgiving mildness expresses his love of God and neighbor (*agape*). But the dynamics of "looking away" are similar in both cases: rather than be diminished by hatred and vengeance, the strong soul "raises higher" and "refuses to become darker" in response to attackers. The looking away is a form of negation, of critique, but especially in Christ's case, this is intended positively to lift others up as well. (Nietzsche seems primarily concerned here with not being dragged down by others, Jesus with building them up.) Ideally, to see Christ look away

---

[44] I owe this observation to Michael Sherwin, O.P.

[45] Friedrich Nietzsche, *The Gay Science*, trans. by Walter Kaufmann (New York: Vintage Books, 1974), Book Four, Sections 276 and 321, pp. 223 and 254. These passages are cited by Michael S. Moore in "The Moral Worth of Retribution," in *Responsibility, Character, and the Emotions*, ed. by Ferdinand Schoeman (Cambridge: Cambridge University Press, 1987), p. 192.

from others, especially from oneself, is to have conscience pricked. In Bosch, indeed, not to see or be seen by the Suffering Servant is not to see, and ultimately not to be, oneself.[46]

Before the disciples and the Romans, both of whom want superhuman control of the world, Christ slowly turns himself into elemental bread and wine. Onlookers must either eat, acknowledging their own animality and sinfulness, or avert their eyes in self-denial. The irony is that the denial of needy finitude, the refusal of apparent cannibalism in turning away from the eucharistic Son of Man, makes one still more inhuman.[47] We torture and murder others because we cannot admit that we fear our own vulnerability and mortality.[48] Another irony, of course, is that by accepting, then sacrificing, his life, Christ proves himself divine. In forgiving sin, he fully shows his sinlessness (Luke 23:34). To fail to see Christ as he is, in turn, is to fail to see oneself as one is or could be: a person before God. Blindness to incarnate beauty, Bosch implies, makes one infinitely ugly.

Perhaps the most singular achievement of Bosch's "Christ before Pilate" is that the observer views the monstrosities encircling Jesus with a measure of compassion rather than mere offense. The bizarre and villainous figures are troubling, but they are also oddly compelling: oneself writ large. In still being able to recognize herself in the "comforters," even if they cannot recognize themselves, the viewer's conscience is humanized by grace. All of us are some degree of monster, one sees, wanting forgiveness.

[46] In the youthful Bosch work, "The Seven Deadly Sins" (ca. 1475), hardened sinners are eyed by a judging (but not mocking) Son. In what is often thought of as Bosch's mature Passion sequence—"The Crowning with Thorns" (1508–1509), a second "The Crowning with Thorns" (ca. 1510), "Christ before Pilate" (1513–1515), and "The Bearing of the Cross" (1515–1516)—sinners are rendered increasingly hardened by not watching, and not being watched by, one and the same Son. See Robert L. Delevoy, *Bosch* (New York: Rizzoli, 1990), pp. 53–64. Wilhelm Fraenger held "The Bearing of the Cross" to be painted prior to the second "The Crowning with Thorns," due to the "calm nobility" attained in the latter; see Fraenger, *Hieronymus Bosch* (New York: Dorset Press, 1989), p. 221. I follow Delevoy's dating, however, which is agreed to by Cinotti but rejected by others.

[47] For more on these general subjects, see William Arens, *The Man-Eating Myth: Anthropology and Anthropophagy* (Oxford: Oxford University Press, 1979), esp. pp. 160–161; and Maggie Kilgour, *From Communion to Cannibalism: An Anatomy of Metaphors of Incorporation* (Princeton: Princeton University Press, 1990), esp. chaps. II and III. Neither Arens nor Kilgour discusses Bosch.

[48] As Ernest Becker writes in *The Denial of Death* (New York: The Free Press, 1973), p. 149: "only scapegoats can relieve one of his stark fear of death: 'I am threatened with death—let us kill plentifully.'"

FIVE
Abortion and an Ethic of Care

Why should I joy in any abortive birth?
—William Shakespeare[1]

Any death that results from predictable and avoidable damage
to a body—whether from war, poverty, social neglect, or
individual abandonment—is a violation of birth's hope.
Precisely because of its commitment to beginnings, its basis
in trust, the concept of "natality" grasps the betrayal in
violent death.
—Sara Ruddick[2]

I came that they may have life, and have it abundantly.
—Jesus (John 10:10)

The issue of abortion highlights many of the tensions surrounding "love" and "justice" with which I have been concerned in this book. If one defines justice, for political and legal purposes, as the public adjudication of the interest-based rights of self-conscious agents, for instance, then the implications for abortion are clear. Since fetuses are not agents with intentional life plans, the necessary condition for having interests, their protection is not a matter of justice. Their parents may choose to value and nurture their lives, but this is a matter of individual preference, an act of political supererogation, and should not be coerced at law. Because the liberal state is commissioned only to uphold justice between self-aware persons, a matter of what I will call "personal dignity," it should not use its monopoly on the legitimate use of force to compel controversial judgments about "impersonal" goods, such as the "sanctity" of human life in utero. The needs and potentials of early human life may suggest to some its intrinsic value, the argument goes, but given that there is no consensus on this point, the laws of a democratic nation must remain neutral and not preclude abortion, at least most of the time.[3] In sum, all three Lockean rights—to life, liberty, and property—apply only to citizens who have acquired self-consciousness.

[1] Shakespeare, *Love's Labors Lost*, spoken by Berowne, act I, scene i, line 104.
[2] Ruddick, "The Rationality of Care," in *Women, Militarism, and War*, ed. by Jean Bethke Elshtain and Sheila Tobias (Savage, Md.: Rowman and Littlefield, 1990), p. 248.
[3] Ronald Dworkin approximates this view in *Life's Dominion: An Argument about Abor-

Within an American tradition that would limit the power of the state, the claim that the province of political-legal justice is achieved dignity, not intrinsic sanctity, is a powerful one. Such an understanding of justice is naturally associated with a privatized picture of agapic love. If justice is limited to the safeguarding of interest-based rights, then love is thought to be concerned with meeting private needs or pursuing idiosyncratic ideals. Love may care for and cultivate the potentials of prenatal lives, but these highly dependent lives are outside the bounds of the political community and its legal protection of autonomous persons. The possibility of a just hope for individuals, as well as of their unjust betrayal, awaits the dawn of robust self-awareness, which is commonly associated with birth or beyond. A Shakespearian concern over "abortive *birth*" is entirely prospective, on this view, flinching at Ruddick's "violent death" only when this is postnatal. A more retrospective concern over birth itself being aborted—call this "abortive *conception*"—may be one of love's labors, but it is not a matter of political-legal justice.

It is my contention in this chapter that the above accounts of love and justice tell an inadequate story about human existence, both individually and collectively. A political-legal ethic of dignity that would attend only to justice between persons must prove both unjust and unloving, precisely because it neglects the dependency and vulnerability of "nonpersons." All finite persons were once nonpersons, in the sense of preautonomous human lives growing and learning, and many finite persons will again be nonpersons, in the sense of post-autonomous human lives aged and declining. The trajectory of human life—from embryo to fetus to newborn to child to adult to elderly to senile—is altogether predictable. To deny this trajectory, or to make only a portion of it subject to legal protections, is to blind ourselves to who we are and what we require. As Eva Feder Kittay has written,

> Interdependence begins with dependence. It begins with the dependency of an infant, and often ends with the dependency of a very ill or frail person close to dying. . . . at some point there is a dependency that is not yet or no longer an interdependency. By excluding *this* dependency from social and political concerns, we have been able to fashion the pretense that we are *independent*—that the cooperation between persons that some insist is *inter*-dependence is simply the mutual (often voluntary) cooperation between essentially independent persons.[4]

---

tion, Euthanasia, and Individual Freedom (New York: Knopf, 1993). I reply to Dworkin below; see also my "A House Divided, Again: 'Sanctity' vs. 'Dignity' in the Induced Death Debates."

[4] Kittay, *Love's Labor*, p. xii.

Relatively "independent" persons do not just happen; they require cultivation and protection, especially when very young. Any society that cannot attend to this dependency will treat autonomous persons like "manna
from heaven" and thereby fail to support the necessary conditions for the
emergence of its own citizenry.

How, specifically, might these observations bear on the question of
abortion? My argument is that duties of justice (based on induced fetal
need) and duties of charity (based on essential fetal potential) ought to
make elective abortion after the first trimester both morally and legally
impermissible. In spite of the minimalism of much recent political theory,
there is ample precedent for this argument even today. Within the United
States, both state and federal governments have a recognized interest in
cultivating and defending "impersonal" human beings, including those
who are *not yet* autonomous persons (infants), those who are *no longer*
autonomous persons (the senile), and those who *never were and never
will be* autonomous persons (the profoundly retarded). All of these groups,
however marginalized, are capable of a "noncognitive well-being"[5] that is
still rightly considered part of the common good. Equal protection under
the law requires that most human fetuses also be included within the
community of those with moral and legal standing, especially when the
neediness of these fetuses has been freely brought into being by accountable moral agents.

As just noted, one can still appeal to legal precedents to support an
inclusive view of community. We stand increasingly at a crossroads, however: if we are to be consistent, either we will move to a political ethic of
pure dignity and exclude *all* nonpersons from the legal community, or we
will acknowledge that the sanctity of human life that has traditionally
been honored by law must also (again) make fetuses the proper subject of
political protection. Much of the balance of this chapter is an elaboration
and defense of the latter course, of a restrictive abortion policy inspired
by a broad understanding of love and justice.

I am well aware that this attempt at a moral and legal reform of abortion policy is no small order in a pluralistic, democratic culture. The Roman Catholic hierarchy considers direct abortions "abominable," even
"unspeakable";[6] many in liberal societies judge them an inalienable
"right," even a "liberation";[7] and despair over compromise often prevails
on both sides. This despair is premature, however. A biblical faith will

[5] I take the phrase "noncognitive well-being" from Stephen G. Post, *The Moral Challenge of Alzheimer Disease* (Baltimore: Johns Hopkins University Press, 1995), p. 9.
[6] See Pope Paul VI, "Respect for Life in the Womb," in *On Moral Medicine*, p. 599; and
"*Gaudium et Spes*," in *The Documents of Vatican II*, ed. by W. M. Abbott, S.J. (Chicago:
Follett, 1966), p. 256.
[7] Kristin Luker, *Abortion and the Politics of Motherhood* (Berkeley and Los Angeles: University of California Press, 1984), pp. 96–97.

articulate, in the end, a distinctive vision of morality. But, whatever divides us, we are all in need of personal care; all of us, no matter what our present condition, have relied on the kindness of strangers. Thus my aim is to spell out what a general ethic of care, coupled with a robust commitment to justice, means for the opposing poles on abortion. Christian faith will inform my position, at times explicitly, but it is not a necessary premise of most of my arguments.

FOUR MORAL DIMENSIONS AND EIGHT ABORTION ARGUMENTS

According to standard theory, there are three dimensions to the moral life: the character of agents, the form of actions, and the consequences of actions. The first dimension is concerned with *who* I would be if I acted with a certain disposition or out of a particular motive, and its study is called aretology—from the Greek word *arete*, meaning virtue or excellence. The second dimension is concerned with *how* I would be behaving (e.g., justly or unjustly) if I embodied a specific action, and its study is called deontology—from the Greek word *deon*, meaning duty. The third dimension is concerned with *what* I would be bringing about in the world if I pursued a distinct path, and its study is called teleology—from the Greek word *telos*, meaning end or consequence. According to religious believers, at least traditional theists, there is also a fourth dimension to the moral life: relation to God. This theological dimension is not antithetical to the other three, but it has pride of place inasmuch as the Creator's holy will defines proper character, action, and effects for creatures. At the heart of Christian ethics, for instance, are divine commands and the Imitation of Christ.

An abortion ethic that would be holistic must address each of the first three dimensions; a distinctively Christian ethic will give priority to the God who is love but also note which virtues, deeds, and consequences are humanly normative. To set the stage for my attempt to do just this, let me now briefly rehearse four specific arguments pro-choice and then follow with four responses pro-life. I will return repeatedly to the concerns raised in these eight arguments as I build my cumulative case for a specific abortion policy.

The "Pro-Choice" Case

A first pro-choice argument is character-centered, an aretological brief. It maintains that elective abortion is or can be benevolent. There can be a conflict of caring[8] in which abortion is sought not out of a flight from personal responsibility or a denial of impersonal value but as an expres-

---

[8] The phrase "conflict of caring" is taken from Noddings, *Caring*, p. 13.

sion of personal care. "How do I, as a single mother, best attend to the two children I already have?" "Especially given that I am unemployed, who has a greater claim on my limited resources of care, my born family or my unborn fetus?" "Might not the future misery of this unwanted child itself justify me in ending its life now—'liberating' it from pain and want—while still in the womb?"

Beyond such concern for others, the option of abortion may also be seen as indispensable to women coming to care for and about *themselves*: elective abortion as an instance of proper *self*-love. Procuring an abortion may be a courageous affirmation of a woman's own worth and claim to respect, the argument continues, a breaking free from repressive stereotypes based on biology and rigid and/or unfair expectations about motherhood. Carol Gilligan describes several real-life examples of how concern for others and taking responsibility for oneself can combine in abortion decisions. Josie, "a seventeen-year-old," is quoted thus: "I came to this decision that I was going to have an abortion because I realized how much responsibility goes with having a child."[9] "Another adolescent" says: "Abortion, if you do it for the right reasons, is helping yourself to start over and do different things."[10]

A second pro-choice argument is deontological. It contends that the autonomy of persons trumps any rights or needs of the pre-personal. The dignity of already existing agents, their right to set and execute their own life plans, is far more weighty morally than any value that can be assigned to fetuses. Because fetal life is un-self-conscious, it has no interest-based rights and thus no legal (and little moral) standing. In particular, to compel a woman to carry an unwanted pregnancy to term is to subordinate her self-determination to the bare biological animation of a life growing inside her. This is an unjust denial of the mother's interest in expressing her own personal integrity via free and heartfelt choices. The dignity associated with self-governance may even override another person's need for life support. As F. M. Kamm puts it, summarizing various "liberal" proposals, "abortion may be permissible to end many pregnancies, even if the fetus is a person, simply because the woman does not wish to share her body or undertake parental responsibilities that cannot be shifted to others."[11]

A third pro-choice argument is teleological. It holds that social utility is served by permitting, if not encouraging, elective abortions. A host of goods—from eugenics, to population control, to women's liberation—is

---

[9] Gilligan, *In a Different Voice*, p. 76.

[10] Ibid., p. 78.

[11] Kamm, *Creation and Abortion: A Study in Moral and Legal Philosophy* (New York and Oxford: Oxford University Press, 1992), p. 166.

promoted when women (if not men) have the option of terminating pregnancies. By keeping abortions "safe and legal," we help avoid the "bad old days" of back alley procedures and unwanted children. In addition, we help avoid unchecked infant deformity and retardation, on the one hand, and spiraling overpopulation, on the other.

On the relation between unrestricted abortion rights and women's liberation, Beverly Harrison is especially uncompromising. She argues that promoting the well-being of women is a moral obligation and that abortion-on-demand is essential to that well-being. She asks, in effect, for a kind of moral affirmative action with regard to abortion: because women's self-respect, as well as procreative choice, have been and continue to be so stifled, it is appropriate to give them the option of elective abortion, although the option is admittedly morally ambiguous. A woman facing the abortion decision is, in Harrison's words, "the most affected party," thus she has the right to be "the moral decision maker."[12] In making the decision, moreover, the woman will be socially empowered, liberated if only slightly from the dead hand of the male-chauvinist past.[13]

A fourth pro-choice argument is theological/biblical. It observes that Scripture is largely silent on the status of fetal life, but that Exodus 21:22–25 evidently draws a qualitative distinction between the fetus and the mother. A woman caused to miscarry must be compensated for the loss of her unborn child, but the induced miscarriage is clearly not equated with the murder of a full-fledged person. Thus, the argument runs, life in the womb is not to be seen as falling (directly) under the "Thou shalt not kill/murder" commandment and its related punishments.

The "Pro-Life" Rejoinder

My first pro-life argument is again aretological. It counters the first pro-choice brief by maintaining that the direct taking of an innocent human life will tend to brutalize the soul of the killer, regardless of any benevolent motive that may seem to be involved. The premise here is the Augustinian one, referred to in chapter 3, that an intentional assault on innocent human life carries with it psychological dynamics that are finally antithetical to charity. To will the death of a fetus is to despise its life, the argument runs, and to despise a life is incompatible with willing its good. If one acts to abort a nascent life ostensibly in order better to care for oneself or others, this is (self-deceptively) doing evil that good might come. One need not think that all direct abortions of healthy fetuses are

---

[12] Harrison, *Our Right to Choose*, p. 226.
[13] Cf. Luker, *Abortion and the Politics of Motherhood*, esp. chap. 5.

prideful or self-consciously malevolent to hold that they are tragically destructive of virtue.

A second pro-life argument is again deontological. It acknowledges the importance of autonomy for persons, as well as the dependency and lack of development of fetuses. The argument insists, nevertheless, that certain exercises of personal autonomy carry moral duties in their train. Specifically, freely to engage in sexual intercourse is seen to entail an implicit promise to nurture any life that might result from that intercourse. To *induce* then *neglect* the dependency of the fetus, even when that fetus was or is "unwanted," is to commit an injustice to another human life. Even though only actual persons can be the *subjects* of promises, potential persons can be the *objects* of the correlative obligations. Think of our responsibilities to future generations and the implicit Lockean pledge that when we use natural resources today we will leave "enough and as good" for those who come after us. To aver that only extant persons have rights and duties, including the right to life, is to deny to others the necessary conditions for personhood that one has enjoyed oneself. It is to embrace, unfairly, what has been called the "winner take all" view of autonomous agency.

A third pro-life argument is again teleological. It takes a very different view of what consequences are likely to result from unrestricted abortion. The thesis here is that social utility is served via expanding the bounds of the moral community to include such "pre-persons" as the unborn, rather than by circling our legal wagons exclusively around healthy adults. Both women and men will tend to benefit, the argument runs, when we honor the sanctity of all human beings and refuse to pit personal liberty against fetal life. The personal only grows out of the fetal, and any society that does not sustain support for early stages of human existence will jeopardize all others. Even if eugenics or population control or women's liberation appears to be served, in the short run, by liberal abortion policies, the long-term costs are too heavy. The general erosion of regard for the weak and dependent implies that the ends don't justify the means. Neither men nor women can be encouraged to take responsibility for their lives and those of their (born) children by permitting the objectification-unto-death of the unborn. If the best of feminism stands for a principle akin to *agape*, then, as Sidney Callahan has written, "women can never achieve the fulfillment of feminist goals in a society permissive toward abortion."[14]

A fourth pro-life argument is again theological/biblical. It points out that, even though Scripture seldom if ever explicitly discusses the morality of abortion, its overall picture of human life is as a good gift (and

---

[14] Callahan, "Abortion and the Sexual Agenda: A Case for Pro-Life Feminism," in *On Moral Medicine*, p. 623.

responsibility) from God rather than a personal possession. The faithfulness that emerges from Abraham to Mary to Jesus is one that welcomes children as an inviolable mystery. Abraham's signal achievement, on this reading, is to overcome child-sacrifice,[15] even as Jesus treats the innocence and vulnerability of children as something due emulation and special consideration. Furthermore, the Bible is not completely silent on the status of the fetus. Psalm 139:13–16 and Jeremiah 1:5 suggest that God cares for the unborn even in their mothers' wombs. Although humans may be blind to the sanctity of developing life, born and unborn, God attends to it with solicitous power.

THE ABIDING CONTOURS OF THE DEBATE

What do these two sets of arguments tell us about the abortion debate? The best of the pro-life position appreciates that personal care is crucial for humanity. It stresses that unearned care is required to nurture inchoate lives into maturity and thus that elective abortion, in particular, threatens a basic human need. Such abortion thwarts an essential potential from which all members of the moral community have sprung, hence any social policy that would condone this practice appears abominable in assaulting a vulnerable and dependent human nature at its root. The problem, moreover, is not simply that fetal life is destroyed in abortion; the thesis of many conservatives is that the social capacity of adults (including women) to care for others and themselves is often profoundly damaged by resort to elective abortion. The best of the more liberal stance, on the other hand, recognizes that individuals already born also require personal care and that, in our society, women continue to be the primary infant-care-givers. Social policy, many who are pro-choice argue, ought to liberate women from an inordinate burden of care and facilitate the whole of society's willing nurturance of individuals already outside the womb. To insist, legally or medically, that women carry fetuses to term, against their will, is to intrude on a matter that is best left to individual conscience and to guarantee that women remain second-class citizens, tied coercively to childbearing and childrearing.

The underlying issue in the abortion debate, then, is primarily a disagreement over the meaning and scope of charity[16]—what does it require of us, and who shall give it and who receive it?—rather than over the relative moral weights of life and choice *in abstracto*. This is not to say

---

[15] See "Is Isaac Our Neighbor?" chap. 5 in my *Love Disconsoled*.

[16] As noted previously, I treat "personal care," "loving care," "charity," and "love" as synonymous. The *New Testament* Greek word *agape* is a more technical noun, suggesting to some a distinctively Christian excellence, but it has sufficiently deep resonances with the more generic terms to be interchangeable with them.

that the quest for a just balance of these competing goods (vitality and autonomy) is irrelevant or that the formulation of moral criteria for occasionally selecting between them is somehow patriarchal. I myself will maintain that the "consideration" represented by the induced dependency of a second-trimester fetus makes it unjust electively to take its life. But in modern contexts justice is largely concerned to distribute preexisting goods between persons, while care, in being productive of personal worth, is the antecedent and (in some ways) superior concern. Thus I make the case in this chapter for *an unabashedly political understanding of love.* Justice (defined as giving each person his or her due) is an indispensable social virtue, but an ethic of loving care attends to the relational needs and potentials of all human beings (welfare rights) rather than exclusively to the autonomous claims of mature persons (liberty rights). Life and choice themselves depend on charity, as does the language of "rights," since without loving care human beings would not emerge or survive as rights-bearers.[17]

The basic issue is not whether to embrace *either* Pauline faith, hope, and love *or* Lockean life, liberty, and property. So baldly put, that is a false dichotomy, although it is sometimes endorsed by both Christian sectarians and secular liberals. Atheism is a possible, but not a mandatory, corollary to democratic sentiments. Certainly no would-be democracy should accept the thesis that the public expression of a robustly "metaphysical" morality is impermissible in a just society.[18] Some substantive

---

[17] Kittay admirably articulates the priority of love, in both private and public contexts:

Principles of right and traditional notions of justice depend upon a prior and more fundamental principle and practice of care. Without practices based on an implicit principle of care, human beings would either not survive or they would survive very poorly—and surely would not thrive. A political theory must attend to the well-being of dependents *and* of their caregivers, and also to the *relation* of caregiver and dependent upon which all other civic unions depend. A principle of care, then, must hold that: In order to grow, flourish, and survive or endure illness, disability, and frailty, each individual requires a caring relationship with significant others who hold that individual's well-being as a primary responsibility and a primary good.

See *Love's Labor,* p. 108. Kittay's is the best—most informed, intelligent, and heartfelt—analysis I know of both sides of the caring nexus, including the ways in which women have shouldered an unacknowledged and unfair burden of dependency work. Although she does not elaborate the reasons why, Kittay does not wish her remarks to be interpreted as support for a pro-life/anti-abortion position (p. 60); for my part, I argue that an ethic of care (partially captured in the phrase "preservative love") does militate for a more restrictive abortion policy than is now the law of the land in the United States. Caregivers (e.g., expectant mothers) deserve much more social support than they currently receive, and no abortion policy can be blind to the gender inequities of a sexist society. Nevertheless, fetuses are among those vulnerable and needy individuals whose neglect or arbitrary killing is unjust: neither feticide nor infanticide is simply a "private" matter beyond the scope of moral reflection and legal regulation.

[18] For a detailed defense of these claims, see my "To Bedlam and Part Way Back" and "The Return of the Prodigal?"

claims about human nature and community will be made, and must be defended, by any adequate social philosophy. The key issue in abortion contexts and elsewhere is not Saint Paul versus John Locke but, rather, how faith, hope, and love, however construed, *bear on* our understanding of life, liberty, and property. To whom does a just love require us to extend the right to life? Is our highest faith to be in human liberty? May we hope for a form of society in which no human being—young or old, male or female, black or white, rich or poor, gifted or handicapped—is treated as property? These questions are not merely legitimate within the public square—they are crucial.

THE TRAJECTORY OF HUMAN LIFE: A SHARED CONTINUUM

In *The Unborn Patient*, Michael R. Harrison, M.D., writes:

> The fetus could not be considered a [medical] patient until it was de-mystified; until the origin and development of the fetus from embryo to neonate could be explained scientifically. It is only with the development of molecular biology in the last century that we have been able to bridge the conceptual gap between the seed and the fully developed and marvelously complex human infant, between subcellular events like DNA-direted enzyme synthesis and subsequent complex biologic functions like the digestion of food. Modern molecular biology provided the conceptual framework for linking the seed to the infant: The seed contains a microscopic blueprint encoded in DNA for the future individual.[19]

If comparatively recent biology has made it possible to relate, with increasing specificity, the unfolding narrative of a human life, that narrative, in turn, must inform our reflections on the morality of abortion. There is as of now no consensus, morally: the inchoate status of the fetus, which for some justifies the elective termination of its life, for many others suggests that such abortion is a grave wrong, the premature silencing of a life story. But there is emerging clarity, biologically, and the relevant descriptive data must fund our normative judgments.[20] Let me now describe the trajectory of human life from conception to birth, thus raising the unavoidable question of the status of the fetus in relation to its mother, father, and the wider society. Modern science is often faulted by conservative thinkers for "disenchanting" the world, thus rendering respectful

---

[19] See Michael R. Harrison, Mark I. Evans, N. Scott Adzick, and Wolfgang Holzgreve, eds., *The Unborn Patient: The Art and Science of Fetal Therapy* (Philadelphia: W. B. Saunders, 2001), chap. 2, p. 14.

[20] I leave aside the endlessly debated question of the exact relation between "is" and "ought." Empirical observations may seldom if ever deductively entail ethical conclusions, but the former are clearly relevant to the latter. It matters for our moral treatment of another, for example, whether she is sentient, can suffer, will grow, and so on.

cultural practices unstable or absurd; however, that same science's "de-mystification" of embryonic and fetal development actually renders reverence for all human life more plausible rather than less, I believe, because it highlights both the complexity and the continuity of that development.

At conception, the two haploid germ cells, sperm and egg, merge to form the diploid conceptus. From the moment of fertilization, the sex and many other genetic traits of the offspring are determined. Barring twinning, the genotype is fixed and unique, with twenty-three chromosomes from the father and twenty-three from the mother together providing "all the genetic information needed for the new individual."[21] During the first four days, the conceptus ("pre-embryo") begins to divide and travel down the fallopian tube, usually being sixteen cells large when it reaches the uterus. At the beginning of the second week (the seventh to eighth day after conception), the fertilized egg implants in the wall of the uterus, and subsequently the placenta begins to develop. With implantation, we have an "embryo" properly so-called. At the start of the third week, the embryo is approximately 1.5 millimeters in length and its cells begin to differentiate. "The beating heart primordium appears between days 22 and 24 [post-conception] as the first intraembryonic functioning organ."[22] Between four and eight weeks, the various other organ systems also begin to emerge, together with arm and leg buds and inchoate eyes, ears, mouth, and nose. The spine and vertebrae appear as well. By the end of the eighth week, there is a readily measurable heartbeat and blood circulation, and all internal organs are present in emergent form, as are hands, fingers, and toes. As Nilsson and Hamberger put it, "The design work is complete; all [the embryo's] organs have been formed."[23] At the start of the ninth week, what was previously called an "embryo" is now called a "fetus."[24]

"The transformation of an embryo to a fetus is gradual," Moore and Persaud observe, "but the name change is meaningful because it signifies that the embryo has developed into a recognizable human being."[25] As

[21] Lennart Nilsson and Lars Hamberger, *A Child Is Born*, trans. by Clare James (New York: Dell, 1990), p. 185.

[22] Jan E. Jirasek, *An Atlas of the Human Embryo and Fetus* (New York and London: Parthenon, 2001), p. 9.

[23] Nilsson and Hamberger, *A Child Is Born*, p. 92.

[24] This number is in terms of "fertilization" or "actual" age, which begins counting from conception. "Menstrual" age, in contrast, begins counting from the woman's last menstrual period. Assuming that conception took place two weeks after the onset of the last menstrual period, fertilization age is two weeks ahead of the traditional menstrual figures, that is, menstrual age is two weeks greater than fertilization age. For more on the two, often confusing, methods of dating, see Bruce M. Carlson, *Human Embryology and Developmental Biology* (St. Louis: Mosby, 1999), p. 22.

[25] Keith L. Moore and T.V.N. Persaud, *The Developing Human: Clinically Oriented Embryology* (Philadelphia: W. B. Saunders, 1993), p. 93.

Jan Jirasek notes, "The fetal face is human in appearance. . . . On the fingers and toes, nail plates are distinct. In the early fetus, well-defined volar pads on the fingers and toes precede differentiation of dermal ridges. Depending upon the location of the volar pads, highly individual dermatoglyphic patterns [i.e., fingerprints] acquire their characteristics."[26] By the end of the ninth week, the fetus weighs roughly 8 grams and is about 50 millimeters long. Other significant benchmarks during the first trimester include: early genital development manifest by the ninth week, with the male scrotum and the female labia typically distinguishable by the end of the eleventh week after conception; brain, liver, lungs, and kidneys measurably functioning at ten to eleven weeks; all major body parts, including toenails and tooth buds, fully in place by the end of the twelfth week. At the end of week 12, the fetus is about 8.5 centimeters long and weighs roughly 45 grams. It remains small but is morphologically quite complex. From this point, fetal development continues, still more plainly, to be a matter of growth in size and strength rather than formation of new systems.

By the end of the fourth month of pregnancy, the fetal heart has a pulse rate of 120 to 160 beats per minute. Myelin appears in the spinal nerves and nerve roots, a sign of increasing development. The eyes are sensitive to light, and the body senses and reacts to cold fluids and tickling. "Shine a light on [the mother's] abdomen, and your baby shields her eyes. Make a loud noise, and she covers her ears. She can also grasp her umbilical cord and suck her thumb."[27] At the close of the fifth month, hiccups and cries may be audible; brain waves are increasingly sophisticated, and heartbeats are audible with a fetoscope. In the sixth month, the fetus nearly doubles her weight. "Her eyelids open and close, and feeble respiratory movements begin."[28] By the end of week 24, the fetus is just under 30 centimeters long and weighs just over 500 grams (1.25 lbs.). Additional benchmarks during the second trimester include traditional "quickening" at around fourteen weeks and "viability" at between twenty-three and twenty-four weeks, depending on available technology.

In the seventh month, the cerebral hemispheres of the fetus expand enormously, and sucking, grasping, and stepping reflexes are all strongly present. The available room in the uterus begins to be filled up, restricting fetal movement. By the end of the eighth month, week 32, eyebrows and head hair appear, and the right and left hemispheres of the brain

[26] Jirasek, *An Atlas of the Human Embryo and Fetus,* p. 33.
[27] Thomas Verney and Pamela Weintraub, *Nurturing the Unborn Child* (Chicago: Olmstead, 2000), p. 93. Verney and Weintraub go so far as to write: "Many experts believe that by the sixteenth week of gestation, your baby is capable of conditioned learning, rudimentary memory, and even intentional behavior" (p. 93).
[28] Ibid., p. 122.

begin working together. The fetus swallows the nutrient-rich amniotic fluid ("fetal respiration") and excretes waste fluid through the alimentary canal. During the last two months in the uterus, the baby's weight increases by almost half a pound per week, including the buildup of a protective layer of fat in the dermis. By week 35 the baby's head usually has descended into the pelvic cavity in preparation for birth. Birth normally comes at 38 weeks after conception or 40 weeks after the last normal menstrual period. "At birth, the baby's brain has hundreds of billions of nerve cells formed and developed throughout fetal life, but it is believed that, after birth, no new nerve cells arise."[29]

This developmental story suggests what is morally problematic about elective abortion. The potential for moral agency inherent in the fetus is destroyed while most vulnerable, such that the unity associated with caring personality is not simply cut short but never achieved. The narrative meaning of a life is thwarted, not merely abbreviated, the thread is unravelled, not just cut off, because the value of the fetus as potential valuer of ends is denied. This implies, somewhat paradoxically, that *the most profound protest against elective abortion is not to equate it with murder*— murder being defined as the unjust taking of an extant person's life. The distinctive horror of elective abortion consists in the fact that it makes murder impossible; it terminates the life of a dependent human being before it can become a self-conscious person with ethical (or unethical) intentions.

Extremely widespread abortion would threaten to murder murder itself, not by schooling all persons/moral agents in virtue or by protecting all persons/moral patients from vice, but by precluding nascent persons from ever becoming actual ones. Elective abortion is not murder, in the technical sense, but what makes it seem unjustifiable (even abominable) homicide to many is that it undermines the prospect of a unique identity that is due reverence precisely because precarious and unfinished. The violence of such abortion is that it assaults *im*personal or *pre*-personal value.

Other biomedical procedures have a similarly troubling connotation. As intimated, there are two possible ways to make murder impossible: first, by making all persons unfailingly respectful of one another, or second, by making all actual persons dispensable or replaceable and all potential persons immaterial or instrumental, and thus beyond both respect and disrespect. The first scenario would be a liberation, but it remains naturally inconceivable in this life; the second scenario would be an abomination, but it is being conceived of more and more these days.[30] Active

---

[29] Nilsson and Hamberger, *A Child Is Born*, p. 137.

[30] See Peter Singer's *Rethinking Life and Death: The Collapse of Our Traditional Ethics* (Oxford: Oxford University Press, 1995), pp. 210–22.

euthanasia for the dependent or disabled (even with their informed consent) would make many persons dispensable; cloning would make all persons replaceable; and elective abortion has already made most pre-persons immaterial. This is not deliverance from murder but murder raised to the second power, the death of death not as redemption of the human condition but as its denial. It is better, some reason, to live with the old-fashioned fear of murder and dread of death than to do away with their very possibility. It is better, that is, to be anxious over radical evil than to put an end to such anxiety by also terminating wonder over the primal good that is an individual human life (for theists, a life given by God).

It is tempting to argue that until an individual is born and welcomed into the community of language-users, there just is no narrative to be frustrated and thus no wrong at all associated with elective abortion. Many who emphasize the "social construction of reality" (including human identity) will reason in this way.[31] But this line of argument is overly subjectivist. Even if the argument allows that reality-construction is communal, it implies either that the stories constructed by human beings establish meaning ex nihilo, rather than discern or cultivate meaning already present (at least in potency) in the world, or that the need-based and potency-based rights of the fetus are unintelligible prior to its delivery. Both of these ideas are highly questionable. The prenatal history of a human life can be documented in great detail, and the language of "the best interests of the fetus," "fetal therapy," and "fetal care" makes perfect sense.[32] Indeed, nascent life's impersonal needs and potentials, distinct from personal intentions, are quite comprehensible from very early on in pregnancy, as are "the potential benefits and liabilities of various interventions."[33] The issue is whether these needs and potentials, and thus the benefits and liabilities, will be allowed to have moral and legal weight.[34]

---

[31] I thank Gene Outka for helping me to see this point more clearly.

[32] See Harrison, *The Unborn Patient*, chap. 1, pp. 6, 3, and 8. Harrison elaborates: "Whether the patient is inside or outside the womb, its care is a continuum that requires the expertise of physicians trained in the care of mothers and babies" (p. 3).

[33] Ibid., chap. 2, p. 16.

[34] Frank A. Chervenak and Laurence B. McCullough defend an approach that "starts with the claim that a human being does *not* always have to possess independent moral status in order to be a patient. Instead, being a patient means that one can benefit from the application of clinical skills of the physician, a form of *dependent moral status*" (*The Unborn Patient*, chap. 3, p. 21). This appears, initially, to be an acknowledgment of the intrinsic worth, yet vulnerability, of human life in utero. But they soon lose track of *who* is being benefited (or burdened) by prenatal treatment. Chervenak and McCullough go on the contend that clinical interventions aim at "a greater balance of goods over harms in the future of the human being in question" (p. 21), thus deflecting attention from the character of the fetus as such. The patienthood of a viable fetus is "a function of [its] biological and technological capacity to become a child with independent moral status," on their view, whereas

THE STATUS OF THE FETUS: RESPONDING TO DWORKIN ON VALUE AND JUSTICE

Is there any adjudication of disputes over the moral status of the fetus? While fetal status does not alone settle the issue, the morality of abortion cannot be fully appraised without considering that status—if there were no ambiguity, there would be a different moral issue—especially in light of our views on value and justice. Those pro-life tend to emphasize the genetic individuality and emerging morphology of the fetus. They point out that (barring twinning) each new life possesses, from conception on, a unique genotype and, from ten to twelve weeks into gestation (shortly after the embryo technically becomes a fetus), a heartbeat *and* a measurable brain wave. The contention is that quite early on in pregnancy there is a second party present whose worth must be weighed and weighed heavily. Those pro-choice, for their part, tend to emphasize the auton-

---

the patienthood of a previable fetus is "a function of [the] pregnant woman's autonomy to take the pregnancy to viability" (p. 21). In the case of a viable fetus, that is, what counts is the child that it can become; in the case of a previable fetus, what counts is whether the mother "has conferred the status of being a patient" (p. 23) on it by agreeing to carry it to term. But why suggest that only present or future persons can be the bases for patient helps or harms? (Do veterinarians have no animal patients, then?) Why not say that the human fetus has (some) independent moral status, here and now, because of its evolving needs and capacities?

Chervenak and McCullough believe that "a principal advantage" of their framework "is that all of the controversy about 'right to life' and the 'woman's right to control her body' is avoided, along with the gridlock these polarizing positions produce" (pp. 20–21). This belief is mistaken, however. To say that "there is no ethical obligation on the part of the pregnant woman or the physician to regard the previable fetus as a patient" (p. 23) is to say that here maternal autonomy-rights trump. To maintain, in addition, that a physician attends to the future person that a viable fetus might (but need not) become is simply to deny that even a viable fetus has a right to life. Their position makes it impossible, for instance, to talk of injuring a fetus unto death—by malpractice, say—because a dead fetus *never* matures into a person with independent moral status and only such persons can be injured. One may wrong a mother who cares about her fetus, of course, but this is not the same as wronging the fetus. Chervenak and McCullough sometimes speak of "beneficence-based obligations to the viable fetus" (p. 21), but these apply only if the mother intends not to abort it. More straightforward is their colleague Howard R. Belkin's concession that "the fetus is not a patient for its own sake" (*The Unborn Patient*, chap. 4, p. 34). Belkin emphasizes that "the interests of offspring to be free of harm caused prenatally is a completely different issue than that of the right of the fetus to complete gestation" (p. 28). Far from avoiding the fetal-life-versus-maternal-control controversy, Belkin, Chervenak, and McCullough all side with those who deny the right of *any* fetus to life. As Belkin puts it: "Prenatal duties to offspring may arise, if at all, only after a woman has decided to continue a pregnancy that she is free to terminate" (p. 35). I will try to show in the balance of this chapter why, especially in light of modern work on "the art and science of fetal therapy," this is an inappropriate stance.

omy of the mother and the radical dependence of the fetus. They point out that respect for the integrity of women requires that they have control over their own bodies (including their wombs) and that, before approximately twenty-three weeks into gestation, fetuses are not viable outside these wombs. The claim is that, because maternal rights immensely outweigh any rights a still-nascent being might have, abortion essentially concerns one "party" only and hence is a matter of personal decision for the mother.

Responding to Ronald Dworkin's recent work helps us move beyond this impasse, I believe. Dworkin has argued that only beings with conscious life (minimally, the ability to feel pain) have interests, and that having interests is a necessary condition for the possession of rights. A fetus, he allows, does not have interests, and thus is not a rights-bearer, at least not until very late in pregnancy—roughly twenty-six to thirty weeks of gestational age.[35] Hence most abortion is not an *injustice* to the fetus itself, not a violation of its rights. Abortion may be wrong on other grounds, such as the violence it does to the intrinsic value or sanctity of the terminated human life. But having intrinsic value does not require or entail having interests/rights, and one must not conflate the two in arguing about abortion. More to the point, law may attend, he contends, only to the protection of interest-based rights.

For Dworkin, even though the liberal-democratic state has an obligation to protect the rights of its citizens from being unjustly compromised, that state has no general mandate to dictate to individuals what has intrinsic value. The state does promote some intrinsic values, Dworkin concedes, as when it uses tax revenues to fund art museums or passes legislation protecting endangered animal species. But Dworkin insists that the promotion of value becomes illegitimate when it works undue hardship on a particular group or when there is no broad consensus on the value in question. How and why to respect the intrinsic value of human life, thinks Dworkin, is a religious question the answer to which must be left up to private conscience. Even if one thinks that abortion is the wicked destruction of a sacred good, the absence of a violation of rights, which are always interest-based, means that one must not appeal to the state legally to restrict the practice. This is implied by the First Amendment's separation of church and state.

I believe that Dworkin misunderstands the relation between intrinsic human value and self-conscious interests, as well as the relation between justice and rights based on extant human interests. Part of a human embryo's inherent worth stems from the fact that it can naturally come to have interests. In addition, there are rights based on *need* rather than on

---

[35] See Ronald Dworkin, *Life's Dominion* (New York: Knopf, 1993), esp. p. 18.

interest; think of the retarded and the senile. Having intrinsic value does not directly *entail* having interests; we think of a beautiful painting or sculpture as valuable (perhaps even sacred), for example, without ascribing interests to it. But human lives naturally grow into beings with interests and therefore interest-based rights, even as those rights develop across time according to the degree of maturation. Human fetuses, unlike material artifacts, have the essential potential for interests, and respecting fetal value involves, in part, anticipating the interests (and related rights) that will grow out of that potential. One way in which we honor early human life, in other words, is as a future-interest-based-rights-bearer. The intrinsic value of fetuses may even be a necessary (but not a sufficient) condition for interest-rights.

Dworkin affirms "that human life has objective, intrinsic value that is quite independent of its personal value to anyone."[36] He explicitly rejects a subjectivism that holds that nothing is valuable save what people want and an instrumentalism that would reduce all goodness to its usefulness to persons.[37] Nevertheless, his position leaves one wondering how abortion can be seen as a harm *to the fetus itself.* Lack of consciousness seems to imply lack of both personal interests and individual vulnerability. Electively killing a twenty-five-week-old fetus seems rather like willfully marring an exquisite diamond or elegant vase given one as a gift: an aesthetic sin, but not something the liberal state may prohibit. Dworkin avers that "the thought of [one of Rembrandt's self-portraits'] being destroyed horrifies us—seems to us a terrible desecration— . . . not just because or even if that would cheat us of experiences we desire to have."[38] He is aware, of course, that "a painting is not a person,"[39] but the appeal to aesthetic categories to explain the sanctity of human life is dangerous. The pope would not have harmed *The Last Judgment* had he cut off Michelangelo's commission halfway through the painting of it, for the work of art has no conative *telos*, even if it has inherent worth. It does not grow, essentially, into and out of needs and interests. Fetuses are different, however.

When Dworkin writes that "the point of laws banning abortion is not to prevent murder but to protect a public sense of the inherent value of life,"[40] the solipsistic temptation is manifest. What are we most centrally protecting: the public sense (us adults) or the inherent value (the fetus)? For all his sensitivity to the issues surrounding life and death, one suspects that a philosopher's valorization of the cognitive is at work here,

[36] Ibid., p. 67.
[37] Ibid., p. 69ff.
[38] Ibid., p. 72.
[39] Ibid., p. 73.
[40] Ibid.

subtly undermining our vision of the psychosomatic self evolving from fetus to person. By insisting that all rights require mental life and that fetal existence largely lacks same, Dworkin obscures the fact that the personal arises out of the impersonal across time, that rights grow naturally out of needs as well as interests. More important, he leaves us without the social means to protect "nonpersons" for their own sakes. If the impersonal as such has no political and legal standing, why should we love the young neighbor into personhood and why should we continue to love the elderly neighbor who has ceased to be a person, that is, an autonomous rational agent?

It is crucial to see that the destruction of a fetus may still be immoral *to it* even if it is not considered a personal-interest-rights-bearer. Even if one accepts a narrow definition of justice as exclusively respect for interest-based rights, such justice does not exhaust ethical obligation and thus does not settle the moral question of how the fetus may be treated. Modernity defines justice as giving individuals their due, and what is due it often defines, in turn, in terms of contract or merit. Love attends to what others basically need and how others might potentially grow, in contrast, and these needs and potentials can be totally independent of conscious mental life. What I have called "duties of charity," that is, stem from impersonal as well as personal considerations. And wouldn't we call "immoral" a person who needlessly chopped down a majestic redwood or gratuitously slaughtered the last snail-darter, to take up one of Dworkin's examples? She would have harmed valuable lives other than her own, would have failed to show them due reverence, even if we decline to say that she has violated any *interest*-based rights. Theists may think it *disobedient to God* to destroy a creature in utero, as Dworkin realizes, but atheists (as well as theists) may think it *cruel to the fetus itself* to take its life, because that life has intrinsic worth the needs and potentials of which ought to be honored.

Even if Dworkin is correct that only persons have interests and thus that only persons have interest-based rights, pre-personal human beings might still have *needs* and/or *capacities* that also translate into rights. Personhood may be a sufficient condition for having certain types of rights, but it is not a necessary condition for having all types.[41] Impersonal values count morally, not just aesthetically, as the examples of endangered species and future generations attest. And there is no in-principle reason why impersonal goods should not be given political protection by a liberal state. To *define* liberal democracy as concerned only with extant

---

[41] For further defense of this view, see Norman C. Gillespie, "Abortion and Human Rights," in *The Problem of Abortion*, ed. by Joel Feinberg (Belmont, Calif.: Wadsworth, 1984), p. 98.

persons' interest-based rights is to beg the question. It is, in addition, untrue to our legal history.

Dworkin maintains that prior to having interests there is no person as such to harm; an impersonal value may be destroyed but no injustice is done (save perhaps to those who have property rights in that value). If one prevents Dr. Frankenstein from throwing the switch that would animate a set of body parts, for instance, this is not an injustice to the creature that would have resulted had he thrown the switch. Again, a real value may be lost, Dworkin grants, but no right of the potential creature itself is violated. A second problem here, however, beyond the neglect of need-based rights, is that Dworkin's analysis fails to attend to the distinction between *a contingent possibility* and *an essential potential*. The animation of a set of body parts is a contingent possibility in Mary Shelley's world, but a normal fetus's growth into personhood is an essential potential in ours. A fetus is deeply dependent and requires care, as Dworkin notes; it does not simply develop on its own. But human fetal life (unlike great paintings and Frankenstein monsters) is "programmed" from the outset to have needs, interests, and rights. There is a recognizable objective *telos* to even a dependent human life that may be immorally thwarted.

Again, pace Dworkin, there is no in-principle reason to limit law to enforcing "duties of justice" alone. Even our liberal, democratic society restricts the destruction of impersonal value in ways that cannot be reduced to the protection of extant interest-based rights. Natural resources are preserved with an eye to the well-being of future generations, if not for the sake of intrinsic beauty. Dworkin would respond that whatever one might think of "duties of charity" to promote value by meeting impersonal human needs, democratic legal sanctions should only be brought against those who violate justice by aggressing against personal human interests.[42] But here the divide that he would assert between value and justice, morality and legality, cannot be sustained.[43]

It is sometimes equally immoral (unloving *and* unjust) for me to fail to protect or to meet a human need as it is to fail to respect a capacity or interest. This is most manifest when I have induced the need myself, as when by my free actions I have rendered another human life dependent upon my own. (Consider the moral and legal obligations of the U.S. government, for example, toward those whom it exposed to agent orange during the Vietnam War.) Now, a fetus has a need, induced by others, to come to have personal capacities and interests; those capacities

[42] See also Dworkin et al., "Assisted Suicide: The Philosophers' Brief," *New York Review*, March 27, 1997, pp. 41–47.
[43] See my "A House Divided, Again: 'Sanctity' vs. 'Dignity' in the Assisted Death Debates" for additional argument to this effect.

and interests are but part of its essential potential as a human life, its normal pattern of growth and development. Fetal need is not the only genuine good—maternal and paternal needs matter profoundly—but it is due recognition and protection for its own sake. It is quite appropriate, then, at least in nonrape cases, to say that the fetus has a prima facie need-based right against its parents (and perhaps the wider community) to acquire interest-based rights. Parents are required, that is, ceteris paribus, to care for their freely conceived young.[44] They have called them into dependency, after all.

To summarize: one's status as a person undergirds a strong right to life (call this "the argument *from* personhood"), but one's essential potential to *become* a person may also ground a prima facie right to life (call this "the argument *to* personhood"). An ethic of care must never lose sight of the fact that persons don't just happen; they must be nurtured into healthy existence. But what is nurtured is a human being already possessed of a unique identity. All things being equal, this identity entails a need-based right of the fetus to the care necessary for it to live and grow to maturity. This latter right may be overridden by other moral considerations, but it may also be violated, a wrong to the fetus itself, as when the induced dependency of the inchoate human being is electively aborted.

If I am correct against Dworkin, then elective abortion is immoral in reducing to mere means individuals whose unfolding stories dictate, by right, that they be treated as ends in themselves. (I would defend a woman's right to a therapeutic abortion, one needed to preserve her life, in that fetal need-rights can be outweighed by personal interest-rights. I discuss this further below.) One need not have conscious ends or interests to be an end oneself; the essential potential of a human life for ends or interests suffices for an intelligible narrative about the intrinsic value of that life. Beyond this, theists have reason to dispute the implicit assumption in many pro-choice arguments that only human beings generate narratives. Hebrew and Christian Scriptures assume that God is both a subject of narration and a narrator, which implies that even unwanted, unborn humanity can literally be "taken into account" by divinity (cf. Isa. 49:1–5; Jer. 1:4–5). Divine care is, for believers, the final source of both full life and right choice. Indeed, the theological reading of "abomination" construes it as what offends God or is without divine blessing (from *absit* + *omen*).

---

[44] Herbert Morris has written: "There is an obligation imposed upon us all, unlike that we have with respect to animals, to respond to children in such a way as to maximize the chances of their becoming persons." I extend this reasoning to fetal human beings. See Morris, "Persons and Punishment," in *Punishment and the Death Penalty*, ed. by Robert M. Baird and Stuart E. Rosenbaum (Amherst, N.Y.: Prometheus, 1995), p. 75.

Managing the Body: The Place of Dependency

The abortion gridlock may be further broken by examining the significance of dependency in light of an ethic of finitude that attends to both needs/potentials and claims/interests. I suspect that we find abortion such a conundrum because we have lost a sense of what human finitude means morally, as opposed to physically or technologically. An intelligent and sensitive professor at Stanford Medical Center once told me that he thought elective abortion was almost always permissible, even into the third trimester, because it was the removal of a deeply needful being from the body of an autonomous person. When I asked the doctor why his principles would not license parents to remove their temporarily impaired child or premature infant from a respirator, he replied that the morally relevant difference is that in the latter cases dependency is on a machine. Although the couple (or their insurance) may be paying for the treatment, the mechanization of its means of delivery makes that treatment mandatory. Use of the hospital equipment does not impinge on the parents' (especially the mother's) freedom the way pregnancy does, thus it may *not* be foregone. If the fetus is still in utero, on the other hand, it can be directly killed, in my former colleague's opinion. With this, I mused, our technological society has come full circle: machines now have more moral obligations than we do.

My Stanford associate (also an M.D.) clearly wanted to draw a plausible distinction between a machine, which one can simply put to work, and a person, whose autonomy must be respected. But the unhappy upshot of this good intention was that he defined human life as what can sustain itself (is viable), at least on artificial life support. The implication was that being dependent does not preclude the presence of human life, *so long as the dependence is artificially sustained*. The *biological* dependence of the fetus on its mother in effect rendered it nonliving (only potentially a human life), but requiring medical *machinery* had no such effect. This is the peculiar reversal, the abominable "liberation," in which biological dependency entails nonhumanity. If the only difference between two fetuses (one a human life, the other not) is that the former is being sustained by a hospital's care while the other is being supported by its mother's body, then the implication is that the physician or his or her equipment is the giver of life, not the parents, much less God. With this, we have moved substantially away from intrinsic properties and potentials and toward external circumstances as definitive of human life. It is impossible to defend an egalitarian social philosophy on the latter basis. The right to life, the very existence of life, turns now on whether others or their machines find one manageable. There are no shared needs, capacities, and histories to appeal to as the bases of human solidarity; there is no imperative to care for others precisely because they are naturally needy.

Widespread adoption of this "ethic of manageability" would entail the death of personal care, for such care aims first and foremost at cultivating the capacity for caring itself—in both oneself and others. This means balancing the ability to give *and* the need to receive care as distinctive human qualities. Many human beings (e.g., the very old and the very young) cannot care for themselves, but this does not mean that they may be killed or would be better off dead. The question for such individuals is: Are they beyond *receiving* care from others, are they unprofited by human sympathy and nurturance? Only then do they cease or otherwise fail to have a place among us as fellow human beings. An ethic of manageability implies, in opposition, that we can (and perhaps should) assert our "independence" of fetuses (as well as of the homeless, the elderly, the retarded, et al.), simply by virtue of de facto technological limitations and our desire to avoid moral obligations that involve self-giving.

There have always been recognized limits to virtuous self-giving; it is undeniable that "care" can become the disguised use of coercive power or plain futility. No one is obliged to prolong the death of a hopelessly ill patient, for instance, in the name of some abstract benevolence. But the manageability ideal would have one's bodily self-control trump even against those whose dependency we ourselves have induced, and this even although all of us once were and may again be similarly dependent ourselves. (Our material creations, to reiterate, would not be equally at liberty; they would have purposes and properties that limit them, that keep them at their posts, so to speak.) Thus the mother-fetus relation, rather than being one of the most profound bonds in nature—demanding yet fulfilling, a trial yet not without its reward—would be less secure than *artificial* means of life support. Under these conditions, it is hard to imagine how care could continue to be *personal*. The requisite commitment to individuals genotypically (and potentially morally) like ourselves would be lacking.

Individual autonomy and technical manageability often go hand in hand in abortion arguments. Among those who defend unqualified elective abortion on the basis of autonomy and manageability alone, procreation of another human being is reduced to something very like the production of an inanimate commodity. The responsibilities of "owners" are lowered, in turn, below what we often expect of things owned. It should be no mystery, therefore, why Pope Paul considered many abortions "abominable."[45] Lost in all of this is an appreciation of the fact that all people, our adult selves included, are finite and needful. As the strong agapist

---

[45] See his "Respect for Life in the Womb."

never tires of reminding us, people only get to be people and only continue to act like people because others have extended to them a self-giving care beyond what explicit contract requires and unfettered freedom desires. There can be conflicts of care, but without an appreciation of the demands (and rewards) of personal care, freedom to contract is a highly contracted freedom. Humanity does not begin with, nor is it reducible to, autonomous willing.

DENYING THE SELF: THE PLACE OF INDEPENDENCE

Once again, the best liberal positions on abortion appeal to more than private freedom and technical competence, and they acknowledge that the fetus is not just a lump of tissue or unproblematically "part of the woman's body." It is instructive, nevertheless, to ask what elective abortion amounts to even if we dwell on the unique *intimacy* of the connection between mother and fetus. It is the case, after all, that (1) the woman contributes half of the chromosomes to the diploid cell formed at conception; (2) barring rape, this contribution (however unintended) is the result of a free act performed in the recent past; and (3) fetal development thereafter takes place within the space of her uterus. These three facts suggest that nontherapeutic abortion (after the first trimester) can be a form of self-denial bordering on the abominable. If abortion stems from disdain for one's own identity or from refusal to take responsibility for personal choices or from rejection of the implications of corporeality, it must be the opposite of liberating. In this case, personal capacities are not expanded but contracted, not merely for the fetus but also for the mother. Both one's genetic legacy and one's temporal history are denied and with them a large part of what it means to be a moral agent capable of and in need of personal care.

It is not uncommon for the abortion experience to elicit a sense of loss, a mixture of guilt and sadness, in both women and men. Often the feeling is one of shame coupled with sympathy for the child who was, as when Linda Bird Francke writes after her 1973 abortion:

> It certainly does make more sense not to be having a baby right now—we [she and her husband] say that to each other all the time. But I have this ghost now. A very little ghost which only appears when I'm seeing something beautiful, like the full moon on the ocean last weekend. And the baby waves at me. And I wave at the baby. "Of course, we have room," I cry to the ghost. "Of course, we do."[46]

---

[46] See Francke, "Abortion: A Personal Moral Dilemma," in *Abortion: A Reader*, ed. by Lloyd Steffen (Cleveland: Pilgrim, 1996), p. 6.

Sometimes, however, reaction to abortion can only be characterized as *self*-alienation: a feeling of self-betrayal rather than breach of contract, a sense of partial suicide rather than accomplished murder.[47] Such a reaction makes sense only if the fetus is thought *not* to be radically autonomous or otherwise independent of the mother. However frequently or infrequently abortion leads to a diminished self-image, it is clear that an argument against the independence of the fetus is not necessarily an argument for the moral permissibility of electively terminating a pregnancy. Elective abortion may be an expression of self-dis-regard. Thus I disagree with Beverly Harrison's claim that "the availability of safe, surgical, elective abortion in the early stages of pregnancy is considered an abomination only by those who value *potential* human life more than they value existing women's lives."[48] Even if one deems the fetus merely a potential human life, as opposed to seeing it as a real human life that is potentially a person (my position), duties that the pregnant woman owes to herself must also be considered and these may very well argue against abortion in a variety of circumstances. I do not value an existing woman's life if I encourage her to think (falsely) that her autonomy is all that matters morally, even to her.

I have noted that the dependency of the fetus may be a compelling reason to extend rather than withdraw care, and nothing in this section gainsays the intrinsic worth of the fetus grounded in its genetic individuality and passive potential for personhood. Neither do I wish to make morality turn on polls, as if the absence of remorse would ipso facto render abortions permissible. My point, rather, is that concern for the well-being of women by no means dictates a broadly libertarian position on abortion. It may be that elective abortions harm women (not only fetuses) in ways that would make absence of regret itself morally regrettable. Even someone as critical of "traditional" (e.g., Roman Catholic) teachings on abortion as Lisa Sowle Cahill writes:

> Abortion as a "means of birth control" is a threat to social support of pregnancy, birth, and childrearing in the family. And when promoted individualistically as a "woman's right," it also detracts from public awareness of the much broader and deeper economic and political supports needed to ensure equality and full moral agency for women.[49]

Cahill is quite clear about the need to "demonstrate strong, practical support for women," and about why abortion is "a symbol of women's

---

[47] In this connection, see Gilligan's description of the "moral nihilism" some women spiral into after abortion: *In a Different Voice*, p. 124. Gilligan makes clear that this reaction is far from universal, but it is not rare either.

[48] Harrison, *Our Right to Choose*, p. 245.

[49] Cahill, *Sex, Gender, and Christian Ethics* (Cambridge: Cambridge University Press, 1996), p. 214.

rights" for many.[50] But her insistence that an acceptable abortion ethic must be holistic, attending to moral virtue and the common good, nicely captures the best in many pro-life arguments. Sidney Callahan is another good example of a pro-life feminist who sees permissive abortion policies as contrary to true female liberation.[51]

THE CONTINUITY OF HUMAN EXISTENCE

How and why do I distinguish between first- and second-trimester abortions? To answer this, I must turn more directly to the dynamic character of prenatal and postnatal life, to the fact that one reaches personhood neither instantaneously nor autonomously. Human lives grow into personal dignity rights only because they are extended unearned (but not undue) care from very early on. Before personal dignity is achieved, that is, various human needs and potentials (what I call "sanctity") must be addressed across time. The most consistent way I know to express this continuity of existence, grounded in love, is to refer to the evolution from "human life" to "human being" to "human person."[52]

The zygote, then the developing embryo, up to ten weeks, is "a human life." It is animate and has the requisite type and number of chromosomes to justify this label; it is numerically distinct and, absent twinning, possesses a unique genotype. After ten weeks, or at the latest after twelve weeks, there is sufficient morphological development (e.g., heartbeat and measurable brain function) to warrant the phrase "a human being," I believe. There is an increasingly integrated and sentient individual, an evolving psychosomatic unity who can readily engage our sympathy as recognizably one of us. At the beginning of the second trimester, a psychological dimension begins to supervene on the biological processes at work, such that the fetus can evidently experience her surroundings. This is not to say, of course, that the twelve-week-old fetus is explicitly aware of her environment, but rather that at a rudimentary, unconscious level her identity is touched and permanently shaped by that environment (including the attention of her parents), with which she interacts.

On the complex nature of fetal experience, Jeffrey Alberts and Catherine Cramer are worth quoting at some length:

[50] Ibid., p. 213.

[51] See Callahan, "Abortion and the Sexual Agenda: A Case for Pro-Life Feminism."

[52] Although individual human *life* begins at conception, with respect to personhood I side with a form of hylomorphism or creationism over strict traducianism: personhood emerges gradually over time. For a discussion of these matters, see Joseph F. Donceel, "A Liberal Catholic's View," in *Abortion and Catholicism: The American Debate*, ed. by Patricia Beattie Jung and Thomas A. Shannon (New York: Crossroad, 1988).

The intrauterine world is commonly characterized as a dark, warm, silent environment, protected and buffered from extrinsic influences. Implied here are homogeneous conditions, continuously bland and undisturbed, perhaps fundamentally comfortable. Most mammals are born at immature stages of sensory development (e.g., sealed ears and eyes). Immaturity often implies lack of function, which can foster the question of whether fetal sensory systems actually transduce much stimulation (experience) at all.

Contrary to some traditional views, empirical studies of intrauterine conditions have revealed numerous forces of change and environmental fluctuation. Moreover, fetal sensory-perceptual systems, though incompletely developed, may be "functionally tuned" to receive particularly important environmental information. Fetal behavior, like postnatal behavior, can be examined for specific adaptive specializations that serve to help the organism both adjust to its immediate environment and prepare itself for an imminent change in its ontogenetic niche. Perceptions of smells, tastes, sounds, and tactile and vestibular events in the uterus can directly affect fetal behavior. These fetal responses can assist in ongoing adjustments to the uterine environment, and they can constitute useful practice for the sensory systems as preparation for later functional demands. Some stimuli, initially experienced *in utero*, will be encountered in postnatal life, so this type of early experience can serve as very specific preparation for later adaptation.[53]

In short, although the fetus cannot yet care for or about herself in substantive senses, she can *receive and react to* personal care from others, which is the minimal mark of a human being. Only with the advent of language use, at roughly one-and-a-half to two years, however, does one have "a human person." Personhood requires consciousness of oneself as a responsible agent, a rationality and intentionality capable of caring about ends as such rather than merely having needs and reacting to sensory stimulation.[54]

[53] Jeffery R. Alberts and Catherine P. Cramer, "Ecology and Experience: Sources of Means and Meaning of Developmental Change," in *Handbook of Behavioral Neurobiology*, vol. 9, ed. by Elliott M. Blass (New York and London: Plenum, 1988), p. 6. William P. Smotherman and Scott R. Robinson observe: "Although the data are incomplete, . . . a continuously expanding behavioral repertoire is . . . apparent in human fetal development. Ultrasonographic imaging during the first half of gestation has revealed that only one behavioral category ('just discernible movement') can be recognized at the onset of fetal movement (7.5 weeks . . .). Within 3 weeks, the number of distinguishable categories increases to 9, and by 13 weeks, 16 behavioral categories are recognizable." They go on to conclude, matter-of-factly: "Behavior and its underlying functional neurology does not suddenly appear at the moment of birth." See "The Uterus as Environment: The Ecology of Fetal Behavior," in ibid., pp. 168 and 188.

[54] The literature on the necessary conditions for personhood is voluminous—for representative discussions related to abortion, see the pieces by English and Lomasky in *The Problem of Abortion*—and I do not claim to offer detailed argument for my terminology. I

These designations are admittedly somewhat artificial, but they are not arbitrary. They are, need I say, cumulative: all human persons are also human beings and human lives, although not all human beings are human persons, and not all human lives are yet human beings. The salient point is that human beings have the capacity for experience and the essential potential for personhood; we grow into relation with ourselves, as well as with others, across time and as a result of our individual histories.

Where is the cutoff point for legal protectability? I side with those who argue that minimal decency dictates that we roll *Roe v. Wade* back (without overturning it completely) and make elective abortions illegal after the first trimester. I realize that the sanctity of human life from its very beginning, its need and ability to receive love, moves some to argue that *all* elective abortion should be outlawed. But the protection of more developed human beings seems the best we can currently hope for within our pluralistic society. Such protection is mandated, moreover, by logical and clinical consistency. If the loss of measurable brain function is the criterion of legal death for human beings (when they are "beyond care"), then the dawn of such function should be the criterion of legally recognized life for human beings (when they are "due care"). As indicated, I judge that "a human life" actually begins sooner than this (i.e., at conception), and because those human lives that are only potential human beings/persons are still exceedingly valuable, "sacred," even early elec-

---

assume, instead, that something like my rough distinctions are intuitively plausible and then ask about the implications for care. I grant that the fetus is not a "person," on most definitions of that term, but I deny that only persons possess rights or are owed duties. My position is somewhat similar to L. W. Sumner's in "A Third Way" (also in *The Problem of Abortion*), in that I take the right to life not to presuppose being a rational moral agent. Life is too weak a criterion for determining when a creature has moral standing, according to Sumner, while rationality is too strong. (Insisting on rationality opens the door to infanticide, for example.) "A criterion of sentience (or consciousness) is a promising middle path between these extremes," he writes, noting later that "when sentience emerges it does not do so suddenly. The best we can hope for is to locate a threshold state or period in the second trimester" (ibid., pp. 83 and 87).

My major difficulty with Sumner is that he too completely conflates early abortion with contraception (e.g., p. 88), thereby ignoring the essential potential even of the zygote not shared by sperm or egg in isolation. I believe he also pushes the advent of sentience farther back into the second trimester than is appropriate. He himself admits that "in all the species with which we are familiar, the components of the forebrain (or some analogues) are the minimal conditions of sentience. . . . [And] at the conclusion of the first trimester virtually all of the major neural components can be clearly differentiated and EEG activity is detectable" (p. 86). Indeed, not only can we get a positive EEG, which represents spontaneous brain activity, we can also detect event-related brain potential (ERP), which is generated by specific external stimuli. For a discussion of ERP, although without overt reference to fetuses, see John L. Andreassi, *Psychophysiology: Human Behavior and Physiological Response* (Hillsdale, N.J.: Erlbaum, 1989), chap. 5.

tive abortion may be morally wrong. One must have a good reason to take the nascent life, to neglect its needs and potentials. For purposes of the law, nonetheless, a compromise that protects human *beings* is now morally legitimate. All human beings ought to be counted in a conflict of care, and only in light of the value of *personal* care can the "right to life" of a person be allowed to trump that of a "mere" human being. Once the fetus reaches the second trimester of gestation it has a basic right not to be electively killed. *Allowing an increasingly sentient creature to remain in relation with oneself as life-supporter, a creature whose dependence is itself partially one's own doing, carries with it an obligation of continued care for its needs and potentials; here love and justice converge.* Thus, while the elective abortion of a pre-personal human being need not be first-degree murder—that designation can be reserved for the premeditated slaying of an innocent *person*—such elective killing should be deemed unjustifiable homicide, a form of manslaughter.[55] The legal sanction involved would be calibrated accordingly.

S. I. Benn, like Ronald Dworkin, has argued that "only persons can be the subject of rights,"[56] because only they can make the intentional demands on which rights depend. For Benn, to ascribe rights to potential persons is akin to the fallacy of believing that because someone is potentially president of the United States he is now commander-in-chief. On my account, however, "mere" human beings can be the bearers of prima facie rights (including the right to life) because *some rights are need- or potential-based rather than intention- or autonomous-claim-based.* (Again, think of the rights of the retarded or senile.) It is not the case that fetuses are *potential* subjects of rights because they are potential persons; no, fetuses (all pre-personal human beings) are *real* subjects of rights because they are in need of and capable of receiving a care that will eventually usher them into personhood. Fetal rights may be overridden in certain circumstances, but they are genuine and significant. As Norman Gillespie

---

[55] My locating the dawn of sentience (and hence the right to life) at roughly twelve weeks into gestation is debatable, as I have noted, but more or less middle of the road. For a defense of a six- to eight-week cutoff point, yet without the attendant terminology outlined above, see Baruch Brody, "Growing into Rights," *Second Opinion* 10 (March 1989): 66–71, and *Abortion and the Sanctity of Human Life* (Cambridge, Mass.: MIT Press, 1975). Philip Devine criticizes Brody's position as too liberal in "The Scope of the Prohibition Against Killing," in *The Problem of Abortion*, pp. 37–38. Ken Martyn argues for "a standard for determining when human life begins based on brain function," but he maintains that "a reasonable estimate is that development of fetal consciousness takes place primarily between nineteen and thirty weeks after conception." See Martyn, "Technological Advances and *Roe v. Wade*: The Need to Rethink Abortion Law," in *Contemporary Issues in Bioethics*, ed. by Tom Beauchamp and LeRoy Walters (Belmont, Calif.: Wadsworth, 1989), p. 237.

[56] Benn, "Abortion, Infanticide, and Respect for Persons," in *The Problem of Abortion*, p. 142.

observes, "being a person is a sufficient, but not a necessary condition, for having rights; . . . less than full persons can have rights, and these rights can be unjustly violated."[57]

An acorn is not an oak tree, but if you want to get oak trees you had better cultivate acorns; similarly, a fetus is not a person, but if you want to get respectable persons, you had better nurture the inchoate beings who grow into them. This means, among other things, limiting elective abortion, not only for the sake of social utility or even for the well-being of the future persons that fetuses may become, but also out of respect for the fetuses alive here and now. Conceiving new human lives may be a pure gift, but carrying those lives to term once they have reached the second trimester is a moral duty, barring a direct conflict of fetal life against personal life. The Congregation for the Doctrine of the Faith overstates the case in claiming that "the human being must be respected—as a person—from the very first instant of his existence."[58] But reverence for the human being as *potential* person, as well as *real* human existent, is ever mandatory.

Why not extend an equal right to life to all sentient animals? Although other creatures are sentient and thus due real consideration, it seems likely that only human beings naturally grow into personhood as a result of the personal care they receive in utero and beyond. I use the phrase "*personal* care" advisedly, meaning by it care *from* persons contributing to the formation *of* persons. Many animals can receive a kind of care from persons, to be sure, but these animals do not themselves become personal; moreover, they do not *essentially* need *personal* care, given that they can (as a species) survive in the wild. Most individual farm animals would now die without human intervention, but as a species even domesticated beasts might endure the demise of humanity (or at least, in theory, be "attended to" by machines). If human babies are not touched and spoken to by persons, in contrast, they all die, even if their grosser physical needs are met.[59] The essential need for, and the essential ability to receive, personal care entails greater intrinsic value in human beings than

---

[57] Gillespie, "Abortion and Human Rights," in ibid., p. 98.

[58] Congregation for the Doctrine of the Faith, *Instruction on Respect for Human Life in Its Origin and on the Dignity of Procreation: Replies to Certain Questions of the Day* (Boston: St. Paul Editions, 1987), reprinted in *Ethical Issues in the New Reproductive Technologies*, ed. by Richard T. Hull (Belmont, Calif.: Wadsworth, 1990). The quotation comes on p. 21.

[59] I believe it was Louis XIV who ordered that several babies in the royal nursery be fed and clothed but not spoken to, so that the king could determine the natural human language. Would the infants, left to themselves, begin to speak French, English, German? Predictably, they all perished. For the poignant story of the terrible impact of verbal and emotional neglect on a modern child, see Russ Rymer, *Genie: A Scientific Tragedy* (New York: HarperCollins, 1993).

in impersonal animals. This is true even of human beings who are permanently retarded or senile. (Again, dependency can be a source, or at least a sign, of value rather than disvalue.) Hence it seems probable that only human beings are due the strong moral and legal right to life that can only be superseded by the rights of persons, and only in direct conflict situations.

My previous remarks notwithstanding, it *may* be that some animals (e.g., chimps and porpoises) possess sufficient linguistic aptitude and/or self-awareness to qualify as nonhuman "persons."[60] If so, they too have a right to life that is due legal protection. We are obliged, in any case, not to visit gratuitous pain on nonhuman animals, and only important human ends can justify the killing of impersonal animals. Whatever status we recognize in animals, of course, this does not imply that pre-personal, nonpersonal, or post-personal human beings do not themselves have a right to life. For *any* sentient creature, to be capable of a noncognitive well-being that benefits from personal care is to possess a range of need-based rights—however prima facie—even as to embody the essential potential for personhood is to possess a range of capacity-based rights.

DILEMMA, PROMISE-KEEPING, AND REFLEXIVE NORMATIVITY

Why isn't abortion a hard dilemma in which the needs of the fetus, the rights of the mother, and/or the good of society irremediably collide unto unavoidable guilt? Describing the female subjects in an abortion study, Carol Gilligan comments that

> the women's judgments point toward an identification of the violence inherent in the [abortion] dilemma itself, which is seen to compromise the justice of any of its possible resolutions. This construction of the dilemma leads the women to recast the moral judgment from a consideration of the good to a choice between evils.[61]

Gilligan is surely right to insist that abortion poses a situation "in which there is no way of acting without consequences to other and self."[62] There is often no avoiding pain to oneself and hurt to others in life. This fact is misunderstood, nevertheless, if it leads us to equate abortion with a moral dilemma in the technical sense: a situation in which, through no

---

[60] I will not attempt here to settle this issue. For arguments that support deeming some nonhumans "persons," see, for example, Peter Singer's *Animal Liberation: A New Ethics for Our Treatment of Animals* (New York: Random House, 1975) and Frans de Waal's *Good Natured: The Origins of Right and Wrong in Humans and Other Animals*.

[61] Gilligan, *In a Different Voice*, p. 101.

[62] Ibid., p. 108.

antecedent fault of one's own, one cannot but do grave moral wrong. This is because, in cases where there is no conflict of life against life and intercourse has been voluntary, it is arguably a matter of promise-keeping for both the mother and the father not to abort but to care for the new life they have created.[63] A duty of justice then prevails that renders talk of "dilemma" unpersuasive.

Parental care is not something above and beyond the call of duty but rather a taking of responsibility for actions precisely by attending to the consequences they have for self and others. Just as the present generation has obligations to future ones (e.g., not to pollute the environment in which they will have to live), so potential generators have obligations to those individuals, as yet unconceived, whose future existence depends upon them. If one ought not to bring another human being into existence when that other will not be able to survive, then to procreate is in fact to give an implicit promise that the new being will be provided for. Generally speaking, if one has an obligation not to do X if it will lead to Y, then knowingly to do X entails an implicit promise that it will not in fact lead to Y. If parents abort a midterm fetus that is the result of voluntary intercourse and represents no threat to the mother's life, for example, then the original conception is arguably an instance of "wrongful procreation."[64]

The language of "implicit promise" may seem anemic in light of the passion that usually accompanies sexual intercourse; the phrase may sound especially inappropriate given the frequently aggressive character of male lust. (Who stops to think about deontology once the clothes come off?) But rejecting talk of "promise" or "covenant" altogether—by suggesting, for instance, that all heterosexual sex is coerced and demeaning[65]— would do a disservice to the moral capacities of men and women. Rape is

[63] Paul Ramsey takes this position in "The Morality of Abortion," in *Moral Problems*, ed. by James Rachels (New York: Harper and Row, 1971). Ramsey locates full "ensoulment" at the moment of conception, and a powerful case can be made, I believe, that the implicit promise entailed by voluntary intercourse is given, in prospect, to the human conceptus. The conceptus has impersonal needs and potentials that require personal care. For legal purposes, however, I propose that the sentient human being is the recipient of the promise, because with sentience (approximately twelve weeks into gestation) comes the psychosomatic wherewithal more palpably to respond to and benefit from care. Once voluntarily conceived and non-life-threatening human life has been allowed to become sentient, that is, it ought to have a legal claim to care from its parents. This seems to me the *minimally decent* political position that a democratic society can and should endorse.

[64] The phrase is from Matthew Hanser, "Harming Future People," *Philosophy and Public Affairs* 19, no. 1 (winter 1990): 69. Hanser's essay is a helpful critique of Derek Parfit's *Reasons and Persons*; Hanser does not directly consider abortion cases, however.

[65] On whether heterosexual intercourse inevitably involves the objectification and exploitation of women by men, regardless of whether the act results in pregnancy, see Andrea Dworkin, *Intercourse* (New York: The Free Press, 1987).

a crime, but it is better to point out the abuses of *eros* as such than to slander genital love by overgeneralizing its "violence" or "irrationality."

The human need for and receptivity to personal care (shared by fetuses, infants, and adults) is such that one can surrender normal entitlements by bringing this need and receptivity into being. Quite generally, to be in need of personal care as a result of another's action is to be due to receive it from him, so long as receipt is possible, even as to be capable of personal care as a result of another's action is to be obliged to return it to her. This contention, what I called in chapter 1 the *reflexive normativity* of personal care, expresses our obligation to our children and parents. It also raises fundamental issues of moral responsibility. How do we acquire obligations and duties toward one another? May we ever become bound to another in spite of ourselves? What is the significance, for example, of failed efforts to avoid conception?

Judith Jarvis Thomson famously suggests that duties must be actively sought or accepted to be binding, and thus that an unwanted child has little or no claim on us.[66] Others insist that this is not so. They ask: Cannot a woman's entitlement to her own body and a man's entitlement to his time and resources be overridden by their voluntary participation in the sexual intercourse that brought the needful (although possibly unwanted) fetal life into being? Thomson contends that even if the fetus is considered a full-fledged person, personal care does not obligate one to be a "Good Samaritan" and to attend to its needs at the expense of one's own interests or preferences. But this is beside the point. The salient fact is that being a Good Samaritan implies caring for someone whose affliction is not your doing, while the dependency of the fetus is an *induced* dependency, the direct result (excluding rape or invincible ignorance) of an action mother and father have freely chosen to perform. Sexual intercourse is plausibly seen as a performative carrying an implicit promise to care, since it is normally both uncaring and unjust to abandon another human being whose vulnerability is the consequence of one's own voluntary behavior. In such a case, even if conception was not the aim, the obligation to nurture can only be overridden when the personal care due to additional others is extremely pressing (e.g., a matter of life against life) and one cannot extend the needed care to all.[67]

---

[66] Thomson, "A Defense of Abortion," in *The Problem of Abortion*, p. 186.

[67] Cf. Thomson on these points in ibid., p. 181ff. For a detailed view inspired by Thomson and in contrast to my own, see F. M. Kamm, *Creation and Abortion*. Kamm, like Thomson, assumes for purposes of argument that the fetus is a person but argues that

we cannot require a woman to abstain from sex during her childbearing years just to prevent a fetus existing that will not have minima[l conditions for a good life]. . . . The reason is that the fetus will be no worse (experientially) off living and dying than it

Consider the following analogy. Suppose that I am the owner of a sailboat and I invite you out on the water for an afternoon's cruise. I know that you cannot swim, but I assure you in good faith that the vessel is seaworthy, all standard safety devices are on board, all reasonable precautions will be taken, and so on. You agree to go, but shortly out of port a squall kicks up that threatens to founder the boat, is so violent in fact that it rips the liferaft from its moorings and washes it and all but one of the lifevests overboard. Would it be moral (either just or loving) for me to claim that, because I conscientiously sought to avoid danger, I may now as owner of the sailboat claim exclusive right to the use of the single means of life support? Presumably not. I have voluntarily put you (and myself) at risk, and this generates obligations even though I have tried by all standard means to avoid having to act on these obligations. Leaving aside any special duties ascribable to a naval captain (e.g., going down with the ship), it would seem that I am bound to share equally with you the available resources for survival (the lifevest). The only plausible scenario on which you would not have a direct claim to share the lifevest is one in which there are several people on board and thus there is no question of trying to share the single vest. Here all must draw straws to see which few have access to the limited means of deliverance.

There are admitted asymmetries between my example and abortion scenarios; the equality of risk of captain and sailing-guest does not seem shared by mother and fetus, for instance. Beyond this, someone may object to my story, intended to be analogous to late abortion after contraceptive failure, because it involves relations between persons, while the fetus is but a potential person. But the point of the tale is to show that obligations to other members of the moral community may come to us unsought.[68] Not all obligations need be matters of just claims between

---

would be if it had never lived, it should bear risks for the chance to gain the benefits of life and also because of the significant size of the sacrifices to the woman. (p. 159)

Kamm is a thoughtful deontologist, but her vocabulary, again like Thomson's, tends to skew discussion. Parents are "creators" and fetuses are "risk bearers." Kamm explicitly claims that creation does not equal ownership (p. 137), but the one is often thought to imply the other. In the absence of any sense that human biological generation—what Kamm calls "creation"—is partially co-creation with God or nature or karma or at least some social reality larger than our individual selves, it seems hard to resist the idea that individual parents possess their children. And if parents possess their children, they need not make sacrifices to cultivate the children's potentials or to meet the children's needs, even if the needs are pressing and have been voluntarily induced. Parents are their children's seemingly omnipotent "creators." In conceiving, parents are generously giving offspring a "chance" at existence, so why should they be faulted if they change their minds after a time and abort their young—rather like an artist leaving a sketch unfinished or a writer tearing up a rough draft? See also Oliver O'Donovan, *Begotten or Made?* (Oxford: Oxford University Press, 1984).

[68] A similar point is made by John T. Wilcox in "Nature as Demonic in Thomson's

autonomous persons, moreover, as some animal rights advocates argue. If elective abortion is judged permissible any time after contraceptive failure, this is not because unsought responsibilities are not binding but because the fetus is judged ab initio to have little or no moral standing.[69]

Bodily Integrity and Biological Pluralism

Patricia Beattie Jung has argued that human need alone is not enough to create an obligation to care if that care involves (as does pregnancy) bodily life support. She writes:

> Persons do not have a right to or a claim upon parts or the use of another's body because living bodies are primordially personal. All objectifications of the body are abstractions from this lived unity. Therefore, while the needy "thief" may have a just right to another's property or wealth, such claims may not be extended to another's body without direct violation of the obligation to respect persons as persons.[70]

Jung supports this claim by drawing an analogy between donating an organ and carrying a fetus to term; neither of these, she contends, can be seen as a duty since this would involve a denial of "bodily integrity."[71] Both organ donation and childbirth must be gifts, on her view, so it is "blatantly inconsistent to grant potential donors the right to refuse to participate in transplant procedures, yet view childbearing as required."[72] Like Thomson before her, however, Jung fails to see the morally relevant difference between the fetus's dependency (which is *induced* by the parents) and a patient's dependency (which is is normally merely *discovered* by the donor). Human freedom expressed in bodily integrity is such a great good that it usually cannot be overridden by need alone, as Jung insists; but, as I have argued, if I am directly responsible for the need of another human being—if the need is *caused* by me—this often *is* suffi-

---

Defense of Abortion," in *The Ethics of Abortion*, p. 219. Wilcox's essay is an excellent critique of J. J. Thomson on rights, duties, and the nature of reproductive responsibility.

[69] As important as the promise-keeping relation is, it must be granted that acknowledging then acting on obligations to others (including unborn generations) requires the schooling of sympathy, not merely the keeping of contracts or the rewarding of merit. We must think of individuals as worthy of respect before we will recognize (much less keep) promises to them. To whom we extend the necessary conditions for fellow personhood, and thus how we draw the bounds of the moral community, will largely determine the way we judge any action. Arguing that parents have no obligations to fetuses is like arguing that God has no obligations to finite persons: a misreading of power's relation to goodness.

[70] Jung, "Abortion and Organ Donation: Christian Reflections on Bodily Life Support," in *Abortion and Catholicism: The American Debate*, p. 153.

[71] Ibid., p. 152.

[72] Ibid., p. 154.

cient to generate an obligation on my part to address that need. Human need *plus personal responsibility* can override normal entitlements, in both organ donation and childbearing cases.[73] If someone's urgent need for a transplant is due to some avoidable harm I have done her or him, for example, then I may in fact have a duty of bodily life support toward that person. Whether or not the harm was intentional, I will, at a minimum, owe that person or his or her family just compensation.

What, more specifically, does this mean for the morality of abortion? In instances of life against life, it seems clearly appropriate to grant priority to the mother; therapeutic abortion is justified, then, in my judgment. It is generally better in other hard cases, however, to err on the side of expanding the moral community rather than contracting it. Individuals are not interchangeable, and even the as-yet-unrealized potential for personal care is an immensely valuable human good. Human resources are limited and overpopulation is a problem, but wisdom aims to make room in the ark for those already living as a result of one's own actions. The drive to bring the needy into secure relation with others seems, in fact, the *telos* of personal care.

Moral maturity is, in good measure, the willingness and ability to recognize others (albeit different) as fellow human beings worthy of reverence and protection. Conversely, a moral abomination involves a basic denial of the humanity of others, or of oneself—not simply the destruction of human beings but the perversion or denial of their distinctive liabilities and prospects. Does the willingness to countenance abortion-on-demand stem not just from a tragic sense of the limits of love but also from an unwillingness to acknowledge the humanity of that dependent minority known as "fetuses"? It seems ironic, in any event, that venereal *eros*, part of the life instinct, should lead to so much killing. But such is often the story of *eros*: when ungoverned by charity, it goes over into its opposite.

Unlike the Catholic hierarchy, I do not think that all direct abortions are abominable or even impermissible. Most involving a conflict of life against life are justified, although tragic. I conclude, in addition, that rape is such a violation of a woman's personhood, including her bodily integrity, that (early) abortion in that instance is morally permissible. Our

---

[73] The physiological fact that pregnancy takes place in a woman's body is not unjust, unless one holds that female procreative power is itself an affliction that can and should be done away with. Jung comes close to such a view in seeming to equate all pregnancies with rape (see ibid., p. 155). Compare also Judith Shklar's discussion of the question, "Is it . . . a misfortune or an injustice to be a woman?" In the name of gender fairness, some (e.g., Shulamith Firestone) suggest that we should strive to remove pregnancy from the female body and place it in machines, but Shklar is not so sure; see her *The Faces of Injustice*, pp. 58–67. For more on the morality of "MEG" (mechanical external gestation), see Kamm, *Creation and Abortion*, pp. 208–20.

society sanctions fetal killing beyond cases of rape or threats to the lives of mothers or even basic conflicts of care, however, and this is ominous both for individuals and for society at large. There is no denying that women have been victimized by Western culture for millennia, and it is understandable that so many insist on abortion as an unqualified right when they have been so wronged. Yet to insist that procreative choice requires unrestricted elective abortion would be to insist on a freedom without responsibility. A just concern for the liberation of women does not imply this. A pillar against such loss of moral reserve is a sense of the equality and accountability of all human beings founded in their need and capacity for personal care, their universal dependence on others.

Such a sense is not easy to cultivate, but the best of feminism itself suggests that we cannot foster social liberation, a sense of the community of all, by denying the integrity of the marginal. The fetus is the least among us, but neither its dependence nor its physical location is morally decisive in the matter of abortion, although both are relevant. A baby out of the womb for twelve weeks has needs and potentials not markedly different from those of a fetus in the womb for twelve weeks; both are radically dependent on others for their survival. (The same can be said, of course, of an adult on a respirator or heart-lung machine.) Yet we generally believe directly killing a babe in arms to be unjust. Moral progress on these issues would mean going forward rather than backward, working for a world that is culturally, politically, *and biologically* pluralistic rather than longing for an inhuman Utopia in which all are sublimely self-sufficient atoms. The challenge is to cultivate an ethos in which the sense of our common humanity, vulnerable yet (for Christians) created in the Image of God, permits unity in diversity, identity in difference, and thus eliminates the need either to swallow up, expel, neglect, or destroy an unformed or ill-formed minority. This ethos begins with the realization that human existence is a continuum; each of us was once a fetus suffered to live by our parents and given the wherewithal to become free by society (and, according to theists, by God). We were all once merely potential persons, and a Golden Rule appeal is often a powerful contraindication to elective abortion.[74]

WHO IS RESPONSIBLE FOR WHOM?

Even if one is convinced that elective abortions are morally indefensible after twelve weeks, one might still contend, on grounds other than those offered by Dworkin, that the state ought not to intervene to prevent the

---

[74] See R. M. Hare, "Abortion and the Golden Rule," in *Philosophy and Sex*, ed. by R. Baker and F. Elliston (Buffalo: Prometheus, 1975), pp. 356–75.

abortions. Alison Jaggar has argued that "the principle that only those who are affected importantly by a decision should share in making it indicates that, in our society, the potential mother rather than the state has the right to decide whether or not she should seek an abortion."[75] She (like Harrison) emphasizes that the woman may make an unjustified decision but that it is hers to make, given that our society expects the mother to be the primary caregiver for her infant—in Jaggar's words, "the primary protector of her child's right to life."[76] This sounds uncomfortably close to a principle of *matria potestas*, unlimited maternal power to dispose of life based on the idea that the mother gives it and therefore may sovereignly take it. The problem is that this (like the more ancient *patria potestas* of Abraham before Isaac) makes the right to life too fragile a reed, ungrounded in passive potential or intrinsic sanctity. In a highly patriarchal culture, for example, it would warrant a husband's right lethally to dispose of his wife since he is expected to bear the brunt of responsibility for her upkeep and thus is "affected importantly" by the decision to let her live. Where women are deemed the least among us and are politically silenced even as fetuses are physically silent, Jaggar's principle would be a chauvinist's license to kill.[77]

Harrison too embraces ideas that undermine her best moral intentions. She uses phrases that cut against taking responsibility for the consequences of sexual intercourse, that tend to support those who would see abortion exclusively in terms of power rather than also as an ethical issue. Harrison is at her best in encouraging women and men to shake off unjust social arrangements that lead to a sense of powerlessness and despair. Yet, oddly, she informs us that "a woman denied access to an abortion she wants is, de facto, *compelled to childbearing against her will*"; the women in her pages "happen to conceive" and experience pregnancy as an "event."[78] There is no denying the contingencies involved in conception, but these phrases do not sit well with the author's proclaimed desire to foster rather than retard moral maturity. Pregnancy does not just "happen" to a woman, unless she has been raped or is invincibly ignorant. Equally troubling is the fact that both Jaggar and Harrison so emphasize moral creativity, the importance of "extending" rights to others in relation, that they come close to undermining moral attention as the recognition of

[75] Jaggar, "Abortion and a Woman's Right to Decide," in *Philosophy and Sex*, p. 331. I alluded above to a similar argument mounted by Beverly Harrison in *Our Right to Choose*; see, for example, pp. 195, 226, and 252.

[76] Jaggar, "Abortion and a Woman's Right to Decide," p. 333.

[77] Lest I be accused of being alarmist, I note that I am making a logical point here about reasons rather than a practical prediction about the actual behavior of husbands.

[78] Harrison, *Our Right to Choose*, pp. 30, 102, and 254; italics in original.

another's intrinsic worth.[79] They lose sight of the fact that, although a passive potential for personal care must be engaged from without and thus is dependent for its realization on relation to others, it is nonetheless a real and valuable feature of a concrete human life. The potential is not the only thing of import, and Harrison cogently maintains that any approach to abortion that attends only to the fetus is sexist. But fetal needs and potentials are ontological facts, neither illusory nor projections of society and/or its machines.

The capacity for personhood is an integral part of the fetus's makeup; it is an *essential* potential, a matter of growth, not simply a contingent possibility (as is the meeting of sperm and egg) or a transformation imposed from without (as is cloning). This means that the death of a fetus is normally a loss to it, a cutting short of the trajectory of its life, although obviously the loss is not self-conscious.[80] Personality only develops as human beings interact with others, but it is not like an injection in a science-fiction scenario that changes kittens into philosophers.[81] The dangers associated with reifying the potential of the fetus must not lead us to valorize the creativity of the parents, the broader community, or technology.

Near the end of her essay, Jaggar writes: "To achieve the legal right to decide about abortion is a first step on the way to women's liberation, but the last step may be the achievement of a society in which the whole notion of individual rights against the community makes no sense at all."[82] I appreciate her suggestion that we focus more on human needs and that current forms of social conflict may be passing, but I believe that this quotation gets things backward. The liberation of women and the justice of society as a whole turn precisely on making and keeping individual rights (both fetal and maternal) intelligible by grounding them in something more basic: personal care. This can be done, to some degree, by perpetually asking whether our social practices are abominable or liberating. More specifically, a community of care will give legal weight to the

---

[79] See ibid., pp. 112 and 218–25; and Jaggar, "Abortion and a Woman's Right to Decide," p. 331.

[80] In responding to Epicurean arguments against seeing death as an evil, Martha Nussbaum notes that "the presence of basic human capabilities, of a functional organization such that, with adequate support, human planning and acting of many kinds would in time take place, already makes death an interruption of a life that is projecting toward a future." Nussbaum has "infants" in mind and does not here mention abortion, but her point is appropriate to second-trimester fetuses as well: their lives can be electively "interrupted" in ways that are bad for them. See Nussbaum, *The Therapy of Desire* (Princeton: Princeton University Press, 1994), p. 211, n. 26.

[81] Cf. Michael Tooley's notorious examples in "A Defense of Abortion and Infanticide," in *The Problem of Abortion*. For more on these issues, see Joel Feinberg's "Potentiality, Development, and Rights," in *The Problem of Abortion*.

[82] Jaggar, "Abortion and a Woman's Right to Decide," p. 336.

right to life by precluding its infringement in many cases, regardless of the benefit infringement might bring in terms of social utility or private autonomy. A society without *any* need for *individual* rights is just as dangerously utopian as a society in which *contractual* rights are *all* we need. Neither is capable of preserving, much less producing, moral persons.

Considerably more elaboration would be required to shape these comments into a fully holistic abortion policy. In particular, abortion-law reform would have to be coupled with sex education in schools, more readily available contraceptives, efforts to hold fathers (in and out of wedlock) responsible for financial support of their offspring, state and business funding for daycare centers, national health insurance, and so on. But the point I want to emphasize is that a position based on autonomy or animation alone is blind to the implications of human finitude. A crude vitalism that makes biological animation the *summum bonum* is no more defensible than a crude voluntarism that worships the free choices of unconstrained persons. The social generation and distribution of personal care is the bedrock issue, rather than any dilemmatic alternative between "life" and "choice."

Most of the 1.5 million abortions in the United States annually already occur in the first trimester, but even a small percentage of 1.5 million represents a sizable number.[83] By more strictly limiting it to the first trimester, we would do to elective abortion what Lincoln hoped, by confining it to the Southern states, to do to slavery: place it "in course of ultimate extinction."[84] At a bare minimum, such a legal reform would reinforce a scruple that was once common sense but has, especially since 1973, been eroded. This scruple insists that abortion is something exceptional, needing special justification, rather than something morally neutral or even normative. The right to elective abortion in the first three months of pregnancy may have to be accepted "on the old ground of 'toleration' by *necessity*," as Lincoln said of Southern property rights in

---

[83] The precise percentage of first-trimester abortions is hard to determine. In 1983, Beverly Harrison wrote that "the overwhelming number of legal abortions in the United States—very conservatively, over 80 percent—are performed during the first trimester of pregnancy." In 1990, she revised that figure to "more like 93 percent." See Harrison, *Our Right to Choose* (1983), p. 226, and "A Feminist-Liberation View of Abortion" (1990), in *On Moral Medicine*, p. 622. Even if the 93 percent figure is correct, this means that approximately 105,000 second- and third-trimester fetuses are legally killed each year in the United States. Assuming that the rates have been constant since 1973, this means that around 3,000,000 fetal "human beings," in my terminology, have been aborted since *Roe v. Wade*.

[84] Lincoln, "A House Divided: Speech Delivered at Springfield, Illinois, at the Close of the Republican State Convention, June 16, 1858," in *Abraham Lincoln: Great Speeches* (New York: Dover, 1991), p. 25.

persons,[85] but the exercise of this right is still unfortunate. It tends to divide the species against itself, to make it blind or unsympathetic to the ways time and chance shape us all.[86] Simply to acquiesce in a jurisprudence that would make the rights of minorities, like fetuses, turn purely on private choices or public plebiscites would be to sever democracy from both love and justice.[87]

CONCLUSION: A RETURN TO *AGAPE*

I end this final chapter where I began the entire book, with the meaning of *agape*. The first usages of the Greek term *agape* evidently carried "the sense of welcome: the surprise of the host who receives a stranger."[88] The fetus is a "stranger" in many ways, not yet fully one of us, but what does this fact require of us? A noted Christian theologian asks how the church can become "surprised hosts," in the sense of a joyful people capable of welcoming new life without fear; while a noted secular philosopher asks how women can *avoid* becoming "surprised hosts," in the sense of an exploited class made involuntary fodder for parasites.[89] The philosopher has a point: love, as I have argued, must neither be equated with masochism nor give succor to sadism. But to affirm the priority of *agape* is, in the abortion context, to side with the

[85] Lincoln, "Last Speech in Springfield, Illinois, in the 1858 Campaign, October 30, 1858," in ibid., p. 34.

[86] Mary Anne Warren's elder-take-all stance is an example of the divisive extremism I would avoid. She writes:

> Neither a fetus's resemblance to a person, nor its potential for becoming a person provides any basis whatever for the claim that it has any significant right to life. Consequently, a woman's right to protect her health, happiness, freedom, and even her life, by terminating an unwanted pregnancy, will always override whatever right to life it may be appropriate to ascribe to a fetus, even a fully developed one.

See "On the Moral and Legal Status of Abortion," in *The Ethics of Abortion*, pp. 232–33. Warren, like Michael Tooley and Peter Singer, provides no substantive moral reason to object to infanticide, save perhaps the property rights of parents.

[87] This would please Stephen A. Douglas and other exponents of "popular sovereignty," but it would contradict much of what Abraham Lincoln stood for. Lincoln opposed slavery, most fundamentally, because he considered it a moral wrong condemned by God, not because it was something on which there was political consensus. For more on the ways in which Lincoln came to see the limits of "liberalism," especially majority rule, and the need for something like theological or natural law arguments, especially in relation to slavery, see Allen C. Guelzo, *Abraham Lincoln: Redeemer President* (Grand Rapids: Eerdmans, 1999).

[88] Ceslas Spicq, O.P., *Theological Lexicon of the New Testament*, trans. and ed. by J. D. Ernest (Peabody, Mass.: Hendrickson, 1994), vol. 1, p. 8.

[89] See Hauerwas, "Why Abortion Is a Religious Issue," in *The Ethics of Abortion*, and Thomson, "A Defense of Abortion."

theologian:[90] the fetus is not simply a parasite,[91] and parental love is a matter of responsibly giving rather than of being unjustly taken.

I have tried in this chapter, as well as in this book generally, to imagine the positive prospects for welcoming and serving life. A fully Christian picture of hospitality will focus on Jesus' self-giving life and love, and this picture will deeply condition one's understanding of moral virtues, principles, and effects. But the dynamics of loving care and carelessness are also intelligible to nonbelievers. If elective abortion is a willed "No" to vulnerability and encumbrance before the stranger, to the fearful fertility of the two sexes, for instance, then it is clearly the opposite of love. That said, the thing most needful in the abortion debate is to become more attentive to our fellows' vulnerabilities, both mothers' and fetuses', rather than less. We must avoid judgmentalism. Shared vulnerabilities should make us aware of the extremity of the demands upon, but also of the resources in, a love extended to all.

We are required by the reflexive normativity of care, for example, not to think of abortion as an intractable dilemma in which innocent human beings must be culpably sacrificed. (Feeling compelled to sacrifice innocent "dependents" is the surest sign of the "primitive" worldview from which Abraham delivered us.) After the first trimester, refraining from elective abortion is rather an enforceable obligation, I believe—*a perfect duty for the parents* (one of justice), based on the induced needs and measured capacities of fetal human beings, and *an imperfect duty for society* (one of charity), based on the natural need and historical capacity to sustain the common good.[92] Anything less is a betrayal of life and love.

In modern theories, justice is typically a matter of adjudicating distrib-

---

[90] I do not limit my appeal to the Christian church, any more than I limit it to pregnant women.

[91] *The American Heritage Dictionary* (Boston/New York/etc.: American Heritage and Houghton Mifflin, 1973) defines a "parasite" as "any organism that grows, feeds, and is sheltered on or in a different organism while contributing nothing to the survival of its host" (p. 952). There is no question but that the human fetus lives off its mother in various ways, sheltered by her abdomen and employing her organ systems for life support. In biological usage, however, a parasite is generally of a different species from its host and is not voluntarily generated or acquired. The fetus is of the same species as its mother, in contrast, and is usually the result of voluntary intercourse. (Even when conception has not been intentional, the dependency of the fetus—its very existence—has, again barring rape and ignorance, been called into being by a free act of its parents.) Moreover, "parasitism" frequently, although not always, implies that some degree of harm is done to the host, while the fetal-maternal relation is typically commensalist and/or mutualist. Indeed, although the survival of a particular mother does not depend on her particular fetus, without viable fetuses the species *Homo sapiens* would die out, thus putting an end to human motherhood itself. Only a highly individualistic understanding of "contribution to survival" will overlook or downplay this obvious fact.

[92] Perfect duties attach to particular agents and require discrete actions on behalf of specific patients; imperfect duties are more open-ended.

utive or retributive claims between free and equal persons, charity of meeting induced or contingent needs of a broad spectrum of human (and possibly nonhuman) lives. As I have insisted, however, this does not imply that our sole obligations are of justice. As Lisa Cahill has maintained,

> The virtue of hope embodied in inauspicious situations enables the perception of at least a *prima facie* obligation to sustain fetal life, even if that life is not clearly of equal value to postnatal human life. . . . If we are able to foster a sense of duty to others and to our common society, a duty that precedes and grounds our own rights as individuals, then it also becomes possible to envision a moral obligation to support the cohesion in the human community of even its weakest members, those with the least forceful claim to consideration, whether they be the unborn, the sick, the poor, or the socially powerless.[93]

Cahill writes of "hope," but she captures the spirit of what I have called "charity," the heart of an ethic of care. The charity/justice contrast I have defended can now be schematized as follows:

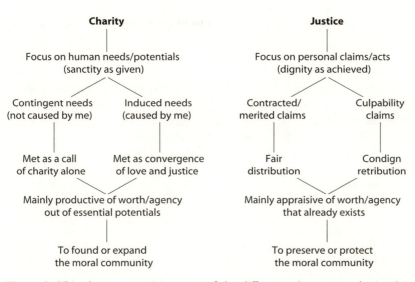

Figure 2: This chart summarizes some of the differences between a charity that largely bestows worth and a justice that largely appraises it. Reading left to right, the chart also helps us to see the priority of love: individuals only become capable of justice (or injustice) after they have been given an unconditional care by their parents and/or the wider society. The care attends to the needs and potentials of human lives (sanctity), rather than merely to their achieved merits (dignity).

[93] Cahill, "Abortion, Autonomy, and Community," in *Abortion and Catholicism: The American Debate*, p. 94.

As always, charity is not antithetical to justice, but it does transcend and transform both contractarian and utilitarian emphases by casting higher and wider the net of moral attention. Love balances the needs and potentials of the fetus, the claims of the mother, the responsibility of the father, and the common good of society in ways not reducible to either contract theory or utility maximization. In particular, love acts to liberate potential persons out of the pre-personal, not merely to respect persons already in existence.

When Peter Singer defends the option of infanticide for babies under the age of twenty-eight days,[94] he is simply working out the implication of an ethic of pure dignity without sanctity, modern autonomy disdainful of human dependency. There is no reason to flinch from infanticide, much less abortion, if a genuine right to life depends on a realized capacity for autonomous choice or a developed sense of self across time. Any liberating abortion policy, in contrast, must aspire to an "equity" that is a synthesis of fairness and responsibility, "a fusion of justice and love," to use Gilligan's terms.[95] We must attend to both human needs and personal claims,[96] both fetal dependency (especially when induced) and maternal autonomy. Indeed, attention to impersonal needs and potentials, what I have called "sanctity," is a necessary condition to the achievement of personal dignity. As I have emphasized, we all grow into personhood through the care of others, both care given *to* us *by* others and care given *by* us *to* others.

Singer acknowledges "the aesthetic, scientific and recreational values of preserving natural ecosystems," and he grants that there are reasons to value inanimate objects like sunsets and nonsentient beings like redwood trees.[97] But moral purposes trump aesthetic, scientific, and recreational ones, and for moral purposes he is ahistorical and hypercognitivist. Ethically speaking, that is, Singer gives real consideration only to *present* consciousness and self-consciousness, thus he can find no substantive reason to object to either abortion or infanticide, even when these are done

[94] Singer, *Rethinking Life and Death*, p. 217; see also his *Practical Ethics* (Cambridge: Cambridge University Press, 1993), pp. 169–74.

[95] Gilligan, *In a Different Voice*, p. 172.

[96] Cf. David Wiggins, "Claims of Need," in *Morality and Objectivity*, ed. by Ted Honderich (London: Routledge & Kegan Paul, 1985), chap. VIII. Wiggins, following H.L.A. Hart and others, sees various vital needs to constitute claims to be met as a matter of "*justice as limitative, protective and remedial*" or "*justice as the keeper and distributor of public largesse*" (pp. 182–83). Again, I reserve the word "love" for the nurturance of human potentials and the meeting of human needs, especially when not induced by others, and "justice" for the adjudication of personal interests and entitlements.

[97] See Singer, "A Response," in *Singer and His Critics*, ed. by Dale Jamieson (Oxford: Blackwell, 1999), pp. 331–32.

for reasons of parental convenience or social utility.[98] This is tragically forgetful of the temporal trajectory of a human life. It is always salubrious, for Christians and non-Christians alike, to remember our beginnings in *the past care of others* (infancy) and to anticipate our likely ends in *the future care of others* (old age). The ethical and legal literature of virtually every civilized society has recognized the obligation to safeguard impersonal goods, both for their own sakes and because some of these goods (e.g., babies) are necessary conditions for the emergence/continuance of personal agents and their rights.[99]

The Judeo-Christian Bible in particular would have us recall that God called creation "good" even before the appearance of sentient beings, including humans (see Gen. 1:4; 1:12), and that God will remain good even after the disappearance of all beings from the face of the earth. Frequently, in fact, "what is prized by human beings is an abomination in the sight of God" (Luke 16:15). To realize this is to approach an humility that puts abortion, and many other moral issues, in perspective. Such humility does not merely "live and let live"; it does not, most characteristically, measure the life or merit of others, in trimesters or otherwise. (Measurement has its place, but in dealing with innocent dependents it is usually a concession to our frailty.) Like Christ, humility would give life "abundantly" and "to the full" (John 10:10, NRSV and NIV); it would sustain fellow creatures, however developed or undeveloped, because its own existence has been sustained by others. This is easier said than done, and it requires concrete actions to assist all who suffer or are at risk in abortion contexts—unwed or unwilling mothers, as well as unwanted or unwell fetuses. When assistance is forthcoming, this is partly out of rever-

---

[98] Singer has endorsed the view that infanticide is "the natural and humane solution to the problem posed by sick and deformed babies," but, beyond this, he has suggested that a small child not wanted by those closest to it may be killed as readily as any fetus is aborted. Because neither fetuses nor twenty-eight-day-old babies are self-conscious, they have no intrinsic value and no real right to life. Both can be killed with moral impunity so long as they are not made to suffer pain and their parents do not object. See *Practical Ethics*, pp. 173–74, and also *Rethinking Life and Death*, p. 217. Singer has recently had second thoughts about the twenty-eight-day boundary; see his comments in "Dangerous Words," an interview with the *Princeton Alumni Weekly*, January 26, 2000, p. 19. The problem, however, is not that infanticide is morally wrong in any substantive sense, but rather that the twenty-eight-day cutoff is "too arbitrary" and thus won't "work" as public policy. Singer's worries are logistical, in sum; he still can offer no in-principle objection to killing healthy babies who are unwanted.

[99] See John T. Noonan, Jr., "An Almost Absolute Value in History," in *The Morality of Abortion: Legal and Historical Perspectives* (Cambridge, Mass.: Harvard University Press, 1970); see also Mary Ann Glendon's *Abortion and Divorce in Western Law: American Failures, European Challenges* (Cambridge, Mass., and London: Harvard University Press, 1987).

ence for the sanctity of human life, partly in recognition of our common dependency on human society, but most fundamentally out of gratitude for the grace of God that makes both life and society possible. The prevenience of divine grace grounds, according to Christians, the priority of agapic love.

Name Index

Subject Index

NEW FORUM BOOKS

New Forum Books makes available to general readers outstanding original inter-disciplinary scholarship with a special focus on the juncture of culture, law, and politics. New Forum Books is guided by the conviction that law and politics not only reflect culture but help to shape it. Authors include leading political scientists, sociologists, legal scholars, philosophers, theologians, historians, and economists writing for nonspecialist readers and scholars across a range of fields. Looking at questions such as political equality, the concept of rights, the problem of virtue in liberal politics, crime and punishment, population, poverty, economic development, and the international legal and political order, New Forum Books seeks to explain—not explain away—the difficult issues we face today.